BORDERS, NATIONS AND STATES

Borders, Nations and States

Frontiers of Sovereignty in the New Europe

Edited by

LIAM O'DOWD
Department of Sociology and Social Policy
The Queen's University of Belfast

THOMAS M. WILSON
Institute of European Studies
The Queen's University of Belfast

Avebury

Aldershot · Brookfield USA · Hong Kong · Singapore · Sydney

Published by
Avebury
Ashgate Publishing Ltd
Gower House
Croft Road
Aldershot
Hants GU11 3HR
England

Ashgate Publishing Company
Old Post Road
Brookfield
Vermont 05036
USA

British Library Cataloguing in Publication Data

Borders, Nations and States : Frontiers of Sovereignty
    in the New Europe. - (Perspectives on Europe)
      1. Territory, National - Europe 2. Europe - Boundaries
      3. Europe - Economic Integration 4. Europe - Politics and
      Government - 1989–
      I. O'Dowd, Liam II. Wilson, Thomas M.
      320.1'5'094

Library of Congress Catalog Card Number: 95-83597

ISBN 1 85972 158 3
Reprinted 1996

Printed and bound in Great Britain by Ipswich Book Co., Ltd., Ipswich, Suffolk

Contents

Maps and tables

Contributors

Susan Baker is Senior Research Fellow at the Department of Social and Administrative Studies, University of Wales, College of Cardiff. Her main research interests are environmental policy and politics and the implementation of sustainable development policies in Europe. She is co-editor of *The Politics of Sustainable Development* (forthcoming 1996) and joint editor of a special issue of *Environmental Politics* (Spring 1996).

Maria Ciechocinska is Professor in the University of Agriculture and Education, Siedlce, Poland. Her main research interests are the policy and politics of regional development in Eastern Europe, collective identity and structural transition in Poland. Her most recently published articles deal with the transition to the market economy and problems of democratization in Poland.

Giovanni Delli Zotti is Professor in the Department of Economy, Society and Territory, University of Udine, Italy. His main research interests are in cross-border cooperation and regionalism. He is co-editor of *International Solidarity and National Sovereignty* (1995) [in Italian] and editor of *Inside the Visegrad Triangle: Civil Society, Politics and Institutions in Central Eastern Europe* (1994) [in Italian].

Henk Driessen is Associate Professor of Cultural Anthropology at the University of Nijmegen, The Netherlands. His current research interests include the Mediterranean Area, particularly Andalusia. He is author of *On the Spanish-Moroccan Frontier: A Study in Ritual, Power and Ethnicity* (1992).

James Corrigan is Research Fellow at the Institute of European Studies, Queen's University, Belfast. His main research interest is a comparative study of the British-Irish and Hungarian-Romanian border zones. His most recent publications include articles on borders, national sovereignty and European integration and cross-border cooperation in Ireland.

Wanda Dressler Holohan is Research Fellow at the Groupe de Recherches sur les Mutations des Societes Europeennes, (G.R.M.S.E.), Laboratoire CNRS, Universite Paris X, Nanterre. Her main research interests are regional policy, transborder regions and the nation-state, European integration, and the process of transition to the market economy in Eastern Europe. Her most recently published articles concern transnationalism and the national question, and national movements and the internationalisation of protest.

Goio Etxebarria is Senior Lecturer in the Department of Applied Economics, University of the Basque Country. His main research interest is in regional and industrial economy with particular reference to the Basque Country. Recent publications include articles on networks and spatial dynamics (with M. Gomez Uranga) and the restructuring process of the Basque economy.

Mikel Gómez Uranga is Professor in the Department of Applied Economics, University of the Basque Country, Bilbao. His main area of interest is technological change and regional development. He has recently published a study on metropolitan concentrations and infrastructure investments in Aquitaine and the Basque Country.

Francisco Letamendía is a Reader in the Department of Political Sciences, University of the Basque Country, Bilbao. His specialist fields are comparative nationalism, political violence adn the construction of Europe. He has written a multi-volume work on the history of Basque nationalism, and has co-edited a study of cross-border cooperation between Euskadi and Aquitaine.

Zdravko Mlinar is Professor of Sociology and Head of the Centre for Spatial Sociology at the Faculty of Social Sciences, University of Ljubljana, Slovenia. His research interests are in the area of socio-spatial development particularly the interrelationship between autonomy and (dis-) integration. His latest books include: *Globalization and Territorial Identities* (1992) [ed.] and *Individuation and Globalization in Space* (1994) [published in Slovene, forthcoming in English].

Liam O'Dowd is Reader in Sociology in the Department of Sociology and Social Policy, Queen's University, Belfast. His main current research interests are the sociology of European integration and border regions. Recent publications include *Whither the Irish Border? Sovereignty, Democracy and Economic Integration in Ireland* (1994) and *Irish Society: Sociological Perspectives* (1995) [co-editor].

Raimondo Strassoldo is Professor in the Department of Economy, Society and Territory, University of Udine, Italy. His research interests include regionalism, processes of localisation and globalisation and European integration. His publications include recent articles on the theory of globalism and localism. He is also joint editor of *Cooperation and Conflict in Border Areas* (1982).

Thomas M. Wilson is Lecturer in European Studies, in Queen's University, Belfast. He is currently engaged in research at the Irish and Hungarian-Romanian borders. He is co-editor of *Cultural Change in the New Europe* (1994) and *Border Approaches: Anthropological Perspectives on Frontiers* (1994).

Acknowledgements

This book originated in a seminar on borders, peripheral regions and European integration held in Belfast in April 1993. This seminar was one of a series under the general heading Peripheral Regions and European Integration, jointly sponsored by Queen's University, Belfast and the University of Ulster. The series was funded by the Department of Education, Northern Ireland and the Economic and Social Research Council ((ESRC Award No. A450 26 4008). Four of the chapters in this volume are much revised versions of papers offered at the original seminar and the remainder were specially commissioned for this volume. We would like to thank our colleagues who participated in, and helped organise the seminar series. In particular, we would like to thank Emer O'Hagan and Zoltán Berenyi for their help in the preparation of the manuscript.

Liam O'Dowd
Thomas M. Wilson
Belfast, November 1995.

1 Frontiers of sovereignty in the new Europe

Liam O'Dowd and Thomas M. Wilson

Border changes in the "new" Europe

There are many versions of the new Europe. The one which most concerns us in this volume is the new Europe of the changing European Union (EU) which is transformed every decade or so through expansion or further integration. But the formal process of EU building has no monopoly on "newness". Other new Europes include those of the post-Soviet Central and Eastern Europe, the new right of the Western European welfare states; the Europes of youth, of global consumer and popular culture, of new immigrants and asylum-seekers, or the Europe of those elites who increasingly see the continent as an economic space which can act as a powerful competitor to North America and East Asia. All of these Europes are interrelated - they find expression in the themes of state sovereignty, transnationalism and cultural adaptation which are central to a social science struggling to come to terms with a period of dramatic flux and transition. This volume's case studies of politics and society at and beyond the borders of the EU seek to demonstrate that international borders are key vantage points from which to view the processes of building and redefining the states, nations and transnational networks which comprise the new Europe.

In many ways, of course, the study of borders reminds us that there is much of the "old" in the "new" Europe. Borders, after all, are reminders of the past - they are "time written in space" (Rupnik 1994: 103), the product of previous conquests, invasions, population movements or treaties. Any redefinition or transformation of borders means engaging with the past. The coining of slogans and catchphrases such as "a Europe of the regions"; "a Europe without frontiers" or "fortress Europe" each in their own way raises questions of how the past is going to be reconciled with the present and married to the future. A "Europe of regions" has meant in part the

1

rediscovering of the outlines of old states and nationalities long suppressed or subsumed within the inter-state system created in Europe over the last one hundred and fifty years. The slogan of the Single European Market, a "Europe without Frontiers", implies, in the first instance, a radical altering of the economic significance of state borders within the EU. Finally, "fortress Europe" raises the perennial question of where Europe's external borders are to be drawn while recalling the many versions of this border which we have inherited from history.

It is scarcely surprising, therefore, that over the last decade borders have become increasingly the focus of political, popular and scholarly attention. The issue of borders is one of definition and construction. In our view, the term "borders" includes both the legal borderline between states and the frontier of political and cultural contest which stretches away from the borderline. The frontier zone is by our definition much wider than the political line in the sand which demarcates state sovereignty, because it encompasses the economic, social and political landscape of borderlands' people. This frontier transcends the borderline, and its width and depth within each state can best be determined through the understanding of border people's behaviour and beliefs. As we and many of the contributors to this volume suggest, the study of borders in the new Europe includes both the geographic spaces contiguous to the borderline as well as the boundary line itself. Some small European states may even be borderlands in their entirety as they are demarcated on all sides by other states' borders.

Although the borders of Europe today are undergoing a series of transformations, it is not the first time this century that European borders have been at the centre of radical political and social change. In fact, the continent is currently experiencing its third major phase of border reconstruction this century. The first two phases followed the ending of two world wars and were at the disposition of a coalition of the victorious states. The current phase which dates from 1989 is somewhat different. It is not the outcome of an all-embracing inter-state war. No victorious states stand ready and willing to impose a "new world order" of national states (Rupnik 1994: 94). Although regional wars play a substantial role in Eastern Europe, to understand what is happening at and to borders we must look more to long-term processes of economic, political and cultural change rather than to single and often cataclysmic events such as a wars, invasions and major peace settlements.

Two somewhat contradictory processes appear to be at work in Europe. In the east, many existing national boundaries are being delegitimised and, in some cases, violently challenged and redrawn. In the EU, on the other hand, it seems that internal (member-state) boundaries, while remaining largely unchanged,[1] are being devalued in the wake of the Single Market and the Maastricht Treaty. Events in the former USSR and Yugoslavia appear to confirm the new salience of borders and the powerful attraction of a bounded homeland for ethno-national groups. EU developments, on the other hand, seem to suggest the opposite, i.e., the diminishing significance of national borders, and by extension, the decline of the national state in a core region of advanced capitalism.

Such a contrast may be superficial, however. It obscures the interconnections and similarities between east and west as shown in the re-unification of Germany, the re-emergence of Central Europe and the debates over the nature and boundary of "fortress Europe". Pressures exist for a form of "balkanisation" or "regionalisation" in western Europe also. As several chapters in this volume demonstrate, these pressures exist even in long-established states such as the United Kingdom (see chapters by O'Dowd and Corrigan and Wilson), Spain (Letemendia et al.) and Italy (Strassoldo and Delli Zotti). Benedict Anderson (1992: 3) has argued that this tendency to fragmentation may be seen by future historians as a long-term process of dis-integration of the "great polyethnic, polyglot, and often polyreligious monarchical empires built up so painfully in mediaeval and early modern times". He traces this process from the American revolution through the collapse of the Spanish Empire (1810-1830), the fall of the Hohenzollern, Habsburg, Romanov and Ottoman empires after the First World War and the period of decolonisation and "proxy wars" in many parts of the "Third World" after 1945.

Attempts to resist this disintegration have had mixed origins and results. They include Hitler's failed attempt to unify Europe under German domination, the collapse of a communist world order under the leadership of the USSR, and the rather more ambiguous attempt to integrate "Europe" under the umbrella of the European Community (EC), now the EU. The latter is caught between two contending pressures: towards "ever closer union", on the one hand, and towards dissolution or dilution by extension on the other. With the collapse of state socialism in eastern Europe, one of the main historical rationales for the EU, as a US-sponsored bulwark against the other major Cold War superpower, the Soviet Union, vanished. Advocates of European unity, on the other hand, see at least two alternative rationales: the long-term processes of global re-integration which are driven by economic and cultural globalisation and the emergence of huge politico-economic trade blocs centred on North America and Japan. Their argument is that Europe, to compete, must unite.

The task of "building Europe" is difficult, however, given the history of internal diversity and warfare within Europe, and the lack of external threat. As Therborn (1995: 244) observes "the unifying Other outside has been distant, weak or nebulous", whereas "the divisive Other within has been close and strong, in many cases stronger and closer than in other parts of the world". In most current debates over the future of the EU, enthusiastic advocates of a supranational EU see the national state (and its attempts to preserve national sovereignty) as the main "Other" of an integrated Europe. From this perspective, in the absence of a major and coherent external threat, the main opposition to a more integrated Union comes from within, from the jealously guarded sovereignties of its own member states.

The "Other without" and the "Other within" immediately raise the problem of borders and borderlands. In other words, where will Europe's external borders rest and, more importantly, will they enclose a "fortress Europe" or one which encourages links with "non-Europe". Alternatively, do the borders of member states and their own internal regional borders reflect a fragmentation or diffusion of

3

sovereignty in the EU, or are they part of a restructured hierarchy of authority. The contributors to this volume address these questions in a variety of ways by examining the development of cross-border cooperation across the external and internal borders of the EU, the re-appearance of old regional and ethno-national frontiers encouraged by transnational networks and the extent to which state (and EU) sovereignty is compromised or reinforced by the management of issues such as the environment, security and illegal immigrants.

Three propositions underlie the following chapters: (1) the old lack of coincidence between nations and states in Europe is manifesting itself in new ways in response to economic, political and cultural change; (2) boundaries are key demarcations of state sovereignty and its relationship to the EU; (3) the border policies of the EU and what happens at the internal and external boundaries of the Community can reveal much about the current status and future prospects of the national state and the European Union.

A spectrum of social scientific interpretations can be constructed on the basis of these shared propositions. At the extremes, these involve contrasting notions of the importance of national borders and, by extension, of the state sovereignty which they de-limit. At one end of the spectrum, the new fluidity, permeability and transcendence of territorial boundaries is emphasised. In this view, the globalisation of economic and cultural life, the revolution in mass communications, the increase in both elite mobility and mass tourism and the alleged transition from modernity to post-modernity all seem to devalue national boundaries both as markers of collective identity and of relatively self-contained and self-governing societies. A potential weakness of this approach is that it is forced to ignore, or to discount, the renewed salience of the politics of borders and identities in both Western and Eastern Europe. Within this perspective much of the research and theorising on the globalisation of economic life has stressed the mobility and increased flexibility of capital and the loss of the national state's economic influence. New forms of capitalism involve spatial differentiation enhancing multi-national strategies, regionalisation and localisation at the expense of state strategies (Harvey 1989).

Applied to Europe, this analysis suggests that the EU is a recognition on the part of national governments that they can no longer effectively control a capitalist order characterised by the competition between large trading blocs, the global strategies of multinational corporations and financial markets. In a capitalist world system based on "free-trade", policy options open to national states are limited and they are forced to join in supranational blocs in order to establish economies of scale and gain competitive advantage. The Single European Act (1986) and its slogan a "Europe without Frontiers" represented the EC's response to competition from North America, Japan and the Far East. A revived neo-classical economics argues that borders are an impediment, a support for protectionism (at least within trade blocs) which hinders market forces and the maximisation of prosperity.

Theorists of cultural globalisation, such as Robertson (1992), pay even less attention to the question of territorial boundaries. While recognising the objective importance of economic and political inter-connectedness as a dimension of globalisation, Robertson (1992: 183) stresses the emergence of a global consciousness and a subjective and cultural dimension to globalisation which is not based on the building blocks of the inter-state system and hence transcends territorial boundaries. Post-modern theorists such as Lash and Urry (1994) see global inter-connections less as structures than as flows. They argue that national structures are being replaced by immense transnational flows of capital, money, goods, services, people, information, technologies, policies, ideas, images, and regulations across national borders. In this view, national governments have diminishing control over activities within their territorial boundaries because of global money markets, huge transnational corporations, new communications technologies and new forms of "sub-politics" (Lash and Urry 1994: 28). This "hollowing out" of the nation-state implies a radical diminution in the significance of national boundaries.

The "post-modern social order" does not necessarily involve the disappearance of territorial boundaries. It may actually lead to their proliferation and, consequently, to the relativisation of all borders, especially those defining the national state. It becomes possible to contemplate, therefore, the proliferation of nationalisms and of new ethnic and regional sub-territories which float free of the sites of economic and political power. Baumann (1995: 247), for example, argues that the durable marriage forged by the "nation-state" between the ethnic and the political nation is now on the brink of divorce, a warning echoed by Mlinar in this volume. Within the new Europe, it is no longer as necessary as in the past for prospective states to pass the "sovereignty tests" of economic, social and even military viability. These functions are now uncoupled and diffused to a wide range of transnational and sub-national agencies. The result, according to Baumann (1995: 247), is that the ongoing erosion of national sovereignty is allowing the forces of ethnicity to roam free and uncontrolled, no longer trammelled by the burden of economic and social management. In this scenario, there is a proliferation of ethnic, military and economic borders, which overlap, co-exist with, and diminish the primacy of national state boundaries.

This image of border flux and volatility is captured well in a British magazine's supplement to a Channel 4 programme, "Borderlands". Referring to Europe, the authors observe:

> As frontier-fixity dissolves, no neat pattern of region and/or nationality seems likely to replace it. Reality is outpacing theory. The feuds of to-morrow are likely to be far more various than has been anticipated: state-nations, long-buried nationalities, immigrants, new regional identities and rising city states are all jostling for houseroom inside the new Europe and its expanding outer rim (Platt and Jones 1992: 2).

Many political scientists, sociologists and anthropologists are less ready to write the obituary of the national state, however (see, for example, Gellner 1983; Anderson,

1992; Mann 1993). At the other end of the spectrum of approaches to national sovereignty, they question the somewhat kaleidoscopic picture of borders dissolving and re-forming. Instead, they see the proliferation of national borders, border disputes, and the emergence of embryonic national borders within existing states as evidence that nationalism and struggles over national sovereignty have retained their significance. Analyses of the alleged retreat of the state can still conclude that it retains immense resources and "an infinite capacity for external and internal adaptability" while remaining for most citizens "a primary source of welfare, order, authority, legitimacy, identity and loyalty" (Muller and Wright 1994: 10). The main potential weakness of this approach is that it fails to address adequately how underlying processes of economic and cultural globalisation are restructuring (perhaps even diminishing) national sovereignty and the borders which delimit it.

One of the more durable priorities of states remains the monopolisation of the legitimate means of coercion within fixed territorial boundaries (Weber 1978: 56). To this Tilly (1990: 85) adds two further reinforcing elements: the monopoly of taxation and access to credit (for expenditure on soldiers, arms and other means of war). The post-1945 settlement in Europe left national borders secure for a time but did not prevent erosion "from within", from secessionist movements, disaffected regions and ethnic minorities. One explanation is that many Western European states moved from relying on mass legitimacy to emphasising the control and surveillance of their populations (Giddens 1985) at the same time as they were advocating giving full rein to free-market forces. Arguably this process of control was even more marked in Eastern Europe, albeit without free-market capitalism. Nevertheless, the roots of de-stabilisation can be seen in the treatment of minorities such as the Basques in Spain, Irish nationalists in Northern Ireland, the playing off of one nationality against another in Tito's Yugoslavia, and the attempt to place a wall around Eastern Germany's experiment in state socialism. Tilly (1990: 203) has even argued that governments became more unstable as their borders became more secure. Not for the first time, state authorities begin to see whole populations as enemies (e.g., ethnic or religious minorities) which means that civil wars can generate huge refugee problems, frequently at or near borders. Widening the scope of the argument to EU level, it is worth asking if the lack of an external and threatening "Other" creates space for movements such as the neo-fascists and neo-nazis to victimise illegal immigrants, gypsies, and other marginalised groups within the EU.

Of course, national boundaries themselves are rooted in coercion, in practices of forcible exclusion and inclusion. Border construction has seldom been a matter of popular democracy. Instead, it has been typically the result of the progressive incorporation of localities, through military conquest, invasion and colonisation interspersed with periods of negotiation, secret manipulations and treaty-making. In other words, international boundaries are the outcome of state-building. Durable states have been able to develop ever more elaborate institutions and more intensive regulation of everyday life. They have been able to mobilise, to a greater or lesser degree, forms of collective identification with both the trappings of state power and with the "nation", which the state purports to represent or which it may even have created. Only in recent times, and in some places, however, has the political *representation* of bounded national territory taken a democratic form.

More detailed studies of what is happening to borders and borderlands can reveal much about the forces impinging on the changing nature of the national state and national sovereignty. In the context of the European Union such studies can also provide clues to the complex processes of European integration. As Wallace (1992: 14) observes: "the question of boundaries is central to any study of political systems, legal jurisdiction, or economic or social interaction".

Borders, nations and states

A variety of social scientific perspectives informs our view of the relationships between nation and state at the internal and external borders of the EU. In his critique of the new myth of a "Europe without Frontiers", the Swiss geographer, Raffestin (1993) insists that borders are a necessary constituent of social life. He argues that they perform four functions, translation,[2] differentiation, connection and regulation. These functions suggest a dynamic social process which, in the case of stable geographical boundaries, becomes frozen in time. Max Haller (1990: 201) has noted the several meanings attached to the terms "borders" and "limits" in a number of European languages. He detects behind this variety a fundamental double meaning (see also Strassoldo 1973). On the one hand, borders may be seen as ends or barriers, on the other as passages, filters or gateways between systems contiguous to each other. This dual meaning is similar to the long-standing distinction made by political geographers between boundaries and frontiers - a distinction traced by Sahlins (1990: 1425) as far back as thirteenth century France when the monarchy began to distinguish between boundaries (definite lines marking the limits of its jurisdiction) and "frontiers" which were zones which "stood face to" an enemy. Historically, frontier or border regions including those between nation-states have been the site of conflicts over territory and are frequently characterised by different ethnic, religious, linguistic or national composition than that of their respective national states - a reminder of the lack of coincidence between national boundaries and other socio-cultural boundaries.

Historically, the allocation and demarcation of borders has been an elite phenomenon where some degree of force or threat of force is usually present. This has meant the forcible inclusion and/or exclusion of several minority ethnic groups or parts thereof. As Hansen (1981: 20) observes, "all the European countries created in the last 150 years have border region problems arising from the demands of minorities seeking to realise their 'national' values within the framework of an organised state". Thus the drawing of national borders in Europe has led to the construction of national minorities many of them located in frontier regions. Of course, national boundaries or the states they enclose cannot be understood merely in terms of elite manipulation or the capacity to coerce. Donnan and Wilson (1994:

7

11), laying out an agenda for an anthropology of frontiers, point out that borders are "continuously negotiated and re-interpreted through the dialectics of everyday life among all people who live at them, but also, to a lesser extent, by those who cross them, and by those people within a state's border who feel in contact with or threatened by outsiders."

The chapters below by Dressler Holohan and Ciechocinska and Driessen underline the role that national borders can play in the everyday life of borderland people. Although in each case they deal with external frontiers of the EU in Upper Silesia and at the Spanish-Moroccan border zone, cross-border interaction is very different in each place. The EU's border seems far more open to Poles of German nationality than it is to Moroccans, despite the latter's strong historical links with southern Spain. In itself this provides clues to the way in which EU identity is being shaped in conjunction with two different kinds of national identity and state formation in Germany and Spain. As Wilson points out in his chapter in this volume, borders are social constructions which are the products of interaction between powerful European and national elites, on the one hand, and people at borders, on the other hand.

Drawing on anthropological literature, Grosby (1995) argues that nation-states have been able to draw on transcendental, primordial patterns of attachment which people in all societies (both pre-modern and modern) have to their homeland. He observes that "throughout history man [sic] has considered, albeit with variations, environments which are considerably more extensive than those of the family or home to be his 'own', hence integral to his life" (Grosby 1995: 144). Bounded territories in this view are not simply a matter of control or access to resources, or of networks of interaction within fixed geographical limits, rather they denote *participation* in a collective consciousness (rituals, customs, traditions, laws, historical knowledge, and even language) associated with a particular territory. Territorial borders are thus sacralised typically *via* nationalism as is shown in the "willingness of millions of Europeans this century to sacrifice themselves for a land and country they believe to be their own" (Grosby 1995: 143).

In sociological terms, therefore, it is as necessary to draw on Durkheimian as well as on Weberian perspectives to understand the combination of coercion and sacralisation which underpins national boundaries. Of course, collective consciousness also includes the existence of a collective, if selective, amnesia, about the origins of borders, which can be a major resource for national institutions and powerholders. Identification with a particular bounded national territory is strengthened to the extent that the memory of shared sacrifice (in war, for example) and inclusion in the nation overrides memories of exclusion, exploitation and coercion which have attended the creation of borders. The prevalence of these latter memories often distinguish border regions from the rest of their respective states.

The political and cultural dimensions of national borders are continually confronted, however, by the universalising thrust of economic development. Hansen (1983: 256), for example, notes that both "growth pole" and modern location theory stress the disadvantages that border regions experience because political boundaries

8

"represent artificial barriers to the rational economic organisation of potentially complementary areas and because both public and private sectors tend to avoid investing in areas where conflicts are likely to arise". The pioneers of modern location theory, Christaller and Losch, assumed that in the case of borders, politics are detrimental to economics and that the political goals of the nation-state are inherently detrimental to border regions. For Christaller, border areas are likely to be subject to the "socio-political separation principle" where the "authority of stately and sovereign might" takes precedence over the "rationality of economic principles" (Hansen 1983: 256; Ratti 1993: 37). O'Dowd and Corrigan's chapter below supports Christaller's argument in the case of the UK-Irish border, despite the precedence given to economic development in border areas by the EU in the wake of the Single European Market.

Indeed, the rationality of economic principles was precisely the means employed by the founders of the EU to desacralise the historically volatile pattern of European national borders - lines that were reforged in the wake of the excesses of territorial nationalism in two world wars, and before that, in the long struggles between European powers in the course of imperialist expansion overseas. Europe has never had settled boundaries, and the borders of what might constitute Europe remain contested today (see also Haller 1990; Lipietz 1993; Pieterse 1990). Only ten states (the largest being Spain) had the same boundaries in 1989 as they had in 1899 - "the nation-states which constitute Europe are themselves almost all imprecise entities with moveable boundaries" (Wallace 1992:14). Germany, at the geographical centre of any definition of Europe, has had particularly fluid boundaries. In many ways the recent unification of Germany underlines the point. Austria, Alsace, Silesia (discussed by Dressler Holohan and Ciechocinska below), Bohemia and several other regions testify to the contingency of German boundaries and the implications of a citizenship regime which continues to be based on *jus sanguinis* rather than *jus soli* (Brubaker 1990).

For the founders of the EU, however, a stabilised pattern of national boundaries was a necessary pre-requisite (what some saw mainly involving the containment of Germany) to generating patterns of economic interdependency which would eventually reduce the significance of existing borders, thereby permanently removing the threat of inter-state wars over territory. This strategy was pursued, however, along with a considerable growth in the economic, administrative and cultural capacity of the state. The new forms of total war had shown the mobilising potential of the nation-state. Translated into peace-time, this potential manifested itself in the growth of what Mann (1984: 208) has termed the "infrastructural power and penetration of the state". Within infrastructural power, he includes the power of regular taxation, a monopoly over military mobilisation, permanent bureaucratic administration, a monopoly over law-making and enforcement, the capacity to store an enormous amount of information, and influence over the economy.

More importantly, in the context of this volume, Mann also argued that growth in infrastructural powers also increased "territorial boundedness", thus strengthening the boundaries of existing states. Tilly (1990: 115-6) links the growth of

9

"infrastructural powers" with the homogenising strategies of state rulers. As the state's sphere of operations expands beyond its military and law and order functions, it begins to employ direct rule and intervention in the everyday lives of its population. This can mean imposing, *inter alia*, national languages, military service, a legal, welfare and educational system, even systems of economic regulation. Citizenship rights are deepened as the population can make claims on the state while sharing certain duties and obligations to state rules. Tilly (1990: 115-6) argues that from the 1850s onwards there was a substantial growth in the rule-making role of the state: "the welfare, culture and daily routines of ordinary Europeans came to depend as never before on which state they happened to reside in." The differentiation and regulation functions of national borders were underlined as states introduced passport controls, employment permits, tariffs and customs as part of economic policy, began to distinguish foreigners within the state as worthy of closer surveillance and more limited rights.

Standardisation of state rules and of the rights and obligations of various categories of people represented a form of social homogenisation. In reflecting on the long rise of the nation-state in Europe, Therborn (1995: 43) points out that it involved a major ethnic homogenisation within state boundaries, especially in the East but also to some extent in the West. This homogenisation, however, seldom went far enough to ensure a co-incidence between the boundaries of state and nation. Furthermore, although the infrastructural powers of states developed substantially after 1945 with the growth of welfare and education systems, the tendency towards intra-state homogenisation was now being challenged. Western Europe was changing from its historic role as a source of emigration to becoming an area of net immigration. Old sub-national, ethnic and regional boundaries showed that they could be politically re-activated given the appropriate socio-economic, political and cultural conditions.

Immigration has become a major issue for most western European states (Baldwin-Edwards and Schain 1994). Driessen provides an anthropological insight below into the plight of North African immigrants at one point of entry to the EU. Immigration threatens some groups of citizens with increased competition for resources and also threatens the process of homogenisation to which national identity is so closely linked. In arguing the case for open borders, Carens (1995: 331) recognises that the most people reject the idea on the basis that "the power to exclude aliens is inherent to sovereignty and essential for any political community". Here the connections between national borders, sovereignty and identity are manifest. Carens (1995: 332) goes on to argue that the moral and philosophical case in favour of restricting citizenship, especially to "third world migrants", is weak: "citizenship in western liberal democracies is the modern equivalent of feudal privilege - an inherited right that greatly enhances one's life chances".

Western European wealth and dominance, once linked to, and frequently dependent on, outward migration as part of imperial and colonial expansionism, is now protected by restricting or denying EU entry to migrants from the ex-colonies of the major EU states (see, for example, Wrench and Solomos 1993). At the core

10

of the debates over EU borders is how the western European "inheritance" is to be protected, who should share in it and who should be excluded. Here, there is a trade-off between constructing common controls at the EU borders and the diversity of citizenship rules and controls which exist among the member states. EU activities directed at standardising immigration and asylum controls have been criticised by human rights' advocates for being secretive and democratically unaccountable (Bunyan 1993). In this, however, they are squarely in a long tradition of border creation in Europe.

EU borders' policies

Despite the attempts of many European states to strengthen or maintain their sovereignty at borders, the EU's drive to greater economic and political integration has complicated these efforts. Evolving border policies within the EU have been shaped by three overriding considerations. The first two seem at first to be contradictory: the abolition of border controls in order to promulgate the "four freedoms" of movement for capital, goods, services and labour, and policing and security. The first suggests the transcendence and porosity of borders, the second leans towards their maintenance and consolidation. Underlying all borders' policy is a third consideration, the potential threat posed to state sovereignty by the lack of coincidence between nation and state. Advocates of a federated "Europe of the Regions", which allows subnational groups more freedom of expression, see "ever closer union" as the means of circumventing existing states without confrontations over territorial borders. On the other hand, proponents of a looser "Europe of the States" insist on inter-governmentalism as a means of preventing the emergence of independent regional voices and international regional alliances which might pose an alternative to the existing inter-state system.

The abolition of internal border controls marks a significant acknowledgement of the weakening infrastructural power of the national state arising from the globalisation of national economies and the loss of state influence over production and over financial markets. With the growing multinational control of the global economy, states lost much of their power of initiation, if not of regulation. Singular national economic interest became more difficult to define, despite the pressures of the Brussels' bargaining tables. Disparities and conflicting interests began to grow between regions and economic sectors within states (see Dunford 1994). These conditions prepare the ground for shifting some elements of economic regulation to the EU level as a way of influencing the continental strategies of multinational corporations. At the same time, by passing economic responsibility upwards, states can attempt to undermine the delegitimising potential of radical economic restructuring and mass unemployment.

The Single European Act (1986) and its compelling, if somewhat misleading, slogan "a Europe Without Frontiers" provided a huge stimulus to European integration. Between 1986 and 1992, the European Commission issued almost 300

11

directives eliminating physical, fiscal and technical barriers to the Single European Market (Williams 1994: 110-115). Significantly, however, national states were given the responsibility for implementing these directives, thus allowing considerable scope for the exercise of national sovereignty and discretion in the long and difficult process of removing internal border controls (i.e., economic and security checks) (Butt Philip 1991; Lodge 1992). Majone (1994) has identified what he terms the "the rise of the regulatory state" in the EU. Thus although the Single Market may have rendered borders more porous by de-regulation, re-regulation is also occurring which is carving out new roles for the national states within their own boundaries through the implementation of directives emanating from Brussels. The Single European Market provided the impetus for the Maastricht Treaty and its three-stage programme for closer economic and monetary union combined with its tentative steps in the direction of closer political union.

The abolition of border controls changed the context for existing regional cross-border cooperation and encouraged the formulation of a positive programme for border regions. As all member states had border regions with problems of adaptation to the new economic regime, this facilitated inter-governmental agreement to include a special initiative on border regions (INTERREG 1 and 2) within the wider framework of the expanded Structural Funds. INTERREG opened up new opportunities for regionalists and federalists to test the limits of national sovereignty by building on cross-border networks (see Baker's chapter in this volume). It also potentially accorded more space to regional and ethnic groupings keen to carve out more areas of economic and political activity in which they would have a greater degree of autonomy from the constraints of existing national borders and inter-state relationships.

The new proactive EU borders' programme was a belated response to the work of the consultative Council of Europe on borders over a thirty year period. The latter sought to develop a triangular borders' policy involving cooperation between European institutions, national states and border regions. From the 1950s onwards a tradition of cross-border cooperation had been developing along the Rhine Axis on the Dutch, German, Belgian, French and Swiss borders (Strassoldo 1973). These attempts were central to the formation of the Association of European Border Regions which was to later become involved in monitoring the EU's INTERREG initiative. The Council of Europe continued to stimulate interest and research on border areas and cross-border cooperation (Strassoldo 1973; Strassoldo and Delli Zotti 1982; Anderson 1982) and promulgated a Framework Convention on Transfrontier Cooperation in 1981 which advanced new models and juridical principles for cross-border links. However, this Convention had little practical effect as the EC/EU remained divided on the precise nature of the links between economic integration and national sovereignty.

INTERREG, which was specifically designated for internal and external border regions, had a dual purpose: to help integrate the economic space of the Community as a whole and to address the negative legacy of border areas, i.e., their isolation from the main centres of economic activity and decision-making, the separation of their commercial centres from their natural hinterland, their inferior infrastructure, their generally poor natural resources, and the specific difficulties arising from having different legal, administrative and social welfare systems, and often different languages and cultural traditions, from their contiguous region across the border (Commission of the European Communities 1991:169).

Overviews of cross-border cooperation, research at borders and EU assessments of the INTERREG programme raise a number of key issues about the changing nature of national boundaries and their durability. Border regions vary widely in terms of their origins, longevity, permeability and history of cross-border contacts, both formal and informal. Moreover, despite suffering in general from the negative economic effects of their marginal location, they nevertheless vary in terms of their potential accessibility to the core regions of economic activity in the EU, and in terms of the immediate benefits to be gained from cross-border links. Internal border regions closer to the geographical and economic centre of the EU may benefit economically to a greater extent by the abolition of internal borders under the Single European Market (see, for example, Nijkamp 1993; Jones and Wild 1994). Finally, the external borders of the EU face additional problems of possible consolidation with the deepening of EU economic integration and the widening of the economic and demographic gaps between the EU and its Eastern European and Mediterranean neighbours (Therborn 1995).

EU borders' policies are in flux, caught between forging links across the external border and policing it. Signs of internal challenges to the bordered sovereignty of member states co-exist with the dynamic and moveable nature of the EU's external borders. The re-unification of Germany, the recent incorporation of Sweden, Finland and Austria into the EU, negotiations for Cypriot and Maltese membership, and German support for the inclusion of Poland, Hungary and Czechoslovakia illustrate the current dynamism of EU borders. Attempts to accelerate the process of creating a common borders' policy through the Schengen agreements have proved very troublesome to implement and have created new distinctions between citizens from EU states belonging to Schengen, those from non-Schengen EU countries, and those who are from non-EU countries (Smith 1995).

Behind the current "official" borders of the EU, new informal borders are emerging, creating new "frontier" or "buffer" zones. As the Oder-Neisse line becomes more porous, the informal EU border is pushed towards Poland's eastern borders. Likewise, there are signs that as the Austro-Hungarian border becomes more permeable the Hungarian-Romanian border is being fortified with EU assistance. These "proxy" borders reflect the long-term strategy of the EU and of its major power-centre, Germany. If there is to be a "fortress Europe" its eastern line has yet to be settled. On this border, small states like Slovenia are seeking to reconcile their new national autonomy with an EU whose general inter-state rules promise to keep large states from arbitrarily controlling their smaller and weaker neighbours. Open borders with the EU, as Mlinar points out in his contribution to this volume, do not necessarily mean less autonomy.

The Norwegian - Swedish border currently marks the northern limits of the EU but here once again the official and informal borders may not coincide in the long-term, at least to the extent that the old Nordic links are maintained across the external EU border (Smith 1995). To the South, the Mediterranean countries are getting EU assistance to fortify their maritime borders against immigrants. Despite the historic inter-penetration of Southern Europe and North Africa, today the latter seems to lie firmly outside the EU. As Driessen notes below, Morocco's admission for membership got scant attention as it was deemed not to be a European country. Similarly, Turkey's application for membership has been put on the long finger, although it straddles Asia and Europe. In the South, the Mediterranean, once the maritime core of a "world economy" before the rise of north-west Europe, is now akin to a moat between rich Europe and the poor Afro-Asian continents. Within the EU itself a band of poorer peripheral regions including southern Portugal, Spain, Italy and Greece acts a further "buffer zone" for the dynamic capitalist core economies, as do the post-socialist central European countries.

Clearly, the buffer and border zones of the EU remain "under construction". With the end of the "Cold War", the eruption of ethno-national border conflicts in the Balkans, and the shrinking of Russia to its seventeenth century boundaries, the designation of "Europe's" external borders has become much more problematical. While the EU lays claim to be the foremost carrier and shaper of European identity, this claim can still be contested by European states which are not members.

The problem of defining Europe's borders and identity remains as formidable as ever. As Pieterse (1990) suggests, the Islamic and non-white peoples are pressed into service to define "Europe's Other". Old fault-lines between Orthodox and Western Christianity and between the old lands of the Ottoman Empire and the rest, have begun to take on new meaning. Borders and borderlands throughout Europe are being re-sensitised in a variety of ways. For the moment, even the advocates of a unified Europe have veered toward emphasising the exclusionary role of borders. Their dilemma is well summed up by the fear expressed by a journalist who is also a supporter of the Single European Market. In an article entitled: "Open borders have their limits", he observes that "building a non-exclusive Europe is equivalent to constructing a home without doors or windows. Pretty soon there will be nothing worth having left" (Millar 1995).

Borders, like the nations and states they circumscribe, are janus-faced. They look inwards as well as outwards; they are inclusionary as well as exclusionary. It is clear from the contributions to this volume that the disposition of borders in the new Europe is far from settled, nor is it clear how functions and meanings will be apportioned to different types of borders within and without the EU. What the contributors do convey, however, is the existence of a sense of transition and change, even if European integration is more easily understood as an ongoing process rather than a set of outcomes. Crucial to the understanding of this process is an appreciation of the ways in which frontiers are zones of contest over sovereignty. It is here too that the changing nature and meaning of national sovereignty may be most transparent.

Borderlands manifest the ways in which inter-state and state-locality relationships have been formed. Both sets of relationships are fundamental to the formation of a "new Europe". Historians show us how the delimitation of national borders often results from great events such as wars, conquests and treaties. Social scientific approaches, while acknowledging the centrality of such events, reveal national borders to be, like European integration itself, a form of social process. This process is bound up with the interaction between power, coercion, citizenship, political representation and identity. In the long-term even great historical events can be read as expressions of this interaction. While the EU is likely to remain the decisive actor in shaping the new Europe, it is too early to judge the nature and location of its external border or to assume that its abolition of internal border controls will be permanent. It seems clear, too, that its borders' policies will continue to shaped by its most powerful member states. In presenting case studies of a variety of borderlands at the internal and external borders of the EU, many of the contributors to this volume point to a co-determination of borders' policies by the EU and member-states. Others point to the unforeseen consequences of further European integration in the form of the revitalisation of old ethno-national boundaries and border identities. All suggest, however, the study of borders and frontier zones can reveal much about the dialectic of fragmentation and integration which is currently reshaping the European continent.

Notes

1. It is worth pointing out that there have been two substantial changes to the national borders of EU states since 1945, the incorporation of Saarland into West Germany and the re-unification of East and West Germany.
2. By "translation" Raffestin (1993:159) means the territorial expression or indication of the wishes and power of those creating the border. While Raffestin's approach is somewhat abstract and functionalist in orientation, he does point to why borders may be a necessary constituent of social order.

References

Anderson, B. 1992. The new world disorder. *New Left Review* 193: 3-13.
Anderson, M. (ed.) 1982. *Frontier regions in Western Europe*. London: Frank Cass.
Baldwin-Edwards, M. and Schain, M.A. 1994. The politics of immigration: an introduction. *West European Politics* 17 (3): 1-16.
Baumann, Z. 1995. *Life in fragments: essays in postmodern morality*. Oxford: Blackwell.

Brubaker, W.R. 1990. Immigration, citizenship and the nation-state in France and Germany: a comparative historical analysis. *International Sociology* 5 (4): 379-407.

Bunyan, T. 1993. Trevi, Europol and the European state. In T.Bunyan (ed.) *Statewatching the new Europe: a handbook on the European State.* London: Statewatch.

Butt Philip, A. 1991. European border controls: who needs them? *Public Policy and Administration* 6 (2): 35-54.

Carens, J.H. 1995. Aliens and citizens: the case for open borders. In W. Kymlicka (ed.), *The rights of minority cultures.* Oxford: Oxford University Press.

Commission of the European Communities 1991. *Europe 2000: Outlook for the development of the Community's territory.* Brussels: European Commission.

Donnan, H. and Wilson, T.M. 1994. An anthropology of borders. In H.Donnan and T.M.Wilson (eds.) *Border approaches: anthropological perspectives on frontiers.* Lanham, MD: University Press of America.

Dunford, M. 1994. Winners and losers: the new map of economic inequality in the European Union. *European Urban and Regional Studies* 1 (2): 95-114.

Gellner, E. 1983. *Nations and nationalism.* Oxford: Blackwell.

Giddens, A. 1985. *The nation state and violence.* Cambridge: Polity Press.

Grosby, S. 1995. Territoriality: the transcendental, primordial feature of modern societies. *Nations and Nationalism* 1 (2): 143-162.

Haller, M. 1990. The challenge for comparative sociology in the transformation of Europe. *International Sociology* 5 (2): 183-204.

Hansen, N. 1981. *The border economy: regional development in the southwest.* Austin: University of Texas Press.

_____. 1983. International cooperation in border regions: an overview and research agenda. *International Regional Science Review* 8 (3): 255-270.

Harvey, D. 1989. *The condition of postmodernity.* Oxford: Blackwell.

Jones, D. and Platt, S. 1992. Introduction. *New Statesman.* Borderlands Supplement 19 June.

Jones, P.N. and Wild, T. 1994. Opening the frontier; recent spatial impacts in the former inner-German border zone. *Regional Studies* 28 (3): 259-273.

Lash, S. and Urry, J. 1994. *Economies of signs and space.* London: Sage.

Lipietz, A. 1993. Social Europe, legitimate Europe: the inner and outer boundaries of Europe. *Environment and Planning D: Society and Space* 11: 501-512.

Lodge, J. 1992. Internal security and judicial cooperation beyond Maastricht. *Terrorism and Political Violence* 4 (3): 1-29

Majone, G. 1994. The rise of the regulatory state in Europe. *West European Politics* 17 (3): 77-101.

Mann, M. 1984. The autonomous power of the state: its origins, mechanisms and results. *European Journal of Sociology* 25 (2): 185-213.

_____. 1993. Nation-states in Europe and other continents: diversifying, developing, not dying. *Daedalus* 122: 115-140.

Millar, P. 1995. Open borders must have their limits. *The European* 5 October.

16

Muller, W. and Wright, V. 1994. Reshaping the state in Western Europe: the limits to retreat. *West European Politics* 17 (3): 1-11.

Nijkamp, P. 1993. Border regions and infrastructure networks in the European integration process. *Environment and Planning C: Government and Policy* 11: 431-446.

Pieterse, J. N. 1990. *Empire and emancipation.* London: Pluto.

Raffestin, C. 1993. Autour de la fonction sociale de la frontière. *Espaces et Sociétés: Identités, Espaces, Frontières* 70-71: 157-164.

Ratti, R. 1993. Spatial and economic effects of frontiers. In R. Ratti and S. Reichman (eds.) *Theory and practice of transborder cooperation.* Basle: Helbing and Lichtenhahn.

Robertson, R. 1992. *Globalization: social theory and global culture.* London: Sage.

Rupnik, J. 1994. Europe's new frontiers: remapping Europe. *Daedalus* 123 (3); 91-114.

Sahlins, P. 1990. Natural frontiers revisited: France's boundaries since the seventeenth century. *American Historical Review* 95 (5): 1423-1451.

Smith, S. 1995. Borders fall to be replaced by queues. *The European* 24 March.

Strassoldo, R. (ed.) 1973. *Boundaries and regions.* Trieste: Edizioni.

Strassoldo, R. and G. Delli Zotti (eds.) 1982. *Cooperation and conflict in border areas.* Milan: Franco Angeli Editore.

Therborn, G. 1995. *European modernity and beyond: the trajectory of European societies 1945-2000.* London: Sage.

Tilly, C. 1990. *Coercion, capital and European states AD 990-1990.* Oxford: Basil Blackwell.

Wallace, W. 1992. Introduction: the dynamics of European integration. In W. Wallace (ed.) *The dynamics of European integration.* London: Pinter.

Weber, M. 1978. *Economy and society.* G. Roth and C. Wittich (eds.) London: University of California Press.

Williams, A.M. 1994. *The European Community.* London: Blackwell.

Wrench, J. and Solomos, J. (eds.) 1993. *Racism and migration in western Europe.* Oxford: Berg.

2 Punctured sovereignty, border regions and the environment within the European Union

Susan Baker

This chapter examines the relationship between border issues and environmental issues in the context of the changing nature of the nation-state within the European Union (EU). At present the function as well as the nature of the state is changing along a number of dimensions (Loughlin 1994). While member states of the EU continue to exercise control over their borders, these borders are becoming more penetrable than before. The area of environmental policy offers a good example of these changes. Pollution does not respect borders and increasingly, environmental policy is becoming internationalised, particularly at the EU level. Furthermore, changes are also taking place at the sub-national level. In recognition of the shared nature of both their environmental and economic problems and the necessity to develop common solutions to them, a number of border regions within the EU have set up transfrontier networks. These exist in both developed as well as under-developed, peripheral regions of the EU and are sponsored by the EU. This chapter focuses on border regions to examine the extent to which the internationalisation of environmental policy has strengthened the policy-making role of the EU and regional interests at the expense of national sovereignty. The chapter is divided into five sections. The first section deals with the growing importance of environmental issues in the EU's policy agenda. Following this, section two considers the way in which internal and external border regions reveal the spectrum of environmental problems facing the EU. Section three outlines the advantages of cross-border co-operation for environmental policy management and some of the barriers to such co-operation. The fourth section assesses the specific EU policy initiatives dealing with the environment, especially those contained within INTERREG, an initiative specifically aimed at encouraging co-operation between border regions within the Single European Market. The chapter concludes by underlining how national borders hinder the development of a coherent environmental policy and how emergent transnational networks impinge on the sovereignty of national states.

The internationalisation of environmental policy and the role of the EU

The Treaty of Rome which established the European Economic Community (EEC) made no mention of environmental protection. Community environmental policy began after the 1972 Paris Summit when it was agreed that economic expansion should also result in "an improvement in the quality of life" (Commission of the European Communities 1986). The ratification of the 1987 Single European Act gave legal recognition to the Community's increased involvement in this policy area, and, under the provisions of the Maastricht Treaty, this involvement has deepened. A number of factors have placed the issue of environmental protection higher on the policy agenda within the EU. In particular, throughout the 1980s, the scale and nature of pollution problems, especially at the international and global levels, became increasingly obvious. One of the lessons learned by the international community in the face of the Chernobyl disaster, global warming, and ozone depletion was that environmental pollution does not respect artificially constructed political and administrative borders. As a consequence, the nation-state was called into question as the most appropriate level for dealing with environmental problems (Weale 1992: 28). It was within the context of the internationalisation of environmental considerations that the EC saw itself as having an important role (Baker 1993a).[1]

The rationale for the increased role of the EU has subsequently widened. By the end of the 1980s and the beginning of the 1990s policy makers had become increasingly aware that the traditional fragmented single-medium responses to environmental degradation, that is, having separate policies to deal with water, air, and land, are also inadequate. The new calls for dealing with "pollution in the round", that is, taking account of the impact of a particular pollution abatement policy on all media, both at the domestic and transnational levels, continued to draw attention away from the nation-state level to international co-operation as the more appropriate levels for dealing with environmental protection. This internationalisation was welcomed by many of Europe's largest firms, especially the so-called 'ecologically modernised" companies. These companies prefer trans-European environmental co-operation leading to the adoption of common procedures, co-ordinated policies and uniform standards as opposed to the fragmentation of the market that can arise from uncoordinated, multiple environmental regulatory activities by numerous nation-states (Majone 1991:26). Increased transnational and cross-border co-operation was also seen as advantageous by environmental groups and other non-governmental organisation concerned with environmental protection.

Thus the last decades of the twentieth century have witnessed the adoption of an expanding EU role in the protection of the natural environment, although the EU has not necessarily confined itself to issues of an international dimension. The increase in policy making at the EU level has substantially reduced the role played by the member-states in shaping responses to global environmental problems. At the same time the EU has been making increased in-roads into shaping member-state domestic environmental policy, as reflected in the substantial body of policy that has now been developed, based largely upon the passage of over 200 separate pieces of environmental legislative, mainly in the form of Directives. Despite this flurry of environmental protection activity, however, the environmental policy of the EU is not above criticism, in particular in relation to the its inability to reconcile its historical commitment to ensuring economic growth with its new concern for protection of the environment (Baker 1993a). This reconciliation is made all the more difficult in the face of the completion of the internal market.

Care must be taken, however, not to overestimate the significance of the internationalisation of environmental policy, lest it should appear that the nation-state has ceased to play a role in shaping responses to environmental degradation. The reason for such caution becomes clear when we focus attention not so much on the global level but on the maintenance of environmental quality at the transnational level. Nature does not always fit comfortably with man-made structures and it is rare for the ecological features of a region to coincide with the administrative and political arrangements of that region. More often than not the ecological features specific to a region straddle more than one political and administrative boundary. This is particularly noticeable in water courses, but also in areas with mountain ranges. Despite the realisation that artificial, human-made political and administrative borders are no barrier to the spread of environmental pollution, borders continue to act as important variables shaping the success of policy designed to address environmental degradation. A good example is provided by the various transnational attempts to co-operate in maintaining adequate environmental quality in river and water basins, such as in the Mediterranean. Such attempts at international co-operation have been hampered by the mismatch between the boundaries of the natural ecosystem and those delineated by the political systems, legislative acts and administrative structures of the many nation-states concerned. The sharing of common ecological features across different administrative and political structures has an important implication for EU policy formulation and, especially, implementation. Furthermore, it also affects one of the original and guiding principles of EU environmental policy, namely the "polluter pays principle" (Baker 1993a). The application of this principle runs up against the problem of frontiers and the related difficulties of ensuring accountability and

21

compensation across different states. However, despite these handicaps, cross-border co-operation in the field of environmental policy is growing and is receiving increased support from the EU. One of the purposes of this chapter is to examine whether this new co-operation at the transnational, particularly cross-border level, is leading to a reduction of the significance of the nation-state in shaping environmental policy. I begin to address this, first, by looking in more detail at the interrelationship between environmental issues and the internal and external border regions of the EU.

The environment and border regions of the EU: Complexity of type

EU internal border regions

Prior to the recent enlargement of the EU in 1995 to include Sweden, Austria and Finland, the EU had almost 10,000 km of land frontier, and borders between member-states accounted for some 60 per cent of this. Approximately 10 per cent of the population of the EU lived in border regions. After this enlargement the importance of border regions has grown considerably. Border regions share a major common feature: they suffer from the juxtaposition of different legal and administrative systems. In many cases these handicaps have been reinforced by poor cross-border communications, a lack of co-ordination in public services, and differences in culture and language (Commission of the European Communities n.d: 1). Despite this similarity, however, border regions vary greatly in terms of population density and levels of economic development (Duport 1994:88).

Peripheral regions, for example, tend to have lower levels of income per head and higher rates of unemployment than other regions, and their peripheral situation has distanced them from the main centres of economic activity and political decision-making. For purposes of environmental contrast, the EU's internal border regions can be divided into two broad types: the first may be termed developed border regions, as is for example found in the regions straddling the Dutch, German and Belgium borders. The second type relates to underdeveloped, or peripheral border regions, such as is found in the border areas between the North and South of Ireland, Portugal and Spain. The environmental problems of these types of border regions may be compared along a number of dimensions:

Ecological vulnerability Unlike the developed regions, it is the geographically peripheral regions of Europe that are chiefly noted for their relatively undisturbed natural areas and habitats. Many of these areas are of international significance ecologically. Yet precisely because these regions have low population density they are often the sites chosen for particularly controversial development projects, such as nuclear power stations and large chemical

22

plants. Low population density combined with weak political influence, for example, helps to explain the fact that most of the member-states of the EU have sited their nuclear power plants in peripheral border regions (Poetschki 1986: 5). Neighbouring states then import the environmental pollution.

Furthermore, it can be argued that because these regions are poor and therefore have to make careful choices concerning budgetary expenditures, the opportunity cost of conservation and environmental protection policies are higher than in developed regions. In other words, money spent on these programmes results in less money being available for other programmes which are perceived to bring more tangible economic results. Despite the incorporation of the philosophy of sustainable development into much of EU environmental rhetoric, many in the rural underdeveloped periphery perceive conservation and environmental protection as offering little tangible economic benefit (Baker et al. 1994). The European Commission's Task Force has argued that further to this, the benefits of conservation are seen as accruing to the Union as a whole, while the costs are borne mainly by the poorer regions or member-states (Task Force 1989: 4.5).

Pressure on the environment The deepening of the integration process and the globalisation of national economies is bringing with it new challenges to both developed and peripheral regions of Europe. In developed regions market forces are strong and there is substantial pressure for development. The region with the greatest pressure for development spreads in a curved shape from Northern Italy, through Germany and the Low Countries, into the British Midlands, the so-called "hot banana". In this region the greatest concentration of population exists, along with the biggest pressures for development and investment. These pressures are expected to intensify through the completion of the internal market. Within the growth zone there are both urban and rural areas where there is pressure for land release for new development. Here many environmental problems are concentrated, including traffic congestion, crowded cities, high population densities and water shortages, coupled with the demand for more airports and other transport infrastructure (Baker et al. 1995).

As the completion of the internal market gathers pace there is also increased pressure within the peripheral regions for a development policy that will enable these areas to "catch-up" with the more prosperous centre, to provide employment, reduce outward migration and increase living standards (Baker 1993b). For example, one of the consequences of the completion of the Single Market is increased expenditure in the regions. The enlargement and reform of the Structural Funds (Regional Fund, Social Fund and the Guidance Section of the Common Agricultural Fund), including the 1994 changes, are of particular importance. As will be seen below, there is evidence to suggest that sufficient safeguards have not been built into the application of the Structural Funds to allow for adequate protection of the environment (Baker 1993b).

23

Types of environmental problems Developed border regions typically have pollution problems stemming from industrialisation and high population density, bringing with them problems associated with air and water quality control. Under-developed regions, on the other hand, typically have environmental problems relating to agricultural practices and land-use patterns, frequently affecting soil quality and water more directly than air quality. For example, grazing of sheep, on poor quality land can lead to intensification of soil erosion. Similarly, drainage schemes, introduced in order to bring marginal lands into production, can destroy important wet-land habitats. In the context of the completion of the internal market, economic development plans for these peripheral regions often add to the environmental problems they experience, as they can include inappropriate tourism, fisheries and forestry development (Task Force 1989: 3.21).

As far as environmental policy is concerned, therefore, different types of regions, while acknowledging that they share many environmental problems in common, typically require different priorities in environmental policy formulation.

Environmental protection policy The environmental policy area attracts a diverse range of interests and requires reconciliation of economic, political, scientific, as well as public health considerations. In under-developed regions the difficulties surrounding the reconciliation of economic and environmental policy can be keenly experienced. It particular, it is here that a sharp trade-off can be felt between the need for economic growth on the one hand and the protection of flora and fauna on the other (Yearley et al. 1994).

In contrast, developed regions may have already gone some way towards reconciliation of environmental and economic needs. The Dutch case provides the most striking example, and can be seen in the adoption of the National Environmental Policy Plan. This Plan is based around the belief that environmental protection is best achieved through a partnership between government, industry and the consumer (Weale 1992: 133). In this context, however, a paradox can develop: while, on the one hand, governments can be favourably disposed, often directly encouraging, the integration of environmental considerations into all policy arcas, the intervention of the EU into the environmental policy arena can also give rise to difficulties. Vested economic interests, including existing policy networks, as well as established patterns of policy intervention can be disrupted by the new environmental imperative of the Union. EU involvement in environmental policy can then begin to be seen as undue outside intervention in a policy area already adequately regulated which, some would say, provides better protection for the environment than that available under EU Directives. This is a criticism often made by the Dutch.

Resource base differences The ability of a region to ensure the maintenance of environmental quality standards through effective implementation of environmental policy is affected by a number of factors. Included in these are administrative capacity, financial resources, the availability of necessary scientific and technical skill and the presence of appropriate institutional structures (Yearley et al. 1994). Meeting these administrative and financial requirements is easier for developed than for underdeveloped, peripheral regions. By virtue of their peripheral status, peripheral regions often suffer from institutional fragmentation and lack the administrative capacity to introduce and enforce environmental standards and often have inadequate resources to remedy these difficulties (Baker et al. 1994). Therefore as far as environmental protection is concerned, peripheral regions can be highly disadvantaged. Lately, these difficulties have been recognised by the EU and reflected in the establishment of the Cohesion Fund.

In short, the regionalised dimension to EU environmental policy is lacking in both developed and peripheral regions of the EU. A regionalised environmental policy is one that arises from consultation with a policy community that includes regional interests, where policy addresses the economic as well as social needs of the region and where the choice of policy instruments and implementation schedules take account of the administrative and infrastructural implementation capacity of Europe's regions.

The EU's external borders

External borders refer to frontiers between the Union and non-EU countries. Concerning peripheral external border regions, three main categories can be identified:

1. regions bordering EFTA countries, some of which have joined the Union;
2. regions bordering Eastern and Central Europe;
3. regions on the Union's southern frontiers, including Turkey and North Africa.

Since 1989 and the break-up of the East-bloc, the frontier regions between the Union and East and Central Europe have taken on a new significance. Here environmental issues are of particular relevance, especially as the full extent of the environmental degradation of these regions has been revealed. Such degradation can effect the Union directly, as in the case of the pollution of shared water-ways, the flow of air pollution and, of course, the spread of nuclear contamination. As far as the EU is concerned its external borders with East and Central Europe typically present it with problems relating to transfrontier pollution effects, especially relating to air and water quality, although the countries themselves suffer an array of pollution problems relating to all aspects of economic activity. The existence of transboundary

25

environmental effects is one of the main contributing factors in the development of EU environmental policy initiatives in East and Central Europe. For example, through the auspices of the PHARE Programme, the Union is currently involved in shaping East and Central European environmental policy and sponsoring projects such as the clean-up of the Danube River basin. Not all of this activity is, of course, purely for environmental reasons, there also being economic arguments underlying EU intervention, such as facilitating the opening of East and Central European economies to trade and inward investment (Baker 1995a).

At first EU involvement in environmental protection policy in East and Central Europe was somewhat ad hoc. However, this involvement has steadily deepened (Baker 1995a). This is significant, especially in terms of trying to understand the changing role of nation-states, including its role in shaping policy. Firstly, despite the claim that the completion of the internal market will lead to the development of "fortress Europe", recent events in East and Central Europe have pointed to the vulnerability of the EU's external borders. As far as the spread of environmental pollutants are concerned, these borders are open, a fact acknowledged by the EU. Secondly, given this openness, environmental policy-making can no longer be confined to neat administrative and political boundaries and the targets of policy have to straddle the external borders of the EU if environmental quality management is to be effectively achieved within member-states of the Union and within the Union as a whole. Thirdly, policy implementation has to be effectively achieved by non-EU states to ensure the maintenance of environmental standards within the EU itself. The delineation of boundaries of policy, especially of implementation zones, is less clearly defined by political and administrative structures than has hitherto been thought to be the case.

Not all of the increased EU involvement in East and Central Europe has been welcomed. There is a fear that this involvement will be at the expense of funding developments within the Union. The Arc Atlantique has, for example, been formed, at least in part as a consequence of this concern (Commission of the European Communities 1993a: 19).

Cross-border environmental policy initiatives: The rationale

In general the Commission sees interregional co-operation as a means of achieving the Union's cohesion objectives (Millan 1994:21). It is also seen as a means of counteracting the negative effects on the regions of globalisation of economies (Kopp et al. 1994: 66). A further rationale for cross-border co-operation has been the Commission's belief that the European integration process had become too remote from ordinary people. The Commission sees the concept of subsidiarity as an important weapon in combating this tendency, the commitment to which was reinforced at the Edinburgh Summit. Cross-border initiatives, they argue, including INTERREG, enable the principle of subsidiarity to be put into practice. Thus the Commission concludes that local agents who co-operate across borders are contributing to the integration process in dismantling internal frontiers and in many cases are reviving historical ties. In INTERREG this is often done through spontaneous actions at grass roots level characterised as "bottom-up rather than top-down" approaches (Commission of the European Communities 1993a: 9).

As far as making the EU appear more relevant to the peoples of Europe, cross-border co-operation in the environmental field is particularly useful. This is because environmental issues receive high media profiling, have mobilised a profusion of groups and interests and environmental protection measures are, by and large, positively received at the local and regional levels. However, the task of environmental protection is made all the more difficult by the mismatch between the political and administrative divisions of the region and its ecological features. With the heightened commitment to environmental protection now prevalent within member-states it makes a great deal of administrative as well financial sense for regions to co-operate in the development as well as the implementation of environmental protection policy. This basis for co-operation is further strengthened by the requirement laid down in both the EU Fifth Environmental Action Programme Towards Sustainability and in the Maastricht Treaty, that environmental considerations be incorporated into other policy areas. This means that environmental considerations have to be integrated into the design, formulation and implementation of all EU policies, including regional policy and the Structural Funds, and across five key sectors, namely agriculture, industry, energy, transport and tourism (Baker 1995b). As a consequence the release of funding for cross-border projects has become, at least in principle, contingent upon sounder environmental management practice.

Ensuring effective environmental management is also seen by the Commission, and increasingly by economic interests, as making sound economic sense. There are a number of reasons for this. First, environmental protection is seen as a way of protecting the resource base upon which future production is dependent. For example, the maintenance of a clean supply of water is seen as essential because water is often vital in the production process. Second, as environmental regulations are tightened and environmental groups increasingly act as watch dogs of the implementation process, government at both the national and local levels, as well as industry face escalating costs in cleaning-up environmental pollution. It is now recognised that preventive measures make greater economic sense. Third, environmental protection is seen as a source in itself of profitable business. Pollution abatement and clean-up technology is much in demand and the Commission believes that through its involvement in environmental protection management it can encourage the development of an eco-industry within Europe. The added advantage of this is that such technology can be exported, especially to East and Central Europe.

Border regions are particularly well placed to take advantage of this, because the development of effective mechanisms and practices aimed at stemming transboundary pollution control is one of the key environmental issues currently on the EU policy agenda (Baker 1995c).

Advantages of co-operation

Existing co-operation between local authorities in frontier regions is grounded on the perception that it brings mutual advantage. Many problems of border regions have accumulated in the past as a result, for example, of the strong national orientation of policies. Instigating cross-border projects can help to shift resources away from policies designed to meet national needs and move them towards those that reflect the needs and interests of the region, including cross-border regions.

Pooling access to technical expertise is a key advantage of co-operation. Given the rapid increase in the volume of policies aimed at environmental protection and that such policies largely involve new, costly, and often highly complex procedures, both developed and underdeveloped regions can gain considerable advantage from pooling resources, skills and expertise with neighbouring regions. For the peripheral region this pooling brings added benefits. In trying to match managerial and financial resources with ecological needs the peripheral border region typically finds itself with administrative incapacities, including inadequate and untrained staff and insufficient or inadequate facilities. Further, many of the basic facilities for data collection and processing are often lacking. For example, it is well known in Ireland that County Councils and other Local Authorities often depend upon firms to undertake their air and water pollution monitoring and that local authorities very often lack adequate skilled personnel to enable them to fully implement EU environmental policy (Coyle 1994).

In peripheral regions, the physical infrastructure needed for compliance with many of the new EU environmental directives is often missing or inadequate. Furthermore, almost by definition, infrastructure is less well developed in the peripheral regions. For example 80% of municipalities in Spain are without sewage plants and in Southern Italy 66% of existing sewage treatment plants do not function (Commission of the European Communities 1990a: 27). Facilities for safe disposal of waste may also be lacking in regions. The pooling of resources across regions can increase access to much needed infrastructure.

Furthermore, as the Task Force has pointed out, many regional underdeveloped economies do not have a strong domestic "eco-industry" so that skills and equipment have to be imported into the regions. As a consequence "meeting environmental responsibilities has the effect that economic activity is transferred from poorer to the richer regions" (Task Force 1989: 4.16). Cross-border co-operation could help in many instances to weaken the spread of this outward flow, containing benefits within a more geographically localised area.

The opposite can be argued for co-operation in developed regions, in particular if those regions are situated within member-states that already have achieved some measure of ecological modernisation: here co-operation, achieved either at the level of the firm or between administrators, can help strengthen an already developed eco-industry, enabling it to develop further its product line or its administrative skills and expertise. It is not difficult to find examples of this type of co-operation. Regions such as Catalonia, Nord-Pas de Calais and North Rhine-Westphalia have long ago realised that in order to compete effectively in the Single European Market is it not enough to rely on the industrial and regional policies of their various central governments. According to O'Sullivan and Lenehan (n.d.: 7) they:

> also need to co-ordinate, direct and market their own resources. These regions have been able to develop successful development plans through their ability to achieve a 'critical mass' - the necessary scale of economic activity governed by new forms of proactive institutional and political management.

However, despite the obvious advantages to all regions of engaging in cross-border co-operation in the environmental field, such co-operation is not without its problems and a number of difficulties have to be overcome if administrative authorities, especially at the regional and local levels, are to engage in successful transfrontier environmental co-operation.

Obstacles to co-operation

Institutional barriers While instigating cross-border projects can help shift the orientation of national policies, the lack of interregional institutional structures makes the establishment of and subsequent administration of cross-border co-operation plans difficult. Furthermore, existing administrative structures on either side of a border may not always be flexible enough to facilitate effective cross-border co-operation. This is often due to the fact that these structures are orientated towards the national administration, especially in terms of command structures, control over resource allocation and are dependent upon central administration to meet funding requirements.

Legal difficulties Cross-border co-operation between local or regional actors, other than that initiated at the nation-state level, usually takes place within the context of legal and institutional restrictions. These restrictions have their origins in the existence of distinct nation-states and the differences between systems of national law, which in effect means that as far as the state is concerned:

Within its frontiers it holds sovereign sway over the legal situation and relations both of individuals and of public bodies and authorities. The geographical region through which a frontier passes is thus subject to two or more fundamentally different legal regimes communicating with each other only via the channels of international law (Council of Europe 1973: 1).

In legal terms, the biggest problem in creating an organisational framework for cross-border co-operation is that it has not been possible to create a legal status which is valid on both sides of the border. This is because:

Normally, legal personality can derive only from one body of law. This is what is meant by the 'loi unique' principle, which applied to legal forms governed by both public and private law. This implies that co-operation - even with participation by members from different Member-States - can be assessed only within the framework of one legal system (Gabbe et al. n.d: 4).

Another legal difficulty is posed by the principle of territorial jurisdiction. This implies the rejection of the use of judicial and legislative powers on foreign soil (Gabbe et al. n.d: 4). There are also differences with respect to the jurisdiction of governmental authorities, especially the division of competencies and authority between local, regional and national authorities. In the context of local and regional authorities becoming involved in cross-border co-operation, these differences can give rise to compatibility problems. The lack of an appropriate legal framework has resulted in problems associated with lack of harmonisation of tax, employment and social regulations, the lack of recognition of diplomas and the absence of legal recognition of the regions making financial accountability difficult to institute.

The obstacles resulting from the disparities between administrative competencies in the various regions has been the subject of debate within the EU. Some resolution of this difficulty has been achieved and since 1992 regional and local authorities have won some right to conclude agreements with their European border regions and set up cross-border joint ventures and syndicates (LACE 1993a:1). Some countries have already begun to address the problems hindering interregional co-operation. The Netherlands and Germany have for example, bilaterally formulated the Anholt Treaty creating a legal basis and granting legal responsibility to regional transfrontier co-operation (Commission of the European Communities 1993a: 11). There has also been a tendency, especially in France, to create cross-border associations based on private law.

Problems with administrative autonomy Legal difficulties, however, are not the only problems encountered in cross-border co-operation. Administratively, local authorities often lack autonomy, particularly financial autonomy and are normally dependent upon central government for funding. While the extent of centralisation differs across different state traditions, nevertheless, all local authorities are supervised to some degree by a higher authority and must abide by the rules and procedures it lays down. Cross-border initiatives within this context normally require the co-operation and approval of central government. Increasingly, however, calls for greater flexibility and the adjustment of specific national structures to facilitate cross-border co-operation at the local and regional levels have been heard (LACE 1993a: 2). A further problem arises in that the time frame used for planning purposes may differ across the regions and this may have implications for project development as well as resourcing.

However, to point only to the difficulties encountered in cross-border co-operation is to ignore the unique contribution that local authorities can make to the development of common policies aimed at dealing with problems specific to a locality. This co-operation can help to counteract the tendency of national policies mainly to benefit the developed centre at the expense of border regions, in economic terms, in the allocation of infrastructure and in the priority given to local environmental protection projects. Furthermore, the local authority is more in touch with the specific interests of its local population, knows more clearly the ecological features of its region and is able to identify more readily its ecological vulnerability in the face of development threats. In the context of environmental policy, cross-border co-operation offers local authorities the possibility of pooling resources and for example, exploiting technological and scientific developments, which are key requirements in modern pollution abatement procedures. Local level, bottom-up input into environmental policy is an essential imperative of sustainable development policy, especially as the successful realisation of sustainability requires integration of environmental considerations into all policy fields. This development is actively encouraged by the EU. The European Commission, in particular, is keen to see the development of inter-regional co-operation as it can make, according to Bruce Millan "a substantial contribution to the process of European integration" (Millan 1991). In particular he argues that, within the context of the Maastricht Treaty and the Conference on Political Union, the EU can now legitimately strengthen its partnership with the regions and allow the voice of the regions to be increasingly heard at Union level (Millan 1991).

A good example of this new co-operation is to be found in recent basin-wide projects for the ecological management of large rivers. In Europe most large rivers have a cross-border character and, historically, basin wide co-operation has been hampered by differences in legislation, governmental organisation and culture between riparian states. Thus it became increasingly obvious that ecological and economic management required the establishment of river basin authorities to which the riparian states assign a certain power. This has occurred in the Rhine, with the establishment of the International Rhine Commission. On other occasions, co-operation has occurred at the regional or local level, an example of which is the new programme of co-operation in the River Scheldt (Smit 1993: 2).

EU policy initiatives

While the EU has played an increased role in shaping international environmental policy, nevertheless it has shown itself to be slow in addressing the environmental policy needs of its own border regions. Furthermore, it has been slow to adequately integrate environmental considerations into its existing regional development polices. EU region policies, in particular the Structural Funds, are an important source of pressure on the environment, especially in peripheral regions. As will be discussed in greater detail below, the failure of the EU to recognise this led them to be subject to severe criticism in a Court of Auditors Report in 1992 (Court of Auditors 1992).

It was not until 1991 that the Union began addressing the issue of environmental management in border regions. The encouragement and sponsorship of cross-border initiatives was not confined to environmental protection policy and thus must be seen in the context of wider development. Prior to addressing issues relating to environmental management, areas such as Catalonia, Nord-Pas de Calais and North Rhine-Westphalia had already been engaged in EU-backed economic co-operation measures for some time. The concept of a regional Europe had also been seen by many within the Commission as an important next stage in the deepening of the integration process. Furthermore, this new emphasis in the integration process had been coupled with the mobilisation of institutional actors in many regions across Europe and the institutionalisation of regional interests at the EU level, including the establishment of a Committee of the Regions (Loughlin 1994).

There are a number of EU initiatives in border regions. Chief among these initiatives are the Observatory, LACE and INTERREG initiatives. The Observatory initiative is run jointly with the Association of European Border Regions (AEBR), an organisation founded in 1971, which brings together over fifty four border areas grouped into thirty four organisations. The aim of LACE is to provide technical assistance for cross-border projects. The second initiative, LACE, is primarily aimed at exchanging information and expertise and the provision of technical advice and assistance. This is also an EU pilot project conducted jointly by the EU and the AEBR. Of the three initiatives, however, it is INTERREG that is of most importance. It receives greater funding from the Structural Funds and has wider aims and goals. INTERREG is project-orientated and its principal aim is to help border areas prepare for the completion of the Single Market within the overall Union commitment to achieving social and economic cohesion. As the Commission itself has stated:

This is to be achieved . . . through the promotion of closer co-operation between regions on opposite sides of national borders and through the revitalisation of the economies of areas on the Community's external borders (Commission of the European Communities 1991a).

It was the intention of the Union that this initiative be implemented with the active participation of the relevant regional and municipal authorities, who argued that "the regional and local authorities must play a major role in the planning and implementation of the programmes" (Commission of the European Community 1990b: 3). Here the principle of partnership is key, especially that involving regional and local levels of government (Millan 1992b: 1). According to Mazey and Richardson, the principle of partnership has acted as a key way in which regional and local authorities have been drawn into the policy process (Mazey and Richardson 1994). This in turn strengthens their links with and subsequent commitment to the integration process. The Commission also stressed that this initiative is unique among EU programmes, in that the budget has been allocated not by individual member-states but by border regions. The hope was that this would "establish and strengthen cross-border partnerships between national, regional and local authorities" (Commission of the European communities n.d.: 2). Similarly, it was planned that through the INTERREG initiative another current aim of the Commission, that of achieving cohesion, would be realised. Specifically, it hoped that the INTERREG initiative could contribute to the achievement of cohesion by helping these regions to overcome the problems arising from their peripheralisation; promoting the development of networks of co-operation on both sides of the internal borders; establishing links between these networks and wider EU networks; preparing external border areas for their roles in the integrated market, and by exploring the possibilities for co-operation with countries outside the EU (Commission of the European Communities 1990b:1).

INTERREG 1, the first of the initiatives, was applied in the main to all regions covered by Objective 1, (regions whose development is lagging behind), Objective 2 (industrial conversion) and Objective 5b (rural development) and supported projects aimed at encouraging cross-border co-operation and development in these regions. By the end of 1993, the EU had contributed ECU 1,034m from the Structural Funds to this initiative, under a scheme of member-state co-financing. The three key objectives of INTERREG 1 were:

* to help develop the internal border regions of the Community and to tackle the problems of economic under-development associated with their border status, especially with the transition to the Single market;

* to encourage cross-border co-operative actions between the internal border regions;

* to prepare the external border regions of the Community for their new role at the edge of the Single Market (Commission of the European Communities 1993a: 7-8).

In establishing this initiative it was envisaged that three types of co-operative measures could be established between participating border-regions:

(1) joint implementation of cross border programmes;
(2) measures to improve relations between public institutions, private organisations and voluntary bodies in border areas;
(3) setting-up of shared institutional structures (Commission of the European Communities 1990b: 2).

The Commission believed that the institutionalisation of cross border relations was a prime method through which cross border co-operation could be strengthened. At the same time they believed that such co-operation had the potential to create alternative jobs in responses to changes in border related activities, thus relieving these regions of some of the pressures that they are experiencing in the face of the completion of the internal market.

Thus it is clear that the INTERREG initiative was not primarily designed as an environmental protection initiative. However, it does include such a dimension and when INTERREG 1 was launched the Commission stated that all the specific measures funded under INTERREG "must comply with the protection of the environment" (Commission of the European Community 1990b: 2). Furthermore in setting up the initiative, the Commission envisaged that INTERREG would directly fund environmental measures aimed at pollution prevention and control, conservation as well as more general environmental protection measures.

In February 1994 the Commission agreed its overall approach on Union initiatives for the period 1994-99. This involved a revision of the Structural Funds, designed to take account of the new social policy priorities and the guidelines for economic and employment cohesion which formed part of the Maastricht Treaty (Commission of the European Community 1993b: 1). As part of these changes, the Commission launched INTERREG II with an overall budget allocation of 2900m ECU.

Due to increased flexibility brought about by the changes in the Structural Funds regulations, all the internal and external land borders of the Union became eligible for support under INTERREG II. To this was added a limited number of maritime borders which have been added to the eligibility criteria (Commission of the European Community 1994: 1). The maritime borders between Greece and Southern Italy and those between Ireland and Wales have

34

been included in this, the latter because Ireland has no land link with the Union. In addition, external land-frontier areas are an important new element is the PHARE budget, the EU programme designed to aid the transition to market economy and participatory democracy in the former Eastern bloc. Under the new changes, 150m ECU will be allocated under the PHARE programme to aid cross-border co-operation with former East-bloc regions bordering on member-states (Commission of the European Community 1994: 1). This will in turn require greater co-ordination between existing EU initiatives, in particular between INTERREG and PHARE, and forms part of continuing Commission efforts to ensure more efficient EU responses to the problems arising as a result of the collapse of the communist states of Eastern and Central Europe. Other changes follow from persistent criticism, including acknowledgement by the EU Commissioner Bruce Millan that "effective participation by regional and local authorities in the design and management of cross-border programmes has not always been evident" (Millan 1994: 21). INTERREG II places strong emphasis on bottom-up involvement in cross-border projects. The Commission has insisted that:

> The participation of regional and local authorities and other local partners, including those representing small and medium-sized businesses, in devising and implementing such measures is clearly very important for their success (Commission of the European Communities 1994:2).

Furthermore, in an effort to take account of the new social priorities of the Union, INTERREG II allows for a wider choice of eligible measures than did INTERREG I. These now include, for example, education, health, spatial planning and measures complementary to Trans-European Networks. The inclusion of spatial planning in INTERREG II reflects the growing involvement of the Union in shaping land-use patterns and policies as a means of environmental management. However, the inclusion of measures complementary to Trans-European networks presents a rather contradictory message, in that the construction of these Networks has been heavily criticised on environmental grounds (Baker 1995b). However, the Commission believes that the new cross-border projects that will be funded under INTERREG II will be more environmentally friendly than they have previously been. This is due to the incorporation of the principles and goals of sustainable development into the 1993 revisions of the Structural Funds. In the past, the primary aim of the Funds was to bring about economic and social development and environmental expenditure was entirely subordinate to this goal (Yuill et al. 1994: 82). In the revised regulations member-states are required to conduct an appraisal of the state of the environment and the environmental impact of the operations envisaged in terms of sustainable development, together with the steps taken to associate their environmental authorities with the preparation and implementation of plans (Yuill et al. 1994:83). Strengthening this resolve is the new Cohesion Fund, intended to aid projects in the fields of transport and the environment in Greece, Ireland, Portugal and Spain.

Operationalisation of INTERREG: Cross-border environmental projects

Much of the basis for cross-border environmental co-operation was already established through projects that pre-date the INTERREG initiatives. Included in these were plans for the establishment of a German/Belgium nature reserve as well as the opening up of "green frontiers", protection of surface waters and projects for dealing with air pollution problems in the Maas-Rhine Euro-Region (Von Malchus 1992: 6-7). The cross-border co-operation in the Maas-Rhine Euro-Region began in 1976. The establishment by the EU of the INTERREG initiatives have not only helped in the provision of further funding for this and other projects but has also institutionalised and therefore legitimated this co-operation. Thus, following the launch of INTERREG I, a basic cross-border ecological plan was drawn up in 1991/92 in the Maas-Rhine Euro-Region leading to the establishment of an action programme and a series of projects. Between 1991-93, 37% of the 20.3 million ECU allocated to it was spent on "environmental protection and farming" (1991 values). In the Rhine-Maas-North Border Region an even smaller percentage of EU assistance was allocated to environmental protection and farming (18%) during the same period. Nevertheless, despite this small allocation, these funds are important in that they were directed at a major source of environmental degradation in these regions, namely agriculture, and included projects in the following areas: training, water protection; clean-up of rivers and rehabilitation of nature and landscape; and waste disposal (Von Malchus 1992: 13).

Other cross-border co-operation in developed regions includes the co-operative agreement signed in 1987 between Kent County Council and the Nord-Pas de Calais Regional Council. Among the aims of this Euroregion is the protection of the natural environment of Kent, an aim which is very much orientated towards developing the tourist trade in the region (Druce 1991: 15). A similar seven point programme has also been established between the Dutch-German border regions of Rhine-Maas North, Rhine-Waal and EUREGIO, which includes environmental protection (LACE 1992a: 1). Similarly, co-operation is taking place between the Belgium and Dutch governments in the Scheldt river basin. The Scheldt is one of the most intensely used river systems in the world and economic returns from industry, tourism, livestock rearing and arable farming in the Scheldt basin is on a par with much larger river basins like the Yangtze and the Nile. However, through this high level of economic activity the Scheldt's ecosystem became so badly damaged that the very basis of economic development in the basin was threatened (Dutch Ministry of Transport and Public Works & Ministry of the Flemish Community 1992: 3). In 1992, the Dutch and Belgium governments signed a management agreement for the Western Scheldt Plan and the regional authorities are also involved in an INTERREG sponsored pollution reduction programme for the river (Smit 1993:3).

The INTERREG initiative has also funded a study of environmental measures in the German-French border region "PAMINA" (Commission of the European Communities 1992a); the frontier region between France and Italy (Commission of the European Communities 1992b) as well as the development of an environmental management programme in the border areas between Belgium and the Netherlands (Commission of the European Communities 1991a).

A similar range of projects has been funded in peripheral regions. This includes the funding of a joint environmental protection project in the Pyrenees. Cross-border co-operation between Spain and Portugal has also received EU funding, only part of which, however, is concerned with environmental protection measures. This includes programmes such as CORINE, the protection of natural areas and the border areas between Algarve and Andalusia. However, much of its emphasis is on the development of road networks and of regional tourism (LACE 1992c: 2; LACE 1993b: 1). Nevertheless, recent developments in this co-operation has led to cross-border measures to protect and develop wetland areas (LACE 1993b: 1). A similar and somewhat contradictory emphasis is also found in recent cross-border co-operation in Ireland. The North-South Ireland programme was approved by the Commission in 1991 and the environmental protection element of the programme focuses on improving and protecting water quality in cross-border areas on the grounds that "the extensive network of rivers, lakes and canals in this region is a valuable national resource which can make an important contribution in advancing tourism, agriculture and fisheries" (Department of the Environment 1992: 11).

Other Irish projects approved include the preparation of water quality management plans for the Erne System and the catchment and estuary of Lough Foyle. According to the Dublin Department of the Environment the plans were prepared under the direction of a joint North/South working group, comprising relevant Departments and local authority representatives. Further to this, in 1992, the Irish Sea Partnership was established between Ireland and Wales, which has identified five areas as having the potential for cross-border projects, including environment and emergency planning such as pollution control and experimental action in coastal erosion (Brinkhof 1993: 2). This became eligible for funding following the inclusion of a number of maritime borders in INTERREG II. Similar co-operation is taking place between Sweden and Denmark along the Baltic sea, under a project known as "Green Migration", whose aim is to increase environmental awareness among tourists to the area and to deal with its growing problem of chemical waste (LACE 1993b: 3).

Increasingly, cross-border co-operation is also taking place along the external frontier of the EU. The areas seeing the most well developed co-operation is along the German-Polish-Czech borders, institutionalised through the Friendship Treaties that have been signed by these three countries. Much of the development is, however, taking place around meeting the infrastructural, in particular the transport, needs of the region. Nevertheless, dealing with the negative environmental legacy of the former regime has also been a pressing task (LACE 1992b: 3), especially as many of these countries have signed Associate Agreements with the EU and seek EU membership. This co-operation is taking place at the state and regional levels and include that established in March 1991 between the state government of Mecklenburg - Western Pomeranian and the *voivodership* of Szczecin, which is included the development of a regional environmental protection policy. Similarly, in the area of Frankfurt on Oder environmental improvement, specifically cleaning the waters of the Oder, is planned on the basis of cross-border co-operation. Many other such examples along the Polish border are also planned and along the "tri-state area" between the three countries, including energy provision, tourist and transport development and environmental protection (Von Malchus 1991: 6).

Not all such co-operation has been welcomed by central governments. Cross-border co-operation along the German-Dutch border initially met with constitutional and budgetary objections from the Dutch and German Ministers of Trade and Industry, with regard to the direct payment of financial assistance by the EU to beneficiaries. This issue was only resolved following laborious and intensive negotiations. This resulted in an agreement that, among other stipulations, cross-border measures under INTERREG would be decided in each region by a steering committee which, as well as including local and regions interests, would also have representatives of the Ministers. This compromise, however, was to result in delays in implementation as well as approval procedures (Von Malchus 1992: 18-19). Later, however, the German Land and Dutch Government signed the Anholt Treaty creating a legal basis and granting legal responsibility to regional cross-border co-operation. This is unique in Europe and it is uncertain whether it will be repeated, even between Holland and Germany. Another problem arose in relation to co-operation with former East-bloc countries. In November 1978 "Alps-Adria", the Association of Border Regions of the Central and Eastern Alps and the Northern Adriatic was established. This co-operation involves members from former east-bloc countries. However, in some cases national governments in these newly forming democracies saw in transboundary co-operation a kind of regional foreign policy which had to be suppressed (Magagnotti 1989).

Assessment and critique of EU policy

A comprehensive assessment of the environmental dimensions of the INTERREG initiatives requires appraisal of both the general functioning and effectiveness of the INTERREG initiative as well as an examination of the specific environmental dimensions of that programme.

Functioning and effectiveness of the initiative.

The INTERREG initiatives have, in general, been well received by regional and local interests. However, they have not been above criticism. In 1992, the Commission published a consultative Green Paper and conducted a detailed analysis of its existing structural policies. The main message, subsequently endorsed at Edinburgh, was that the principles of the 1988 reform of the Structural Funds, namely, concentration, programming, partnership and additionality should be maintained in any future developments (Commission of the European Communities 1993b: 3; Loughlin 1994). Yet it is precisely these that have proved problematic in the operation of the INTERREG initiatives. The problems associated with INTERREG can be grouped under the headings of eligibility, partnership and management (Commission of the European Communities 1993a: 7-8).

Eligibility   In terms of eligibility, arriving at a proper definition of what constitutes a frontier zone has proved problematic, and in particular the question of whether or not maritime borders should be taken into account was repeatedly raised under the INTERREG I initiative, especially by Greece. This problem arises as a result of the narrow coverage of the initiative. Cross-border co-operation under INTERREG I has not extended to all border areas of the EU and, as we saw above, there were a number of particular gaps that the Commission subsequently closed (LACE 1992c: 1). Furthermore, clarity was needed as to the extent of coverage along the external borders of the EU. INTERREG I for example did not apply to the new German Länder and the extension of coverage to include cross-border initiatives with countries which are not yet members of the Union as yet remains unclear. The picture was even more vague for those states that could only envisage joining in the longer term but who already enjoy a special relationship with the EU through European Agreements, including many Central European countries. The extension of the eligibility under INTERREG II to include the new German Länder dimension to PHARE has gone some way to addressing these criticisms.

Furthermore there have been discussions as to what kind of intervention should be supported by the Union. Under INTERREG I major emphasis was placed on infrastructural projects, while there was a growing body of opinion that support should also be extended to other areas, such as social integration and health. This was later reflected in INTERREG II.

Partnership   Cross-border co-operation, especially within the context of the INTERREG initiative, has evolved from three sources. First, it has stemmed from governmental or intergovernmental decisions to seek closer co-operation between two or more border regions. A good example of this is to be found co-operation between Spain and France in the Pyrenees. mentioned earlier. A second source is that of the EU itself, and in particular the Commission, which sees cross-border co-operation as an essential component of the deepening of the integration process. These two sources can be grouped under the heading of "top-down" pressure. The third source of pressure shaping the evolution of European cross-border co-operation stems from the "bottom-up", and involve projects promoted by border regions themselves. The classic example of this co-operation is found in the EUREGIO. Thus there was substantial variation in the way that the INTERREG I initiative was run in the individual member-states of the EU. Priorities, content and the forms of institutional co-operation chosen differed widely. According to Santos (1993: 1):

> Whereas INTERREG action between Spain and Portugal, for example, and France and Italy, was mainly organised by the central authorities, co-operation between the Benelux countries and Germany fell to regional authorities on one side (Belgium and the Netherlands) and the Länder on the other (Germany), and made use of innovative financial engineering techniques (joint bank accounts etc.).

As a consequence, regional and local authorities in some areas have been critical of the domination of these co-operation programmes by central government, as indeed was the Commission itself. This has been stated clearly by Jordi Pujol, President of the Assembly of European regions:

> Interreg is an excellent Community initiative but is also necessary to change it so as to make it even more regionally-minded, more efficient, more flexible because at the moment the programmes have to be approved by the respective member states and this gives rise to difficulties that are particularly large in those member-states where, whatever the reason might be, they are rather reluctant to recognise the regional nature of the frontier areas (Pujol 1994: 86).

Furthermore, because of the weak participation of local and regional authorities there has been a tendency, particularly in Objective 1 regions, to focus on national infrastructures at the expense of regional cross-border co-operative action (Millan 1994: 22). The funding of specific central-government originating projects under the INTERREG initiative has been a source of controversy. This is seen as incompatible with the encouragement of local and regional autonomy and one of the most serious criticisms that has been made against the INTERREG I initiative concerns the lack of autonomy for border regions themselves in formulating policy and in subsequently implementing projects. This led to the Association of European Border Regions arguing that the major problem with INTERREG I was that it was managed by the member-states themselves. In its review of this initiative, LACE has argued that since in many cases there were no existing cross-border plans, development strategies and institutions, many border regions were unable to take part as partners in the preparation of INTERREG. This was the case in particular of border regions in Spain, and Portugal, Greece and France They go on to argue that:

> A particular problem of Objective 1 areas was that programmes and individual projects prepared and implemented in the border regions were largely defined by national authorities, even through the nature of the measures were intrinsically regional. In addition, supra-regional national infrastructure projects were granted top priority (LACE 1992c: 1).

In the face of such criticisms the Commission has argued that in INTERREG II the requirements to put the principle of partnership into practice are more stringent. It is believed that INTERREG II will provide future opportunities to local and regional authorities to deepen their autonomous involvement.

Management The problems associated with management are related to the difficulties in institutionalising interregional co-operation. During the first INTERREG initiative it emerged that a major obstacle to transfrontier co-operation was the lack of a clear legal framework. In their investigation of Objective 2 and 5b border areas LACE found that unexpected institutional and procedural or technical difficulties emerged which in many cases have not yet been resolved. They found that "these are primarily due to the difference in status of the regions in either side of the border. This in turn has an effect on the eligibility of measures and the level of participation" (LACE 1992c: 1). Other general criticisms concerned with management have been made. In particular, the initiative has been criticised for its excessive bureaucratic procedures.

The environmental dimension

Both the INTERREG initiatives as well as individual programmes funded under INTERREG have been subject to criticism on environmental grounds. The INTERREG initiative is financed under the Structural Funds and may be subject to the same environmental criticisms as them. Environmentalists generally believe that the type of regional development promoted by the EU's structural funds has until recently taken little account of the environment (Robins 1994: 96). In particular, environmental groups have been critical of the failure of the Union to address adequately environmental issues in its development programmes aided by the Structural Funds (Baker 1993c). The World Wide Fund for Nature, for example, critically examined structural fund expenditure in all member states. In their examination of the Irish case they were critical of:

* Centralised planning and a sectoral approach, resulting in limited local and regional input;
* the lack of adequate project appraisal procedures to ensure that only projects compatible with the sustainable use of natural resources will receive funding;
* the lack of adequate environmental monitoring (World Wide Fund for Nature 92:4).

This lack of consultation in the planning stages was found in Northern Ireland as well as in many other member-states (Borooah 1993: 13).

In 1992, a coalition of 66 environmental groups across the EU come together to press the case for reform at the European level (Robins 1994: 98). Their environmental concerns were to be echoed in a series of official reports in the early 1990s, including in the Task Force and the Court of Auditors Report. As a consequence of these pressures, the Commission expressed concern about the negative environmental impact that may arise as a result of the reform of the Structural Funds. Since then they have, for example increased seven-fold the environmental component of the Structural Funds, from 100 Million ECU per year in the years 1985-87 to 730 Million ECU per year since. Furthermore, they have placed three demands upon member-states seeking funding for projects under the Structural Funds. These demands are: that the project to be funded conform with environmental legislation; that the legislation's objectives be met where it has not yet been implemented; and that applications for funding include information about the likely environmental consequences of the project (Commission of the European Communities 1992c: 71).

However, the Commission is far from pleased about the efforts made by member-states to meet its demands (Commission of the European Communities 1992c: 71). In many ways its demands can be seen as a testing ground for the methods by which the Union ensures the integration of environmental considerations into other EU policy areas. According to the Commission's own admission "The results of the exercise have been mixed" (Commission of the European Communities 1992c: 71). Furthermore, judging by the past record of the Community in safeguarding the environment in the face of economic development pressures, for example through its Integrated Mediterranean Programme, it is unlikely that adequate environment protection will be achieved. The Task Force argues that "The manner in which environmental considerations are integrated into the Structural Funds is highly unsatisfactory" (Task Force 1989: 4.17) A look at specific projects funded under the INTERREG I initiative shows that environmental protection measures form just one small part of the projects funded. Furthermore, most cross-border areas have been funded for more than one project type, typically for tourist development, infrastructure and environmental protection measures. Thus environmental protection measures usually form part of a wider package of funding proposals. The compatibility of measures to protect the environment in the face of new development plans remains unspecified and furthermore it remains unclear how these two developments intend to be co-ordinated. However, the establishment of a new Directorate-General, DGXXII (Co-ordination of Structural Instruments) may help to ensure greater co-ordination and the further integration of environmental considerations into the allocation criteria for the Structural Funds.

INTERREG I, for example, has funded a cross-border canal linking waterway systems in Northern and Southern Ireland, which has been subject to criticism on the grounds that it disturbs bird habitats. A more general look at the projects funded under INTERREG also points to the lack of progress in integrating environmental considerations into other EU policy areas. In terms of general funding, 45% of the funds have been given to aid substantial road-building in the border regions of Spain/Portugal and Greece, while only 10% of all funding has gone to environmental protection activities (Commission of the European Communities n.d: 4). While funding levels are only one indicator of action priority, it is important to note that road building projects are among the most environmentally damaging activities that can be undertaken in peripheral areas and that, furthermore, many of the major environmental problems arising at both the Union as well as the global level arise as a result of transport, particularly road transportation, methods. By sponsoring such developments the INTERREG initiative has actually contributed to environmental degradation while at the same time providing funding for environmental quality improvement. This tension, between on the one hand, encouraging economic growth and, on the other, contributing to environmental degradation points to a contradiction that lies at the heart of EU policy (Baker 1993a).

In his analysis of the objectives of the different cross-border programmes, including INTERREG, Von Malchus has shown that when we compare the objectives under the programmes, some 30% to 50% of the goals are allocated to "integration" categories, 40% to 60% to "regional economy" and only 5% to 20% to the "environment" (Von Malchus 1992: 8). This weakness, furthermore, should be set against the background of the point mentioned above, that, as far as the Commission is concerned, the introduction of programmes targeting border regions is primarily aimed, not so much at the development of these regions per se, but at ensuring that their fuller integration into the Union can be realised through effective economic growth. To add to this, local and regional authorities by and large see cross-border co-operation as a means for bettering the economic situation of the regions, a goal that is not always compatible with the maintenance of environmental quality in these areas.

The 1994 revision of the Structural Funds included a number of new environmental features and these are generally regarded as marking an important step forward for the integration of the environment into the EU regional policy (Robins 1994:101). As a result of these reforms environmental considerations must now be incorporated into each stage of the planning cycle for the Structural Funds and an overarching commitment to the goal of sustainable development is contained in the preamble to the framework regulations. Member States, for example, are required to provide more information about the environmental impact of their plans, and to ensure that the appropriate environmental authorities are included in Monitoring Committees (Commission of the European Communities 1993b:4)

Weaknesses remain, however, in the new regulations, including the absence of any formal requirement for the monitoring committees, which oversee the management of the Structural Funds in each member state, to include environmental performances. It has been argued that some member states will seek to minimise the role of their environmental authorities in reviewing the performance of the Funds (Robins 1994: 102). Environmentalists also argue that there are inadequate provisions for public participation in the design of projects. However, it is generally recognised that underlying these changes in the rules governing the Structural Funds has been a pronounced cultural shift within the Commission wherein environmental scrutiny is becoming more and more an automatic part of the management of the Structural Funds (Robins 1994: 102).

Conclusion

This chapter examined EU environmental policy particularly in border regions in order to illuminate the changing role of the nation-state in formulating and implementing policy. I conclude by examining the effectiveness of the European nation-state in ensuring environmental protection and the nature of the changes that have occurred in its functions and roles.

As far as environmental protection is concerned, this chapter has argued that national-borders are a hindrance not an aid to ensuring environmental quality management. The incompatibility between the borders of political and administrative systems and those of ecological systems is especially visible at the implementation stage of the policy process. Effective maintenance of environmental quality requires transnational, and increasingly international, co-operation. In this context national state sovereignty is threatened by the rationale of a coherent environmental policy which, almost by definition, could not respect national borders. It may be argued that, even in countries like France, the region is the appropriate level for environmental management (Bodiguel et al. 1994). However, in the face of such threats, nation-states have a number of structures and features that serve to protect them from threat. In particular they are protected by the juxtaposition of incompatible legal, administrative and political structures in border regions. These, as we have seen, have acted as a hindrance to the development of cross-border co-operation, ensuring that the sovereign nation-state continues to exercise authority in its border regions and over key policy areas. The extent to which border regions have been successful in exercising policy autonomy differs across countries. In particular it is influenced by the extent of state decentralisation and regionalisation. Many of the most successful examples of cross-border environmental co-operation have occurred in regionalised, central developed border regions and some of the least successful examples are to be found in peripheral, underdeveloped border regions where the contiguous states are most centralised, for example, Greece and Ireland.

Furthermore, this chapter has found that the establishment of effective cross-border co-operation is in itself no guarantee of effective environmental protection. First, there is a deficit, or gap, between EU directives and the implementation of environmental policy (Baker et al. 1994). This implementation deficit is particularly noticeable in peripheral regions. Second, in the light of the development needs of border regions and the weakness in the integration of environmental considerations into its other policy areas, the capacity of programmes like INTERREG to deal with the environmental problems of border-regions remains somewhat limited. In fact, in the face of the development pressures that the completion of the internal market is placing upon these regions it would come as no surprise to find that the environmental problems of border regions will deepen in the coming decade. The reconciliation of the Union's historical commitment to economic development with the new concern with environmental protection may indeed be hard to achieve in these regions.

I conclude by asking whether the institutionalisation of transfrontier co-operation, as seen for example in the INTERREG initiative, has changed the function and role of the nation-state, particularly in the policy field? In many ways the answer to this question remains ambiguous. On the one hand, as has been seen in the INTERREG case, its operations programme is run in many instances in conjunction with national and regional authorities, not with regional authorities alone. Indeed this co-operation, particularly at the planning stage, sometimes only involved national authorities. Furthermore, the extent to which interregional co-operation is successful is in itself limited by the extent of state centralisation and regionalisation and by the attitude of national governments to this development. Thus, the existence of cross-border co-operation is not necessarily an indicator of increased autonomy at the sub-national level.

On the other hand, the fact that the EU funds this co-operation on the basis of cross-border and not interstate co-operation forces us to modify our initial answer somewhat. We are at present witnessing a Europeanisation of environmental policy, that is, a shift from the nation-state level to the international, EU level coupled with a regionalisation, a shift from the nation-state level down to the sub-national level. Both of these parallel phenomena would seem to indicate a reduction in the significance of the nation-state, what, borrowing from a metaphor used in the theory of the firm, can be called a "hollowing-out" of the nation-state, a shift of its functions upwards and downwards, to high and lower levels respectively.

This makes for a somewhat confusing picture - sometimes cross-border co-operation is by-passing the nation-state, other times it is done directly by the nation-state. Thus it would appear that contradictory tendencies are present: both an expansion of the competencies of the nation-state as well as that of local and regional authorities. Putting these two pictures together suggest not so much a weakening of the centrality of the nation-state as a change in its roles and functions (Loughlin 1994). It would appear that the rationale of effective and efficient environmental management is leading to the Europeanisation of environmental policy. Given this, the nation-state is playing less of a role in formulating and implementing policy in this arena. Future research needs to reveal whether this reduction in one set of roles is off-set by a rise in another set of roles: that of the regulation of the framework within which the policy process operates. The extent to which we are witnessing a rise of the regulatory state, and how national regulations relate to EU regulations, especially in the environmental field, would form a useful subject of further research.

Notes

1. Of course the EU also became involved in regulation of environmental management for other reasons, including the concern that member-states' own policies could distort EU-wide competition, see Baker 1993a, for a fuller discussion.

References

Baker, S. 1993a. The environmental policy of the European Community: A critical review. *Kent Journal of International Relations.* April: 8-29.

____. 1993b. *La Politica medioambiental y las regiones periférica de La Comunidad Europea* (Environmental policy and peripheral regions of the EC). In Arenilla, N., Loughlin, J., and Toonen, T. (eds.). *Europe of the regions: An intergovernmental perspective.* Granda: The University Press. (In Spanish)

____. 1993c. The impact of recent EC policy on the environment in the west of Ireland. Unpublished paper, Annual Conference of the Irish Association for Cultural, Economic and Social Relations, Derry, October

_____. 1995a. Environmental policy in East and Central Europe: the role of the EU. In Glasbergen, P. (ed.). *Environmental policy in an international context*. Utrecht and London: Open University.

_____. 1995b. The evolution of European Union environmental policy: From growth to sustainable development. In Baker, S., Kousis, M., Richardson, D., and Young, S.C. (eds.). *Sustainable development: Theory policy and practice within the European Union*. London: Routledge.

Baker, S., Milton, K., and Yearley, S. (eds.). 1994. *Protecting the periphery: Environmental policy in peripheral regions of the European Union*. London: Frank Cass.

Baker, S., Kousis, M., Richardson, D. and Young, S. 1995. Sustainable development: The northern challenge. In Baker, S., Kousis, M., Richardson D., and Young, S.C. (eds.). *Sustainable development: theory policy and practice within the European Union* London:Routledge.

Bodiguel, M., and Buller, H. 1994. Environmental policy and the regions in France. In Loughlin, J. and Mazey, S., (eds.). The end of the French unitary state? Ten years of regionalization in France (1982-1992). *Regional Politics and Policy* 4 (3) 92-109 (Special Issue).

Borooah, V. 1993. *The second round of the reformed Structural Funds: The case of Northern Ireland*. Unpublished paper, the Regional Studies Association and the European Society for Irish Studies, Queen's University Belfast.

Brinkhoff, A. 1993. Irish Sea partnership. In *Info* 3: 2. Gronau: LACE and Association of European Border Regions.

Commission of the European Communities. n.d. *Info Background: INTERREG Initial assessment*. Brussels: Commission of the European Communities.(Info Background, file Series B).

_____. 1986. *The state of the environment in the European Community*. Brussels: Commission of the European Communities EUR 10633.

_____. 1990a. *Environmental policy in the European Community*. Brussels: Commission of the European Communities, European Documentation 5/1990.

_____. 1990b. *Community initiatives: INTERREG* .Brussels: Commission of the European Communities. Info Technique files T-501.90.

_____. 1991a. *Regional policies: Approval of two INTERREG programmes for the border area between Belgium and the Netherlands*. Brussels: Commission of the European Communities IP/91/1113.

_____. 1991b. *INTERREG*. Brussels: Commission of the European Communities IP/91/1161.

_____. 1992a. *Regional policy: INTERREG Community programme for part of the German French border region programme "PAMINA"*. Brussels: Commission of the European Communities IP/92/372.

_____. 1992b. *INTERREG programme - ECU 25 million for the frontier region between France and Italy.* Brussels: Commission of the European Communities IP/92/284.

_____. 1992c. *Report from the Commission of the European Communities to the United Nations Conference on the Environment.* Brussels: Commission. March SEC (91) 2448 final.

_____. 1993a. *European regions in partnership: Interregional co-operation and the future of the Interreg Programme, a synopsis of the onference Interregional Co-operation Regions in Partnership held in Brussels December 1992.* Brussels: Commission of the European Communities.

_____. 1993b. *Background report: The Structural Funds for 1994-99.* Brussels: Commission of the European Communities ISEC/B16/93.

_____. 1994. *Community initiatives 1994-99.* Brussels: Commission of the European Communities IP/94/145.

Council of Europe 1973. Co-operation between local authorities in frontier regions. *Study series, local and regional authorities in Europe. 6.* Strasbourg: Council of Europe.

Court of Auditors 1992. Special report no. 3/92 concerning the environment together with the Commission's replies. *Official Journal 92/C245/01.* Vol. 35: 23 September.

Coyle, C. 1994. Administrative capacity and the implementation of EU environmental policy in Ireland. In Baker, S., Milton, K., and Yearley, S. (eds.). *Protecting the periphery: Environmental policy in peripheral regions of the European Union.* London: Frank Cass.

Department of the Environment (DOE) 1992. *Environment bulletin* January-March. Dublin: Department of the Environment.

Druce, D. 1991. Kent county council: Kent cross border activities. In *Information* 1. Gronau: Association of European Border Regions.

Duport, J. P. 1994. Conclusion: Internal borders. *Proceedings of the Conference on Interregional and Cross-Border Cooperation in Europe - Regions in Partnership, Brussels, 14 and 15 December 1992.* Brussels: Commission of the European Communities.

Dutch Ministry of Transport and Public Works & Ministry of the Flemish Community. 1992. *Prospects for the Scheldt Estuary.* Den Haag: Dutch Ministry of Transport and Public Works & Ministry of the Flemish Community.

Gabbe, J., Broos, L., and Von Malchus, V. n.d. *Institutional aspects of cross-border co-operation.* Gronau: LACE, Cross-Border Cooperation in Practice Series.

Kopp, R., Leygues, J. C., and Chatfield, J. 1994. Introduction and issues. *Proceedings of the Conference on Interregional and Cross-Border Cooperation in Europe - Regions in Partnership, Brussels, 14 and 15 December 1992.* Brussels: Commission of the European Communities.

LACE 1993a. *Info* 2. Gronau: Linkage assistance and co-operation for the European border regions and association of European border regions.

_____. 1993b. *Info* 3. Gronau: Linkage assistance and co-operation for the European border regions and association of European border regions.

_____. 1992a. *Info* 1. Gronau: Linkage assistance and co-operation for the European border regions and association of European border regions.

_____. 1992b. *Info* 2. Gronau: Linkage assistance and co-operation for the European border regions and association of European border regions.

_____. 1992c. *Info* 3. Gronau: Linkage assistance and co-operation for the European border regions and association of European border regions.

Loughlin, J. 1994. Nation, state and regions in western Europe. In L. Beckemans (ed.). *Culture: the building stone of Europe 2004.* Brussels: Presses interuniversitaires.

Magagnotti, P. 1989. Alps-Adria: A success for "micro-diplomacy": Exemplary co-operation between differing social systems. *Information* 1. Gronau: Association of European Border Regions.

von Malchus, V. 1992. *INTERREG: Germany/Netherlands Issue Paper.* Gronau: Linkage assistance and co-operation for the European border regions and association of European border regions.

_____. 1991. Important initiatives for cross-border co-operation on the Eastern borders of the European Community. *Information* 1. Gronau: Association of European border regions.

Majone. G. 1991. Regulatory federalism in the European Community. Paper presented at the Annual Meeting of the American Political Studies Association, 29 August - 1 September.

Mazey, S. and Richardson, J. 1994. Policy co-ordination in Brussels: ernvironmental and regional policy. In Baker. S., Milton. K., and Yearley, S. (eds). *Protecting the periphery: Environmental policy in peripheral regions of the European Union.* London: Frank Cass, London.

Millan, B. 1991. Extracts from the address by Mr. Bruce Millan to the Conference of the Association of European Border Regions on the Role of Border Regions in the Europe of 2000, Ledgen, Germany, 25-27 September 1991. Brussels: Commission of European Communities, IP/91/865.

_____. 1992. With the signing of the Maastricht Treaty. *Info* 1. Gronau: Linkage assistance and cooperation for the European border regions and association of European border regions.

_____. B. 1994. Opening speech. *Proceedings of the conference on Interregional and Cross-Border Cooperation in Europe, - Regions in Partnership, Brussels, 14 and 15 December 1992.* Brussels: Commission of the European Communities.

O' Sullivan, B., and Linehan, D. n.d. *Towards a new regionalism in Ireland: opportunities and constraints.* Unpublished paper, University of Leicester.

Poetschki, H. 1986. *Report on transfrontier co-operation at the internal borders of the European Community*. Strasburg: European Parliament, Working Documents, A 2-170/86.

Pujol, J. 1994. Conclusion: The role of the regions. In *Proceedings of the Conference on Interregional and Cross-Border Co-operation in Europe - Regions in Partnership, Brussels, 14 and 15 December 1992*. Brussels: Commission of the European Communities.

Robins, N. 1994. The EU Structural Funds and environmental policy. *European Trends*. 1st quarter: 95-104.

Santos, P. 1993. AEBR/LACE Annual conference on European Border Regions - Dividing Lines or Meeting Points. FARO. *Info 3*. Gronau: Linkage assistance and co-operation for the European border regions and Association of European Border Regions.

Smit, H. 1993. Cross-border co-operation in large rivers, a key to sustainable economic and ecological development. *Info 2*. Gronau: Linkage assistance nd co-operation for the European border regions and Association of European Border Regions.

Task Force 1989. *1992: The environmental dimension: Task force report on the environment and the internal market*. Brussels: Commission of the European Communities.

Weale, A. 1992. *The new politics of pollution*. Manchester: Manchester University Press.

World wide Fund for Nature. 1992. The environmental effects of the EC Structural Funds in Ireland. In Meldon, J (ed.). *Structural Funds and the environment: Problems and prospects*. Dublin: World Wide Fund for Nature.

Yearley, S., Baker, S., and Milton, K. 1994. Environmental policy and peripheral regions in the European Union: An introduction. In Baker, S., Milton, K. and Yearley, S. (eds.). *Protecting the periphery: environmental policy in peripheral regions of the European Union*. London: Frank Cass.

Yuill, D., Allen, K., Bachtler J., Clement K. and Wishlade, F. 1994. *European regional incentives, 1994-95*. 14 edition. London: Bowker Saur.

3 Transfrontier co-operation at the external borders of the European Union: Implications for sovereignty

Giovanni Delli Zotti

Nothing is more hateful than frontiers, nothing more stupid. They are like guns, like generals: when reason and humanity rule, we do not perceive them, we laugh at them, but, as soon as war and madness break out, they become important and sacred. Herman Hesse, *Wandering*.

The Founding Fathers of the European Community were motivated by distinguished ideals that were well in tune with the spirit of their times. In a Europe which was just emerging from a world war, means were sought to bring the nation-states responsible for such tragic deeds to a mutual understanding. Over the last generation the supporters of an integrated Europe, well aware that national egoism would slow progress toward unity, have proposed a variety of models for the a united Europe. One of these ideas was to build a "Europe of the Regions", as opposed to a "Europe of the States".

More recently, Europe has taken convincing steps towards economic, monetary and political integration, and thus our judgement of the role of the states in creating a new Europe cannot be completely negative.[1] One can maintain that member states of the European Union (EU) have accelerated the drive to integration as a result of necessity, rather than because of a sincere wish to devolve some portion of national sovereignty to a supranational institution. The moves to widen and/or deepen the EU reflect growing national awareness of the international challenges of economic interdependence, environmental menaces and security problems, among others. Regardless of motives, however, the devolution of power to the European Union will happen at the expense of the competencies which are at present attributed to nation-states. Growing identification with this supranational entity will perhaps leave space for the creation of new local identifications and socio-political

51

movements. Regions, whatever their definition, may stand to gain from the loss of power by nation-states. A Europe of the Regions may be perceived by public opinion to be a more attainable goal.

Without engaging in a thorough discussion of the social and political architecture of the new Europe, it is possible to agree, in general terms, with Toniatti's (1992) contention that inter-regional co-operation contributes to the integration of civil society in Europe, confirming and extending what has been achieved at the level of inter-governmental co-operation. In several parts of Western Europe today the phenomena of concerted action, collaboration and exchange of information among regions belonging to different states are resulting in a number of very interesting developments. Regional co-operation is being carried out on an unprecedented level within the EU, and represents one of the most efficacious forms of international and transnational co-operation between Western and Eastern Europe. Moreover, it is also becoming clear that inter-regional co-operation has become a precious instrument in the promotion of harmonious relations, particularly in border areas, among the ex-communist states of Central and Eastern Europe.

This chapter examines the process of inter-regional co-operation in an area where old internal EU borders are losing some of their significance, where new national borders have been recently established, and where the external border of the EU is moving eastwards. The primary focus is on inter-regional and transfrontier co-operation within the Alps-Adria Working Community. Here both inter-regional and inter-governmental co-operation overlap within a growing profusion of transfrontier links. In the second part of the chapter analogies are drawn between the process of transfrontier co-operation and the wider process of EU integration involving national and sub-national units. The chapter concludes by advocating a variable geometry of transfrontier links which would transcend the limited and limiting frameworks of national sovereignty as traditionally understood in Europe.

Transfrontier co-operation and the Alps-Adria Working Community

One of the main axes where co-operation of frontier regions developed after the war is along the French-German and German-Dutch borders. One can speak, in fact, of a "Rhine axis". Local authorities along the Rhine river institutionalised forms of co-operation which sought to oversee the economic exploitation, regulation and protection of the river. Other examples of transfrontier political and economic co-operation are to be found in the Scandinavian region and in the Alpine region.[2] In the latter region one of the most interesting outcomes is undoubtedly the "Alps-Adria Working Community". The Working Community was founded in Venice on 20 November 1978 and its promoters were the Italian Regions of Veneto and Friuli-Venetia Julia, the Yugoslav Republics of Slovenia and Croatia, and the

Austrian Länder of Carinthia, Styria and Upper Austria. The Länder of Salzburg and Bavaria assumed the role of "active observers". During the following years many other regions applied for admission to the Working Community. A few years after the constitution of the Community the Italian Regions of Trentino-Alto Adige, Lombardy and the Austrian Land of Burgenland were admitted. In 1986, in a development which anticipated historical changes that followed only three years after, the Hungarian regional Committees of Györ-Sopron and Vas were included, to be followed in 1988 by Somogy and Zala and, later, by Baranya and by the Swiss Canton Ticino.

With the Agreement signed in Venice the Alps-Adria regions joined together to "deal in common, at an informative and technical level, and to co-ordinate problems that are of interest for its members" (art. 3). Its six Standing Commissions deal with matters of co-operation in:

1. territory and environmental protection,
2. transport,
3. culture, sport, science,
4. economy and tourism,
5. agriculture, forests, zootechnics, mountain economy,
6. public health and hygiene.

The Alps-Adria Working Committee is principally a "forum" of discussion rather than an executive body, but it is responsible for the realisation of support, organisation, and implementation of such activities as meetings, research, the publication of books and reports, and common participation in promotional events and informational exhibits. [3]

As an institution the Alps-Adria Working Community can be considered a public transnational actor. The strategic choice of its organisers was to keep a low profile and reduce the levels of organisation to a minimum. It was only after many years that the Community provided itself with a permanent Documentation centre. In part, the delay was in order to avoid opposition from the more centralist states. Throughout its history it has experienced a wide range of relationships with the nation-states of its member regions. At the beginning Italy, for example, looked at the external activity of some of its regions with suspicion, while Austria's foreign policy was to build Working Communities because its central government could not take on a more direct role due to international pressures (Morrow 1992).

The foundation of Alps-Adria Working Community was based on a number of existing links between regions, as well as new forms of co-operation created by the Working Committee.[4] Many contacts already existed at various levels and among different actors and the creation of the Community provided a wider context to their activities. This was done without interfering with the spontaneous and rich experiences of bilateral co-operation. The latter is a preoccupation clearly expressed by the first article of the Agreement Protocol:

"The activity of the Working Community should not hinder the bilateral and multilateral contacts already existing among the Länder and Regions". It is thus an interesting initiative, which has certainly met with limitations and difficulties (Delli Zotti and De Marchi 1985). Several problems have not yet been completely removed and some are, paradoxically, a direct consequence of the success of the initiative. One of the objectives of this chapter is to review some of these problems and to suggest strategies which may help to overcome them.

To begin with, the independence of the ex-Yugoslav republics has caused some embarrassment to the Alps-Adria group. The presence of the Yugoslavian members, initially regions but now independent states, contradicts the original aim that motivated the creation of the Working Community, i.e., co-operation among regions. At the Plenary Assembly (November 1992) of the Presidents of Alps-Adria regions, Slovenia and Croatia reinforced their intentions to co-operate with the organisation even though their international status has dramatically changed from regions to sovereign states. This statement has been highly appreciated by the other regional members. It seems advisable, however, for the Working Community to insist that, as soon as these newly recognised independent states achieve the foreseen regionalisation of their territory, the new regions (or whatever will be the name of the new sub-national entities), or some of them, will take the place of their states in the Alps-Adria Working Community. The need for introducing such correctives was clear when, following the change in the Yugoslavian members' status and after the outbreak of war, instead of their regional Presidents the Ministers of Foreign Affairs of Slovenia and Croatia participated in the Plenary Assemblies.

Intergovernmental co-operation and the Central European Initiative

Another problem which the Alps-Adria Working Community is now facing comes from the existence, in that area, of alternative forms of international co-operation. One of these is the recently established Central European Initiative. With the fall of communism in Eastern and Central Europe new opportunities opened up for co-operation at the governmental level. The prevailing idea was that of building an area of intergovernmental co-operation in Central Europe. The Alps-Adria example, whose impact was at first underestimated, was later much more positively evaluated and was considered a forerunner of greater inter-state co-operation in the area. An important recognition came from the Milstatt declaration,[5] where the representatives of the states to which the Alps-Adria regions belong, after congratulating the regions for the successes achieved, underlined that "inter-regional collaboration . . . contributes in a significant way to the strengthening of mutual understanding and trust, and to promote friendship and collaboration among the peoples" of the different states involved.

At the Conference of the Ministers of Foreign Affairs and Heads of Governments held in Budapest on 10 and 11 November 1989 the decision to promote a permanent form of co-operation (the so-called Quadrangolare) among Austria, Italy, Hungary and Yugoslavia was taken. In May 1990 Czechoslovakia was officially accepted as the fifth member of the newly named Pentagonale, which became Hexagonale one year later with the admission of Poland. In 1991 the Yugoslav crisis broke out and this fact cast dark shadows on the future of this form of co-operation. At an extraordinary conference of five members held in Venice on 30 November 1991 (Yugoslavia was not present although it was the state holding the Presidency), it was decided to change the Presidency at the beginning of each calendar year. Thus Yugoslavia's Presidency expired in a few months and Austria assumed the Presidency for 1992, as the first country in alphabetical order.

In regard to the current status of the states belonging to ex-Yugoslavia, Croatia, Slovenia and Bosnia-Herzegovina were admitted as full members in July 1992, while Macedonia submitted an application for membership, which has been accepted after international recognition of its independence. It is as a consequence of all these changes in membership, plus the division of Czechoslovakia, that the Hexagonale assumed the final name of Central European Initiative (CEI).

Because the CEI is new, it would be more appropriate to analyse it as both ideas and ideal rather than to concentrate on its efficacy to date as an institution. It certainly has proved to be a popular initiative. Applications for admission have already been submitted by Byelorussia, Bulgaria, Romania and Ukraine. However, it was decided by the CEI to offer them only co-operation on a pragmatic basis, principally through the activities of selected Working Groups on matters of mutual interest. Bavaria assumes the same role in the organisation that it holds in the Alps-Adria Working Community, that of "active observer".

The areas of co-operation have been extended from five in 1989 to thirteen today, and are represented by the presently standing Working Groups: Environment, Transport and Traffic, Small and Medium-Sized Enterprise, Information, Telecommunication, Culture Education and Youth Exchange, Science and Technology, Migration, Energy Production and Transport, Disaster Relief, Tourism, Statistics, and Agriculture. In these areas of co-operation 119 projects have been discussed, fifteen of which, by mid-1993, were reported as already completed and sixteen were partially implemented. As one can see it seems to be a rather ambitious program of work and, although a full critique of the CEI is beyond the scope of this chapter, it seems clear that a wiser strategy for the CEI would have been to concentrate efforts on carefully selected issues. This should have led to pragmatic results that would have been better advertising for the relevance and efficacy of this form of intergovernmental co-operation.

I am more concerned here, however, with the relations between Alps-Adria and the Central European Initiative, where difficulties can arise in spite of well motivated and proclaimed intentions (Bonvicini 1992). In fact, the Alps-Adria and the CEI have overlapping but often opposing agendas, which in the long run may threaten the existence or success of the Working Community, in part because of the threat it may pose to the competing national sovereignties of the CEI.

The main danger to the Working Community is the possibility that the Alps-Adria initiative will be levelled off and somehow absorbed into the Central European Initiative. This is a real danger especially because of the powerful resources that the nation-states are able to mobilise and which can be easily transformed into much more effective action. The regions should be very careful because the praises they have received from their nation-states may hide the will of political expropriation. Some ideas, born at a regional level, have, very recently, been accused of provincialism by those who then converted these ideas to serve state political agendas. As a result, the regions should be jealous of their own initiatives and the spaces for external action which they acquired with difficulty.

The logic underlying the action of governments can be partly different from that of Local Communities. One example is that of the Italian government during the Yugoslav crisis. Its centralist logic led, at least during the first phases, to privilege relations with Belgrade, while Italian regions were more sensitive to the needs of Ljubliana and Zagreb. This was motivated not only by a generic feeling of togetherness (belonging to sub-national level), but also by the strength of the relations developed inside the Alps-Adria Working Community.[6]

These external threats notwithstanding, the most immediate danger to the Working Community seems to come more from the inside than from the outside. Some of the persons engaged in the Alps-Adria Working Community feel that an historical goal has been already achieved, with the readmission of Eastern Europe regions. These parts of Europe are seen by many of their people to belong to a common Central European cultural and social area. Now that regions in Central and Eastern Europe are not only in contact but are co-operating on a number of formal and informal levels, there is a temptation to allow the more powerful Central European Initiative to take over. Croatia and Slovenia, for example, have partly lost their motivation to co-operate in a transnational form (i.e., through co-operation among regions), as they can now co-operate directly with states in an inter-governmental form. The Austrian Länder as well may have lost the support of its government because Austria, as already mentioned, used to promote transfrontier co-operation as a substitute for foreign policy (Morrow 1992). As a consequence of the changes in East-West relations, Austria no longer needs to continue these practices.

The problem of financing their activities is another predicament that has to be solved by Alps-Adria and other similar Working Communities, and, in this case, the Central European Initiative's entrance on the scene may be a positive event. In the Alps-Adria it has been agreed that each participant meet its own expenses. This means, of course, that it is very difficult, if not impossible, to engage in long range projects. In 1991 the Plenary Assembly in Linz established a common budget made of fixed quotas for half the amount, while the rest depends on the number of inhabitants of each region. But greater efficiency is only to be expected by the implementation of the Milstatt Declaration. In Milstatt the state governments recognised the role and importance of the activity of Alps-Adria and announced their "availability . . . to support and develop inter-regional collaboration within Alps-Adria".

For the Central European Initiative the financial resources available are those of the member states. Moreover, they also have easier access to institutions like the European Bank for Reconstruction and Development, which can be very useful, especially in financing projects related to transport and infrastructure. These economic capabilities are different in magnitude from those that the regions of Alps-Adria could mobilise, but a properly regulated form of co-operation between the two organisations could make resources available in order for Alps-Adria to implement its own projects. However, caution has to be exercised on the latter point because it is not so long since the Italian state vetoed attempts by its regions to promote laws which would allow for the funding - however modest - of their participation in the activities of the Working communities.

The juridical framework of co-operation

A further, fundamental, problem with which Alps-Adria is confronted - a problem common to other similar experiences of transfrontier co-operation - refers to the different degrees of autonomy and different competencies enjoyed by participants, according to the different constitutional frameworks to which they belong.

In the Alps-Adria there are Regions (Italian), Länder (Austrian), Republics (ex-Yugoslavia, now independent states), States (Bavaria), Cantons (Ticino) and Committees (Hungarian). In the Italian case there is a difference between the Ordinary Regions and Special Statute Regions, with the addition of the unique situation of the Trentino Alto-Adige Region and its two Autonomous Provinces. This situation means, first of all, that there is an imperfect match among the matters that can be discussed among the participants, due principally to a lack of specific competence by one or more of them. Secondly, and this is probably the worst problem, there is a different degree of capacity - if any - to act internationally, especially to sign treaties. Pernthaler recalls, for example, that "since 1989 the Austrian Länders - as well as the German Länders and the Swiss Cantons - can sign international agreements with bordering Länders and States, whereas the Italian Regions are allowed to do so only after authorisation from the State and within very limited spheres" (1992: 39).[7]

At a broader level of European integration the non-uniform and heterogeneous regionalisation of the member states has had a partial influence, at least, in that it excluded every explicit involvement of the territorial autonomies in the institutional structure of the Community (Toniatti 1992: 75). In transfrontier co-operation this asymmetry meant that the Alps-Adria capacity to act has been relegated to the lower level, that of recommendations to the different regions to be active in presenting and supporting the solutions and indications jointly put forward to the respective governments. To solve this problem the support by the nation-states of the Council of Europe's policy of harmonisation of regionalism in Europe may be of paramount importance. This is a proposal which sets a regionalist standard that the contracting states might decide to adopt in their centre-periphery relations. However, the Council of Europe does not have an exemplary record in its implementation of its policies regarding regionalism, which creates some grounds for scepticism. One can have the legitimate impression that the nation-states do not object to the will of the Council of Europe to foster and proclaim very general principles. However, after the proclamation of these principles, the political will to actually implement the decisions taken is frequently lacking. This is the case, for example, of the "European Charter of Local Government", promoted in 1985, whose impact on the process of regionalisation is not much in evidence at the moment.

Another example of the lack of efficacy and strength of the action of the Council of Europe is the "Declaration on the legal aspects of transfrontier co-operation" issued in 1988. After a reaffirmation of the relevance and absolute necessity of transfrontier co-operation, this declaration seems to withhold any possibility of actually reaching the harmonisation of the relevant competencies: "the harmonisation of the allocation of powers within the various national systems or the concentration of powers relating to a particular field of transfrontier co-operation, is often not possible, nor is it indeed always advisable". After this declaration of powerlessness it is added that "transfrontier co-operation must be allowed to take place despite these differences", with the recognition that "it therefore requircs collaboration between the various levels of public authority and assumes co-operation between these levels in the various states" (Council of Europe 1988: 10). The conclusion I draw, based on the Italian experience, is that active co-operation among different levels is something which is not easy to achieve.

The promotion of the homogenisation of the competencies of the regions is not the only field where the action of the Council of Europe proved to be ineffective. More directly related to the problem of transfrontier co-operation are the efforts of the same Council to give a juridical framework to this type of transnational co-operation. The juridical instrument proposed, signed and ratified by many member states is the "European Outline Convention on

Transfrontier Co-operation between Territorial Communities or Authorities" (Council of Europe 1982). Although this instrument is well intentioned, its promise has not resulted in concrete applications. Even though several contiguous states have already signed and ratified this Convention, we have no news of international treaties concluded through the use of this instrument (at least in the Alpine Region).

The Central European Initiative also proposes its own plans for more effective co-operation between regions, even though the frameworks of agreements, statutes, and contracts enclosed in the Convention, and which envisage common action in the area of information exchange, the provision of services, and the realisation of joint ventures, are already available. These treaties could give transfrontier co-operation a more stable and juridically recognised status. What is lacking, of course, is the political will by the central governments to give away even a small part of their reserved competence in dealing with international affairs. The problem will be presumably solved in the context of a real European Union, because in this case the harmonisation of local government structure will become a necessity.[8]

Sovereignty, inter-dependence and transfrontier co-operation

Transfrontier co-operation represents, in fact, a potential "attack" on state sovereignty. However, it has also become almost commonplace to notice that state sovereignty has been put into question by a phenomenon defined as "globalisation". As a consequence Langer, for example, maintains that "in an increasingly inter-dependent world one cannot legitimise a substantially privatistic concept of sovereignty (*usque ad sidera, usque ad inferos*, like the property right of the Romans)" (1993: 37). The concept of internationally legitimised intervention in national affairs is becoming more widely accepted in Europe [9] in particular circumstances. Here we may recall the Gulf War, the polemics about the non-intervention in the old Yugoslavia, the ineffectual intervention in Bosnia and the more recent positions taken by the Pope. Human rights and monetary policy are two further areas where an absolutist adherence to the doctrine of national sovereignty does not appear feasible. The European Convention on Human Rights necessarily limits national sovereignty. The latter is also limited by monetary inter-dependence. As Padoa Schioppa states: "the monetary autonomy of a small EEC country lasts for the few hours (or few minutes) between a Bundesbank decision on, for example, discount rates and the measures that the small bordering state is forced to adopt not to endanger the stability of its own currency" (1992: 119).

The fact that the threat to sovereignty comes from a number of directions does not mean, however, that the problem of the international role of the regions does not have to be addressed with the utmost attention. In this regard it is appropriate to remember the role played by at least some of Alps-Adria partners in the crisis of ex-Yugoslavia. In a recent, very critical, pronouncement Sema (1994) - after examining the backstage intrigues and the activity of Alps-Adria which, according to him, consented to Ljubliana's games aimed at making the situation appear more dramatic than it was in order to favour their autonomistic demands - concludes that "it would be advisable to reconsider the regions' competencies and pretences in foreign policy, in order to avoid transforming too easily regional segments of the Italian political and administrative apparatus into efficient bases which are controlled by external interests, as was the case with the Northeast of the country during 1991" (Sema 1994: 228).

Globalisation processes and the activity of border regions undermine substantive sovereignty. Formal sovereignty, as Esterbauer states, does not change in these cases, nor does it change when transfrontier co-operation finds its own international juridical framework, for example through the drawing up of bilateral or multilateral agreements. In the much more important case of European Union treaties it is certainly not formal sovereignty which has been brought under discussion, as "it is . . . willingly ignored that a treaty may transfer competencies only, not sovereignty. The transfer of sovereignty - and not its limitation - would require a constituent assembly" (Esterbauer 1992: 20). In a further clarification, Falcon (1992: 54) points out that:

> today the European Community is not a federal state, because . . . it is not a state, and it lacks statehood not for reasons of principle, but because it continues to be founded not on its own sovereignty, but on the devolution of specific "sovereign" powers . . . The European Community thus carries out the apparent paradox of exercising sovereignty without having (its own) sovereignty.

Thus, it is once more confirmed that the activity of the European Union limits the substantive, rather than the formal, sovereignty of the member states.

In regard to transfrontier co-operation, the gradual assertion of power by the European Union is changing the nature of the relation between at least some of the sub-national partners. Falcon (1992) recalls that the Community Charter on Regionalisation of the European Parliament (1988), which as a political recommendation for the member states, sets some objectives:

> transfrontier co-operation among the regional bodies of the member states in the areas of their competence [forms] a co-operation which has to be understood as neighbourhood relations and not as external relations (art. 20, co. 3).

the whole of the EEC common policies cannot be defined as "external relations" according to classical international law, and consequently it is appropriate not to assign them to the exclusive competence of the States (art. 24, co. 1).

the Regions will contribute to the States taking sides as regards the Community requests which fall within their competencies when the matters under consideration directly concern their interests (art. 25, co. 1) (Falcon 1992: 63-64).

With the first two principles mentioned above "the territorial bodies will realise a sort of extension of the principle of "free circulation", although "the principle of the "internal" nature of inter-community space - established in the doctrine, and sometimes applied in reality - has, so far, not been codified in positive Italian law" (Falcon 1992: 65).

Thus the crucial distinction is that between internal and external EU borders. Co-operation among border regions belonging to the internal EU space becomes, in fact, normal inter-regional co-operation, like that between regions of a single state. Although this generates a considerable asymmetry, it is the type of transfrontier co-operation not uncommon on the external borders of the EU.

Co-operation across internal EU borders, which have been increasingly losing their importance in the single European market, may in due course be transferred to borders which are now external, as they become internal ones in a widening European Union. When applying these considerations to the Alps-Adria case, one can notice remarkable changes. The borders separating the Alps-Adria members were, in origin, all external borders of the European Union. But Austria is now in the EU and it is possible that, in a not too distant future, so too will Hungary. Thus the borders with these countries have become, or they might become, internal borders. While waiting for the accession to the EU of Slovenia (more likely) and Croatia (less likely), it is appropriate to notice that the administrative division between Slovenia and Croatia has changed its nature: in practice a new frontier has been added.

The definition of borders: widening vs. deepening

The clear definition of stable borders for Alps-Adria is another unresolved problem that, as we have seen, makes its situation similar to that of the Central European Initiative. It is not without significance that the European Union as a whole is also searching for the right balance between widening and deepening. A viable unified Europe may not be possible if too many new states apply for membership both from the area of the EFTA and from the area of the ex-communist countries, and if this happens at a moment when the existing member states are insufficiently integrated in an economic sense.

As reviewed above, the Working Community grew substantially during the 1980s towards both the East and West. The reasons were largely political - the expansion provided the opportunity to integrate regions belonging to the communist area into a form of co-operation with the West. For the same reason regions from the West applied to get into the Community. This was seen as one of the means of coming into closer contact with the East which was opening its borders to a modest degree even before the historical watershed of 1989.

The danger now is that the Alps-Adria's success, together with the new opportunities offered by events after 1989, may lead other regions to request joining it. This "geographical" success of the Working Community is dangerous because its extension, without limits, means a dilution of its initial goal, which was to co-operate and exchange information among regions that have common problems, especially of a transfrontier nature. Widening the Alps-Adria Community has been done at the cost of a reduction in its collective identity and a loss of specificity. It is hard to say what certain regions of Hungary have in common with Lombardy, and which problems are shared by Canton Ticino and Croatia. Of course, certain economic actors of Lombardy might be interested in investing in Baranya (Hungary), but this has little to do with transfrontier co-operation as it involves normal economic transactions. There is a danger too that many transfrontier co-operative actions within Alps-Adria may disappear in the *mare magnum* of the activities carried on inside the Central European Initiative.

An examination of cases of transfrontier co-operation reveals that the most successful experiences are those comprising a few partners devoted to solving a number of well defined practical problems. Transfrontier workers, the common management of services, and the fight against pollution are good examples of problems that can be addressed jointly while Euregio, Regio Basiliensis, or the Geneva transfrontier region are probably examples of successful institutions engaged in transfrontier co-operation. The success of issue-oriented transfrontier co-operation does not undermine the importance of the general political thrust of attempts to link the EU with parts of the East, but it seems advisable to underline the initial and more limited aims of transfrontier co-operation in the Alps-Adria Working Community.

The present set up of Alps-Adria evokes more properly a definition of a multi-transfrontier region that could split for functional reasons into the constituent dyads or triads more appropriate to carry on a genuinely transfrontier activity of co-operation. Alps-Adria could take on the role of a wider framework of co-ordination for other purposes to provide a common image and identity, and deal with problems that interest all partners, such as building infrastructure networks. However, here there is a risk of an overlap with the activities of Central European Initiative.

There is another problem which both Alps-Adria and the European Union share. Widening creates problems of management, as an increasing membership makes decision-making more complex, thereby risking paralysis. Thus, it is necessary to find correctives because, as Padoa Schioppa ironically points out: "the Pope is elected with two-thirds of the Cardinals' votes, and the believer is convinced that through the vote of the Cardinals, assembled in Conclave, the Holy Spirit operates. Then, why should the EU's Council of Ministers not take its decisions by majority vote (simple or qualified) on all subjects which are under its competence?" (1992: 126).

In the Alps-Adria case the decisions are obviously less binding, as they are mainly recommendations. In finding a solution to its functional problems (i.e., competencies, the international legal framework, and sources of funding), more adequate forms of management will have to be found. For example, the possibility of abandoning, or at least limiting, the principle of unanimity in the decision-making process will have to be considered. There is also the possibility of adopting a strategy of "variable geometry", that limits the number of partners (thus making the group more homogeneous) per initiative undertaken.

Thus an antidote to the excessive geographical expansion of the Union and the Working Community might be provided by two potentially complementary strategies. Firstly, small-scale bilateral and multilateral initiatives should be encouraged, so as to leave to the EU the role of an overall political actor. The other strategy should be that of functional differentiation, which should include not only what is being done already through the activity of the Alps-Adria Commissions, but which also should promote as much as possible the activity of specific actors inside the borders of Alps-Adria. The EU and the Alpe Adria, instead of acting on their own, should become more and more a container of activities of other actors. The already existing activity of the Standing Conference of the Rectors of the Universities of Alps-Adria or the activities of its Chambers of Commerce are good examples of such activity.

Internal functional differentiation may be useful for deepening relations particularly where the differential participation of members in specific projects is foreseen. In this case a further analogy can be drawn between Alps-Adria and the European Union. In order to overcome the problem of different levels of economic development, the possibility of variable integration was advanced. Stronger association at a political level could co-exist with less developed economic integration in the case of countries that cannot keep up with the others. In the same way, in the Working Community, regions could participate in initiatives which they consider to be in their interest at a particular time. As mentioned above, a form of collaboration of this kind has been offered already to some of the states applying to join the Central European Initiative.

The intersection of political units and the permeability of frontiers

The depoliticisation and the desacralisation of frontiers is a valuable goal for Europe, even if one cannot deny that borders continue to play some vital roles.[10] Borders will continue to mark the limits of territory, where the legislative remit of a clearly defined political unit applies. But it is not necessary for frontiers to have a strong political character; some might continue to lose their political significance and assume a more administrative character. On the other hand, the frontier between Croatia and Serbia used to be administrative but its creation as an international border heralded serious ethnic and national strife.

This last point is relevant to the potential dangers involved in the rush to become a member either of the Working Community or of the Central European Initiative. The spirit of transfrontier co-operation seeks to render the existing borders more permeable, not to create new ones. Yet, if it is perceived to be so important to be in and so penalising to be out, then inevitably new borders are created which may become a source of problems.

Together with the strategy of geographical and functional fragmentation, the creation of similar organisations should be favoured, and the collaboration between different organisations for particular aims and objectives should be encouraged. This already happens in the Alpine Area where some regions belong, at the same time, to the Alps-Adria Working Community and to the Alpine Region Working Community - Arge Alp. Other Working Communities could be created, especially to take into account new regional actors in Eastern Europe eager for this form of co-operation. At the intergovernmental level, the Central European Initiative has on its agenda the task of finding useful forms of co-operation with other, often overlapping, inter-governmental organisations such as the Black Sea Economic Co-operation, Working Communities of the Danubian Countries and Balkan Co-operation.

Obviously, it is better to proceed with caution, because there are cases in which clear borders and tasks are important. In the management of the Yugoslavian crisis the overlapping of roles has, together with other factors, contributed to making EU action ineffectual. "The Yugoslav conflict revealed almost a plethora of organisations with often overlapping membership, each with responsibility or potential role in preventing conflict and/or seeking its resolution. They ranged from the pan-European CSCE, via the European Community, NATO, and the WEU to the Pentagonale, now Hexagonale" (Edwards 1992: 162-163, quoted in Donini 1993: 16).

However, promoting forms of collaboration at different levels and managing crises may require completely different attitudes. In the case of the management of crisis, effectiveness and speed are absolutely necessary. In the case of co-operation, effectiveness is not to be undervalued as, otherwise, there would be a waste of all kinds of resources. However, speed is not as important. Efficacy may also be served by more participatory and democratic procedures, although this requires more time and effort. It should not be forgotten that the consultation procedure is in itself valuable.

What I am suggesting could be theorised as the strategy of cross-cutting cleavages, which renders fractures - that are an integral part of social life - potentially less dangerous. Coser (1967) concludes his work on the functions of social conflict by stating that the intensity of a conflict is connected with rigidity. The latter encourages sentiments to accumulate and, once the conflict breaks out, they confront one another along a single cleavage. Cross-cutting cleavages could also ameliorate ethnic and national antagonisms creating a "process which leads to multiple belonging that modifies the psychology, the feelings as well as the actions of the new European citizen, who has to learn to be faithful to different masters at the same time" (Martini 1993: 54). Multiple belongings make impermeable borders more unlikely because "the real de-construction of antagonistic nationalism either takes place at the border or it does not take place at all" (Hilf 1993: 81).

The reasons for more transfrontier co-operation

Having examined the problems of transfrontier co-operation, and having suggested some solutions, it might be asked how worthwhile is this form of co-operation. At one level it is essential as it is the most suitable form of co-operation for solving problems of ethnic and national revival which are highly dangerous and menace the stability and harmonious development of several European countries. Only in a Europe of the regions, where local authorities gain ever more strength - inside their states and as actors of transnational co-operation - can the ethnic problem be reduced, if not solved. Moreover, it is clearly at state borders that many ethnic minorities are situated.

The possibility of keeping intense local exchanges, at the cultural, social and economic levels, with people of the same language and ethnicity who live across the border, should render citizenship less important. The fact that Italy does not have a "Slovene problem", when in other countries the presence of ethnic minorities means a society full of tensions, is evidence of the role that transfrontier co-operation can play.[11]

The alternative to the pursuit of transfrontier and inter-ethnic co-operation is, as Langer (1993: 36) says: "to resign oneself to the fact that inter-, super- or trans-national ideas of aggregation are residuals from the illusions of the Enlightenment, types of rationalistic inventions without life, and to pursue the objective of creating nation-states with clear borders from the ethnic point of view". According to Willms (1994: 62) one can find an alternative to this form of resignation:

Against the epidemic of a once again virulent nationalism there is but one possibility. European integration has to be developed with firmness, by strengthening, especially, one component of the process which has been unforgivably neglected: culture. European identity is not based on coal nor on steel, still less on beet-root or colza, but only on its cultural traditions, that are intertwined thanks to a continuous process of exchange.

Unfortunately, however, the cultural dimension of European integration remains underdeveloped. Some observers saw in the Danish people's initial refusal to ratify the Maastricht treaty, and the difficulties that the overall EU unification process still encounters in different parts of the continent, an indication of the dissatisfaction with an EU which is too restricted to economic issues. The EU may in fact be defined as a technocratic structure strongly weighted towards the economic and financial fields.

The Alps-Adria experience, which was quite unsatisfactory on the economic level because of the limits that it encountered in mobilising resources, was much richer under the headings of cultural exchanges, co-operation of voluntary associations, and personal direct contacts that developed among administrative and political personnel of the local authorities.[12] If one would ask the functionaries of the Working Community of Alps-Adria what are its most important achievements, many would stress the experience of co-operation per se rather than the substantive content of the projects accomplished. The most precious achievement is the development of a mutual understanding, the formation of a co-operative culture, something that is much needed throughout Europe.

Transfrontier co-operation may also be a valid instrument to foster the development of the new democracies in Eastern Europe. The development of human resources is considered an essential step for the changes in the economy and society in Central and Eastern Europe. If this development is achieved by training carried out in the West the danger is that a brain drain might undermine the Eastern countries. Transfrontier co-operation may help to guarantee that the growth of human resources is achieved on a reciprocal basis through the exchange of information and experiences, while people keep their positions of responsibility inside the institutions of their own country.

Co-operation with the countries of Central and Eastern Europe requires an imaginative effort, and co-operation among regions provides a partial answer to the need for discovering new strategies and institutions to achieve this. Other models of international co-operation may be instructive, but in the European context they may not be as instrumental or effective. For example, it is not possible to apply, in a uncritical way, the model of global North-South co-operation, which has shown its limitations within its own orbit of application. North-South co-operation is in fact highly asymmetrical in its nature: some states play the role of donors and others play that of beneficiaries.[13] This model is thus not applicable because it denigrates the role of the ex-communist countries.

Another model of co-operation is that of regional (sub-continental) international co-operation . In this case the partners are at least formally equal and co-operation develops to the advantage of all members: the EEC and Benelux, for example, may be useful models for the countries of the Visegrad Triangle (Czechoslovakia, Hungary and Poland).[14] The Central European Initiative provides an intermediate formula and foresees, as an end result, symmetrical co-operation among equal partners which, by means of a long process of convergence, have reached a similar level of development. However, at the beginning there is a situation of relative asymmetry inasmuch the Western partners play the role of promoters of the development, since they are the purchasers of the economic resources for the realisation of the projects that are launched. In this framework it is really important that a considerable space is reserved to the encouragement of co-operation among local authorities, because at this level the capability of mobilising economic resources is not so important. Far more important is the fact that every actor is the bearer of a culture, i.e., experiences, intuitions and solutions that can be exchanged for reciprocal benefit that, from the very beginning, affirm the equal value and dignity of each partner.

The future of transfrontier co-operation: the Euro-regions

The subsidiarity principle should guide the future action of the EU. If it is correctly understood and implemented, it is the principle which gives legitimacy and strength to the transfrontier Working Communities. If the specific problems proper to frontier regions are recognised, then the subsidiarity principle implies the existence of institutions with their own specific competencies and autonomy spanning frontiers. The role of subsidiarity as a solution to a real problem is confirmed by the recent proposal to constitute Euro-regions,[15] which can be seen as the institutional reinforcement of the Working Community experience. This proposal is recent and suggests a return to the genuine spirit of transfrontier co-operation. The proposals put forward concern the central-eastern sector of the Alps and suggest establishing the Euro-regions of Tyrol and Istria, that is, specific sub-regions of the Working Communities to which they belong.

The ideal behind the Istrian Euro-region is clear from Bogliun-Debeljuh's (1994: 270) proposal:

the ideal normalisation of the Istrian region, understood as a Euro-region to be included in the wider Central European context, should follow these phases of realisation: a) attainment of a maximum level of regional autonomy in Croatia and Slovenia; b) an international agreement between Croatia and Slovenia for the official recognition of the status of autonomy in Istria; c) an agreement between Croatia, Italy and Slovenia for the constitution of an Istrian Euro-region: d) the inclusion of the Istrian Euro-region in the sphere of the Alps-Adria macro-Euro-region.

The Euro-region is an open window on the future evolution of a system of co-operation which has to develop at all levels. It also must promote regional autonomies and the homogenisation of competencies. This chapter predicts and anticipates that the proliferation of co-operative organisations will not necessarily be a major hindrance to further European co-operation.

Conclusion

The experience of the Alps-Adria Working Community and related examples of transfrontier co-operation are important not just in their own right but as an indication of the complexities and difficulties of European integration. A "Europe of the States" co-exists and interacts with a "Europe of the Regions" which is struggling to come into existence. New forms of transfrontier co-operation can be a useful antidote to existing and potential conflicts over territorial sovereignty between ethnic and national groups. Such co-operation also helps to correct the imbalance between the economic and cultural dimensions of EU integration and suggests a variety of models for forging links with the countries of Eastern Europe.

The discussion of transfrontier co-operation in this chapter indicates that it is necessary to move beyond old conceptions of national sovereignty of the kinds mentioned in the quotation from Hesse at the beginning of this chapter. As Bocchi and Ceruti remind us (1994: 205):

> our current representation of borders and the interaction between nations are too limited and too limiting. We need new representations which, sometimes, require overlapping and multiplication of sovereignty. With a new sensibility for multiple and collective identities, we have to look for new opportunities, exactly where the risks and the dangers of conflict look more likely.

One can certainly agree that the only alternative to these opportunities for solidarity and civilisation is brutality, which Europe today witnesses with growing dismay.

Notes

1. The recent expansion of the EU to include the membership of Sweden, Finland and Austria is certain to have some negative effects, some of which will affect the Alps-Adria Working Community.

2. The Council of Europe publishes updated lists of international, inter-regional and local agreements related to co-operation of frontier regions.

3. For further information on the origin, activities, structure and perspectives of the Working Community of Alps-Adria, see Fedrigotti and Leitner (1993) and Poropat (1993). The latter also includes useful information on the Central European Initiative.

4. For a research work that shows the richness and complexity of contacts that developed in the area well before the founding of the Community, see Delli Zotti (1983). A summary of the research can be found in Delli Zotti (1982).

5. The representatives of the governments that eventually gave birth to the Central European Initiative met for the first time in this town.

6. See Sema (1994) on the negative reactions to the divergence between national and regional levels.

7. All translations from the original Italian in this chapter are my own.

8. See, for example, the contributions submitted to a conference promoted by the Trentino-Alto Adige Autonomous Region and published in 1992, both in Italian and German (Berti 1992).

9. See, for example, Bobbio 1990 and the proceedings of a Round Table devoted to the relationship between "International solidarity and national sovereignty", which are in Papisca 1993.

10. On types and functions of boundaries see, for example, Strassoldo (1982).

11. On the role of the Slovenes see, for example, the volume edited by Delli Zotti and Rupel (1992) and, more generally, on ethnic minorities in the area, see the volume sponsored by the Working Community of Alps-Adria (1991), also published in German, Slovene and Croatian.

12. However, the economic aspects of co-operation within Alps-Adria are not negligible. See, for example, Cappellin (1990), Inotai (1992) and Senn (1993).

13. This has to be said leaving aside the discussion on the real nature of the asymmetry: one can maintain that, when the relations are neo-colonialist, the roles of beneficiary and donor are completely reversed.

14. On models of co-operation among ex-communist countries see Tonzar (1992) and Marasà (1993). On the perspectives of development of these countries, see Delli Zotti (1994). Visegrad is the town where the Heads of Government of these three countries met in 1991 to agree on some form of co-operation. The triangle metaphor is now vanishing, due to the division of Czechoslovakia into the Czech Republic and Slovakia.

15. On Euro-regions see, for example, Korinman (1993).

References

Berti, G. et al. 1992. *Posizione delle regioni italiane nella prospettiva del Trattato sull'Unione europea* (The position of Italian regions in view of the European Union Treaty). Trento: Regione Autonoma Trentino-Alto Adige.

Bobbio, I. 1990. *L'età dei diritti* (The age of rights). Torino: Einaudi.

Bocchi, G. and M. Ceruti. 1994. *Solidarietà o barbarie. L'Europa delle diversità contro la pulizia etnica* (Solidarity or barbarity. The Europe of diversity against ethnic cleansing). Milano: Cortina.

Bogliun-Debeljuh, L. 1994. Come faremo la nostra euroregione Istria (How we will build our Istria Euro-region). *Limes* 1: 263-270.

Bonvicini, G. 1992. Gli aspetti politici dell'interrelezione fra Esagonale e cooperazione regionale intrafrontaliera (The political aspects of the interrelation between Hexagonale and regional transfrontier co-operation). In Istituto Affari Internazionali (I.A.I.) *Le interrelazioni fra Iniziativa esagonale e Alpe-Adria in un Europa che cambia.* Trento: Regione autonoma Trentino-Alto Adige.

Cappellin, R. 1990. *L'internazionalizzazione delle economie di Alpe-Adria e la cooperazione interregionale* (Internationalisation of the economies of Alps-Adria and interregional cooperation). Milano: Ispi (mimeo).

Comunita di lavoro Alpe-Adria. 1991. *Le minoranze nell'ambito di Alps-Adria* (Ethnic minorities of Alps-Adria). Triest: Regione autonoma Friuli-Venezia Giulia (also published in German).

Council of Europe 1982. *Convention-cadre Européenne sur la coopération transfrontaliére des collectivités au autorités territoriales.* Série des Traités européens 106. Strasbourg.

_____ . 1985. *European Charter of Local Autonomies.* Strasbourg:

_____ . 1988. *Declaration on the legal aspects of transfron tier co-operation.* Strasbourg.

Coser, L. 1956. *The functions of social conflict.* Glencoe: Free Press.

Delli Zotti, G. 1982. Transnational relations of a border region: The case of Friuli-Venetia Julia. In R. Strassoldo and G. Delli Zotti (eds.). *Cooperation and conflict in border areas.* Milano: Angeli.

_____ . 1983. *Relazioni transnazionali e cooperazione transfrontaliera. Il caso del Friuli-Venezia Giulia* (Transnational relations and transfrontier co-operation: The case of Friuli-Venezia Giulia). Milano: Angeli.

_____ . (ed.). 1994. *Dentro il triangolo di Visegrad. Società civile, politica e assetti istituzionali nell'Europa Centrale* (Inside the Višegrad Triangle. Civil society, politics and institutions in Central Europe). Gorizia: Isig

Delli Zotti, G. and B. De Marchi 1985. *Cooperazione regionale nell'area alpina* (transfrontier co-operation in the Alpine Area). Milano: Angeli.

Delli Zotti, G. and A. Rupel (eds.). 1992. *Etnia e sviluppo. Ruolo della presenza slovena nell'area goriziana* (Ethnicity and development. The role of the Slovenes in the province of Gorizia). Gorizia: Isig.

Donini, G. 1993. Il ruolo della Cee nella crisi dell'ex-jugoslavia (The role of EC in the ex-Yugoslavia crisis). *Isig* 2: 16.

Edwards, G. 1992. European responses to the Yugoslav crisis: An interim assessment. In R. Rummel (ed.). *Toward political union: Planning a common foreign and security policy in the European Community.* Boulder and Oxford: Westview.

Esterbauer, F. 1992. Regionalismo e federalismo: idea e realtà in Europa (Regionalism and federalism in relation with the European right). In F. Esterbaurer et al. (eds.). *Regionalismo e federalismo nella costruzione della nuova europa.* Trento: Regione Autonoma Trentino-Alto Adige.

Falcon, G. 1992. Regionalismo e federalismo in rapporto al diritto comunitario (Regionalism and federalism in relation with the European right). In F. Esterbaurer et al. (eds.). *Regionalismo e federalismo nella costruzione della nuova Europa.* Trento: Regione Autonoma Trentino-Alto Adige.

Fedrigotti, A. and G. Leitner (eds.). 1993. *Alpe Adria. Idenhta e ruolo* (Alps-Adria. Identity and role).Trento: Regione Autonoma Trentino-Alto Adige.

Hilf, R. 1993. I progetti tedeschi di regioni transfrontaliere (The German projects of transfrontier regions). *Limes* 4: 79-84.

Istituto Affari Internazionali (I.A.I.) (ed.). 1992. *Le interrelazioni fra Iniziativa esagonale e Alpe-Adria in un Europa che cambia* (The interrelation between the Hexagonale initiative and Alps-Adria in a changing Europe). Trento: Regione Autonoma Trentino-Alto Adige.

Inotai, A. 1992. Aspetti economici della cooperazione nell' area Centro-Europea (Economic aspects of co-operation in Central Europe). In I.A.I. (ed.). *Le interrelazioni fra Iniziativa esagonale e Alpe-Adria in un Europa che cambia.* Trento: Regione autonoma Trentino-Alto Adige.

Korinman, M. 1993. Euroregioni o nuovi Lander? (Euro regions or new Länders?). *Limes* 4:.65-78.

Langer, A. 1993. Diversità, autodeterminazione e cooperazione dei popoli (Diversiry, self determination and co-operation of peoples). In *Localismi, unità nazionale ed etnie. Diritto all'autodeterminazione e rischi di guerra.* Martini, G. S. Domenico di Fiesole: S. Edizioni Cultura della Pace.

Marasà, B. 1993. *Oltre Maastricht. Il futuro dell'Unione europea e i nuovi paesi dell'Est* (Beyond Maastricht. The future of European Union and the new Eastern countries) Roma: Ed. Associate.

Martini, G. 1993. La costruzione dell'Europa comune (the construction of the EC). In Martini, G. (ed.). *Localismi unità nazionale ed etnie. Diritto all'autodeterminazione e rischi di guerra.* S. Domenico: S. Edizioni Cultura della Pace.

Morrow, D. 1992. Regional policy as foreign policy: the Austrian experience. *Regional Politics and Policy* 2: 27-44.

Padoa Schioppa, A. 1992. Federalismo e coscienza europea (Federalism and European conscience). In F. Esterbaurer et al. (eds.). *Regionalismo e federalismo nella costruzione della nuova Europa.* Trento: Regione Autonoma Trentino-Alto Adige.

Pernthaler, P.   1992.   Esperienze e prospettive del regionalismo e del federalismo nell'area centro-alpina (Experiences and perspectives of regionalism and federalism in Central alpine area). In F. Esterbaurer et. al. (eds.). *Regionalismo e federalismo nella costruzione della nuova Europa..* Trento: Regione Autonoma Trentino-Alto Adige.

Poropat, L.   1993.   *Alpe-Adria e Iniziatia Centro-Europea* (Alps-Adria and the Central European Initiative). Napoli: Ed. Scientifiche Italiane.

Sema, A.   1994.   Estate 1991: gli amici italiani di Lubiana (Summer 1991: The Italian friends of Lijubliana). *Limes* 1: 215-228.

Senn, L.   1993.   *Rapporto sull'economia di Alpe Adria* (Report on the economy of Alpe-Adria). Trento: Regione Autonoma Trentino-Alto Adige.

Strassoldo, R.   1982.   Boundaries in sociological theory: a reassessment. In Strassoldo, R. and G. Delli Zotti (eds.). *Cooperation and conflict in border areas.* Milano: Angeli.

Toniatti, R.   1992.   Ipotesi e progetti di unione europea e ruolo delle regioni (Hypotheses and projects of European Union and the role of regions). In F. Esterbaurer et al. (eds.). *Regionalismo a federalismo nella costruzione della nuova Europa.* Trento: Regione Autonoma Trentino-Alto Adige.

Tonzar, O.   1992.   Organizzarione internarionale e cooperazione nell'Europa centro orientale (International organisation and co-operation in Central Eastern Europe). *Isig Working Papers 92.1. International sociology.* (Section on international relations).

Willms, J.   1994.   L'Europa come antidoto alla balcanizzarione (Europe as an antidote to balkanisation). *Limes* 1: 61-62.

4 Ethnic-regionalism versus the state: The case of Italy's Northern Leagues

Raimondo Strassoldo

Except for its small French, German, and Slovene border minorities placed along the Alpine arc, Italy has usually been thought of as an ethnically homogeneous nation. Thus, the explosive rise of the Lombard League since the late 1980s has been a surprise to everyone. The Lombard League, enlarged in 1992 as the Northern League, was one of the key factors as well as symptoms of the sudden dissolution of the exceptionally stable party system that had ruled Italy for forty years. The League questioned the very idea of Italian national unity, at one point proposing the break-up of the country into three sovereign, albeit confederate, Republics. Some feared that Italy might go the way of Yugoslavia, The Caucasus and Ireland. Calls to arms, more or less metaphorical, were heard.

One of the issues raised by this phenomenon is the place of the Lombard/Northern leagues within the ethnic-regional or mini-national movement which has characterized some modern Western societies in the 1970s (Smith 1981). The Lombard League certainly started out as such a movement, as the very name implies; it is also clear, although usually supressed by League leaders and overlooked by observers, that it took the lead from earlier ethnic-regional movements in other parts of Northern Italy (*Movimento Friuli* and *Liga Veneta*)

A second issue, not unrelated to the first, concerns the role of space (place, territory, region) in shaping this political phenomenon (Agnew 1987), in particular, the extent to which it can be seen as an example of the centre-periphery opposition (Shils 1975; Gottmann 1980). Most ethnic- regional movements develop in peripheral areas. The Lombard League is no exception: the electoral force of the Northern League climaxes in the border areas. The connection between ethnic-regional movements and peripheral location is often seen in economic and other material disadvantages such as "marginalization"

73

and "internal colonialism". But this is not the case with the Lombard and the Northern leagues: their home districts are socio-economically the most developed in the country. They were, however, or were believed to be - which in politics does not make much difference - peripheral in reference to the national political system, centered in Rome and perceived as largely shaped by Southern mores and interests. The role of the Leagues in shaking and perhaps renovating the Italian political system reminds one of Ibn Khaldoun's ancient theory on the cycle of corruption of the centres and regeneration from the periheries.

Much less attention has been given so far to the linkages between the Leagues and international affairs, besides the rather obvious observation that they reaped large electoral benefits from the end of the "communist threat" and therefore also of the use of the "anti-communist dam", the Christian Democratic party (DC). No sytematic studies are at hand on the linkages between the Leagues and the process of European integration and the ensuing changes in the role of borders; linkages which are rather well established in the case of European ethnic-regional and of "frontier regions" movements (De Rougemont 1968; Strassoldo 1973). The fact that the strongholds of the Leagues all lie along Italy's Northern boundary is certainly meaningful, but liable to different explanations. The European rhetoric was quite prominent in the early stages of the movement, when the cultural differences between North and South were emphasized and traced back to the historical, geographical and even racial proximity, respectively, of the North to Central Europe and of the South to the Mediterranean. One of the main models for a Federated Italy was Germany, and for Lombardy, the Free State of Bavaria. One of the chief arguments for the threatened secession was that the North was already fully equipped for European Unity, and did not want to "lose the European train" because of Rome's and the South's backwardness. Thus, the Leagues can be seen, to some extent, as a dislocation of domestic political equilibria brought about, quite unwittingly, by the process of European integration. On the other hand, the abandonment of the separation hypothesis has certainly something to do with its clear unacceptability by the rest of Europe.

In this chapter I provide a sketch of the Italian ethnic-regional movements and politics since 1945, an analysis af the general conditions and causes of the rise of the Lombard/Northern League, and a discussion of its changing ideology, strategies and tactics, up to the end of 1994.

Methodologically, this study is based on the sociological literature already accumulated in Italy and elsewhere on the subject (Mannheimer 1991; Diamanti 1993; Schmidtke 1993, Cartocci 1994, Poche 1994); and on several years of attentive scrutiny of the phenomenon as it appears in the daily stream of information from general media. Of this, however, no formal record has been taken nor evidence or reference given.

Ethnic regionalism in Italy, 1945-1980

Italy is a rather elongated country, with a 2500 year history. Its different parts have been subject to a wide variety of demographic, cultural and political influences. When, towards the middle of the nineteenth century, times were ripe for political unification, it was generally held that the new state should have a federalist character, in order to take into account the deep regional differences. Unity was instead achieved in 1861 through sheer diplomatic-military means. Piemontese centralism prevailed, and an encompassing "nation-building" effort was set in motion. Fascist nationalism was only a culmination of this process. All through these obsessively patriotic eighty years the rule was enforced that every Italian citizen should also be or become culturally Italian. The larger border national minorities (French, German, Slav) were subject to ruthless de-nationalization policies (suppression of any outer signs of culture, interdiction of institutions and associations, prohibition of language, change of personal and local names, dilution through planned immigration from other regions, etc.). With Fascism, open violence against them (especially against the Slovenes) was let loose. Regional-ethnic variation within Italy was denied or ignored, except as a dying object for folkloric studies.

By 1943, the unity of the Italian nation was strong enough to survive the experience of the splitting of the country into a Fascist "Socialist Republic" in the North, under German rule, and a "Kingdom of the South", supported by the Allies. The experience was universally interpreted as due entirely to military contingencies, with no relation to deeper socio-cultural features.

Of the political forces that replaced Fascism some, like the Christian Democrats, were genuinely opposed to nationalism and centralization, and favoured a regional reform; others, like the Marxists, held more ambiguous and instrumental views. The post-war coalition governments recognized the four autonomous regions already set up under international or local pressure: French-speaking Val D'Aosta, German-speaking South Tyrol, plus the two island-regions of Sicily and Sardinia. The new republican Constitution of 1948 provided for a fully regionalistic state structure. Besides the four already in existence, a fifth "special autonomy" region was provided for, Friuli-Venezia Giulia, where the Slovene minority lived. The rest of the mainland was subdivided into fourteen "ordinary autonomy" regions. However, the constitutional provision was not implemented for many years; Friuli-Venezia Giulia only came into existence in 1963, and the "ordinary" regions had to wait until 1971. This staggering is due basically to the reluctance of the governing parties (Christian Democrats and their allies) to devolve central powers; especially unsettling was the perspective of having the middle section of the country (Emilia-Romagna, Toscana, Umbria) ruled by the Communists. Other arguments against the regions - threat to the national unity, politicization of administration, inefficiency, waste - were variously used by different parties.

While the three "special autonomy" border regions were the result of international pressure to protect national minorities, Sicily and Sardinia were granted their special autonomy on the bases of their insularity. But this geographical, spatial feature is inseparable from some feeling of cultural identity. For example, during the Allied military government a separatist movement arose in Sicily. This movement had dubious social, political and ideological bases, linked in part to the mafia, but it was snuffed out with the implementation of the regional autonomy. Since then there have been no signs of a Sicilian ethnic party or movement. In Sardinia, on the other hand, a "Sardinian Action Party" was established right after the fall of fascism, whose political fortunes have oscillated with each election, reaching at times even the highest posts in the regional government. It strives for ever more autonomy from Rome, sometimes with separatist overtones, and is engaged, with various degrees of intensity, in the protection and development of the Sardinian cultural and linguistic heritage. As in Sicily, however, one basic problem in this field is that both islands lack a really unitary "regional language", and no internal "dialect" is acceptable to the speakers of other varieties.

As a consequence of international treaties and moral support from "mother" nations beyond the state border, ethnic/national parties command a large majority of voters in the two areas where the French (Franco-provencal) and the German minorities live, i.e., Valle d'Aosta and Alto Adige (South Tyrol) respectively. In the latter case, the situation is a bit confused by the fact that officially there is one autonomous region comprising two autonomous provinces, Alto Adige / South Tirol and Trentino; but since 1972 the Region is only an empty shell. The German minority in South Tirol - which is a solid majority in its own province - is clearly of the national, and not of the ethnic-regional, type, and after a long and hard struggle has been granted a large degree of autonomy. The Trentino question is less well-known and less linear. This is an Italian-speaking mountain area which only came under Italian administration in 1918. Nostalgia for the higher degree of local autonomy enjoyed under the previous Austrian rule lingered on, and re-surfaced after 1945 in the form of a strong localist-autonomist movement, which cannot be called ethnic-regional because of the lack of distinctive language claims. In the following years it was subsequently mostly swallowed up by the Christian Democratic party, surviving only as a splinter party (*Partito Popolare Trentino Tirolese*, PPTT). In the last few years it has flourished again.

Also in Friuli-Venezia Giulia one has to distinguish the two parts of the region. Venezia Giulia is a misnomer for the city of Trieste, an ethnically mixed city of the Hapsburg empire where Italians always held the dominant position. Since the late nineteenth century they grew nervous about Slovene encroachment, and developed ever stronger pro-Italy attitudes. In 1945 the city suffered a brief but murderous occupation by Tito's troops and received about 60.000 nationals displaced from Istria and Dalmatia. To this day, Trieste's political life is marked by an almost paranoid, Slav-hating form of nationalism.

Friuli (population 900,000) has long nurtured a cultural-historical identity, but this was translated into political terms only after 1945. A Society for Friulian Autonomy was active from 1945-53. But the inclusion of Friuli among the "special autonomy regions", requested by only a few local Christian Democrats, was bitterly opposed by many local nationalists, fearful that autonomy would foster secessionism and give leverage to Yugoslavian claims over parts of the region. This fear also helps to explain the fifteen year delay in implementation of the Region. In fact, the autonomist feeling has always been very weak, and limited to a handful of lay intellectuals (like Pier Paolo Pasolini) and lower clergy. With the setting up of the regional institutions, ethnic-regional awareness was reactivated; a *Movimento Friuli* was founded in 1964, which at the 1968 elections won twelve per cent of the vote. Its platform included: more autonomy for Friuli, from Rome as well as from Trieste; protection and development of the ethnic-linguistic heritage: European federalism (the "Europe of the Regions" model); environmental conservation, and prehaps most important of all, social and economic development. Its ideology was significantly influenced by local "revisionist" historians and literati, extolling the values of ancient local automous political systems (the Friulian "patriarchal state") and literature; by the contemporary foreign and Italian writers on ethnic-regional matters (G. Heraud, R. Laffont, S. Salvi, etc.); and, later, by some ideas from the New Left. With this mixture, the Movimento Friuli managed to become a significant political force, but in the late 1970s its fortunes declined, due basically to a cleavage between the older clerical-moderate-conservative and the younger marxist-revolutionary wings. In the 1980s it was reduced to about three per cent (Strassoldo 1985) and in the 1990s it dissolved. Other political formations took its place (*Lega Autonomia Friuli*), with about the same low level of electoral turnout.

The example of Friuli was probably not without significance for the neighboring, much larger Veneto (population 4,300,000). In the late seventies, a *Liga Veneta* (Venetian League) was founded. While Veneto had a much more glorious history (for example in the Republic of Venice), the main initial motivation of the *Liga Veneta* was simply the percieved threat to local culture and way of life posed by recent immigration from the South, both in the public service sector and in private industry, spurred by the region's lively rates of economic growth. One of the more characteristic rally cries of the Liga was *Fuori i terroni*, (Southerners go home). The *Liga Veneta's* electoral support was modest, hovering on the 3-4 % of the regional vote. Finally, in the 1980s mighty Lombardy also got the ethnic-regional message.

The case of the Lega Lombarda - Lega Nord

Since Late Roman times the region around Milan has been one of Italy's powerhouses. This was originally due to the exceptional productivity of its irrigated agriculture in the plains, to the ironworks in the mountains, and to its position along one of the great commercial channels between the Mediterranean and the North (the Genoa-St.Gotthard-Rhine valley axis). In Roman times, Milan had been one of the imperial capitals; after its decline, neighbouring Pavia was chosen as the capital of the Goths' and then the Lombards' (Long-beards) Italian kingdom. In the new milennium Milan again became again one of the major economic and political powers. Its strong ties with transalpine Europe are witnessed by its Dome, one of Europe's grander gothic cathedrals. Lombardy managed to retain its economic and civil leadership even during the centuries of foreign domination , and in the nineteenth century was ready for the industrial revolution. By 1980, it was by far the largest (9 million), richest and most modern region in Italy and one of the world's great industrial regions.

That an ethnic-regional movement would sway such a region is certainly a rather intriguing event. In the early 1980s Mr. Umberto Bossi, a restless young man from the a village north of Milan, developed some interests in vernacular poetry, culture and ethnic regional movements. Formerly, he had tried his hand as a pop singer, enrolled in a medical college and worked briefly for the Communist party. He established ties with a mentor of the small Piedmontese ethnic movement, B. Salvadori, and called at the *Venetian Liga* and the *Movimento Friuli*. He saw some scope for such an inititative in his home region and, with a handful of cronies, founded the Lombard League. In 1985 they ran in the municipal elections in a few communes of the province of Varese, getting about 2.5 % of the votes. Two years later (1987) the League participated to the electoral contest in the seven northernmost Lombard provinces; again, its overall turnout was around 2-3%, enough to stimulate some political and scholarly interest. In the following two years, its share in the whole of Lombardy increased to about 6%: in the highly fractured Italian political system, it had become the fourth major party (after the Christian Democrats, Communists and Socialists) and an unsettling political phenomenon. At the European elections of 1989 it won 16.4% of the votes, becoming the second major party in Lombardy and attaining national prominence; the following year its vote reached 18-20%, and the first place in many townships. In 1992 it formed a coalition with the other regional leagues, named *Lega Nord*. The result was, in comparison to the glacial pace of Italian electoral change, a true landslide north of the Po: 25-30% voteshare in Lombardy, Piedmont, Liguria, Veneto, Friuli.

Sources of success

This success has many sources. As with the older Leagues and regional movements, it provided a new political message. For the first time in modern history, the Lombards were declared a nation different from the other Italians, with full rights to self-government. A complete break with tradition was carried out also in its form of political discourse. In contrast with the convoluted, often byzantine, highly sophisticated style of political communication prevalent in Italy, League leaders adopted an elementary, uncouth linguistic code. Mr. Bossi perfected the art of speaking like the common man, someone with whom the populace could completely identify. In contrast with the word ballets of established politicians he used the bludgeon. His speeches were full of macho expressions (the most famous being "the League has it hard") outrageous invectives ("Rome, the Great Robber") and violent metaphors (including references to Kalashnikovs and "cutting throats from ear to ear"). He also shows an utter disregard for consistency in thought and proposals; his dramatic announcements and sudden about-faces are so frequent as to legitimize the suspicion that they are carefully planned to keep the public constantly dazzled. In some ways, he embodies the ancient figure of the rabble-rouser; in others, the consummate post- modern politician.

In contrast to the novelty of its contents and communication form, the organizational style of the League seems quite traditional. It has been criticized for being a "Leninist" type of party, in its high degree of centralization (Mr. Bossi is unquestionably the Boss), the tight gatekeeping and the merciless suppression of internal dissent. Also traditional is the building of a system of specialized "collateral" agencies aimed at different social groups and interests (working class, businessmen, youth, women, Catholics, etc.). Like the other parties, the League also uses all the traditional propaganda and fund-raising techniques, from party "festivals" to marketing gimmicks. In the early years it suffered from very low exposure in the larger, national media; its growth relied almost exclusively on personal networks and local press and electronic communication. Finally, the Lombard knack for hard work, discipline and efficiency, allied to the organizational skills of Mr. Bossi's clique, his personal capacities and finally the considerable technical and economic resources of the region, help explain why the Lombard League took off, while the others had stalled or failed.

Favourable structural conditions

Wider structural conditions were also conducive to the growth of the League. In the late 1980s, the moral basis of the two main national parties, the Christian Democratic and the Communist, was dissolving. Their ideological "raison d'etre" had slowly eroded respectively with the secularization of society and the withering away of revolutionary, millenaristic expectations. The PCI, *Partiti Communista Italiano* (now PDS, *Partito della Sinistra*) had long ceased to appear as a "threat to Western Civilization". Correspondingly, also the Christian Democratic party lost its function as the "dam" and "shield" against Communism. This process culminated in 1989, as an aftershock of the destruction of the Berlin Wall and the ensuing collapse of the Soviet empire. It is paradoxical that in Italy one of the main consequences of the fall of Communism has been the crumbling of the system erected against it. The Communist Party adapted swiftly to the new circumstances, changing its name to Democratic Party of the Left, and jettisoned most of its old doctrine, while keeping its organization and its multifarious structural roots in society. It suffered sizeable losses, but was able to hold its heartland (the regions of Emilia-Romagna, Tuscany and Umbria), thus containing the League steamrollers north of the Po river.

The presence of a powerful Communist Party had resulted, for several decades, in a "blocked" party system in which there was no acceptable alternative to the Centrist governments. This inevitably lead to "consociativist" practices (i.e., the parties in power "buying out" the opposition) and widespread corruption. Italians have always been cynical on the honesty of their administrators, but only after the Milan "Clean Hands" operation started (February 1992) was the incredible extent of corruption fully exposed to public opinion. The ensuing disgust gave a huge boost to the League, seen then as the only wholly uncompromised and clean political force. But it cannot be ruled out that Milan's prosecutors had been encouraged by the winds of political revolt already raised by the Lombard League.

Italy's fiscal system had been reformed in the early 1970s, and by the end of the decade small businessmen, who until then had largely skirted taxes, began to feel increasing pressure. By the mid 1980s, the pressure on Italian taxpayers in general had reached Scandinavian levels; while the services rendered by the state, it was felt, remained at a "third-world" level. Moreover, the procedures for paying taxes were becoming ever more difficult, time-consuming and uncertain due to a continuous outflow of new fiscal measures. Paying taxes had become a torture. As is well-known since the Boston tea party, this is the surest recipe for revolution.

There was also a general feeling, in the productive North, that the Italian central state, occupied by the corrupt party system, wasted hard-won taxpayers' money in an inefficient public sector, in excessive welfare and in ill-conceived aid programmes in the South. Deficit spending and a mounting national debt - in the late 1980s getting close to one year's GNP - raised nightmares of state bankruptcy and general financial catastrophe.

In the minds of a growing number of Northerners, one cause of inefficiency and corruption in the public sphere was the fact that the public service, at all echelons, was occupied overwhelmingly by Southerners. This is due to the national competition system for public jobs, and the much higher quest for such jobs in the South, where opportunities in the private sectors are fewer. Thus the proportion of Southerners in such services as the military, police, elementary and secondary schools, health service, judiciary, mail, rail, revenue, and others are much higher than their share in the population, and many of them have moved to fill such posts in the North. Southerners are also accused of having a special inclination to such low-paying but often non-demanding jobs, and better connections to get them ("clientelism"). The state was increasingly seen by Northern productive classes as a huge machine to create jobs for Southerners and funnel them to the North. And they grew all the more impatient of being vexed, or at least ill served, by a State that spoke with a distinct Southern accent.

This linked with a lurking "anti-Southernism", that had already emerged at the times of the great immigration (1950-1970), when hundreds of thousands of Southerners had come to work in the fast developing industrial North-West (the triangle between Turin, Milan and Genoa). As usually happens in such conditions, the indigenous populations showed some hostility against the newcomers. Such feelings hardened in the 1970s, when the immigrant communities were considered breeding grounds of both petty and organized crime (encroachment of Mafia, launching of the "kidnapping industry"). Anti-southernism, an undeniable ingredient of both the *Liga Veneta* and the *Lega Lombarda* in their early stages, has in several ways been muffled as they grew. It must be noted that in the League country, so far, there have been no recorded incidents between supporters and immigrants; on the contrary, many of the latter have joined the League.

Another early target of the Leagues was immigration from less developed countries. In the late 1970s, Italy, long a country of emigration, began to house growing flows of immigrants from the Third World. This aroused xenophobic and racist feelings especially in large cities. Undeniably, the early League rode this wave of unrest; but, as in the case of anti-southernism, the anti-immigration argument has also been toned down in more recent years.

In sum, the Northern Leagues may be interpreted as a manifestation of, or reaction to, a number of grievances of the Northern productive strata over many general features of the Italian socio-economic and political system. At the beginning it had a markedly lower-middle-class basis; then it expanded in both directions, among workers (especially self-employed artisans) and among the upper-middle professional class. Some of its features - social bases, strong centralization, aggressive style, early "racist" veneer - have elicited fears that the League embodies a new form of fascism; but differences are deep. To begin with, throughout its career the League has scrupulously shunned recourse to any violence other than verbal. Secondly, its central official values, like federalism, localism, autonomy, anti-etatism, are squarely opposite to those of fascism. Thirdly, events in 1994 amply demonstrated the incompatibility between the two. That its anti-fascist stand is earnest has been now amply acknowledged also by most of its political opponents, and all studies show that the support does not come primarily from the traditional right, but from the entire political spectrum, perhaps mostly from the centre (from former socialists and Christian Democrats). The League is now usually defined as a populist protest movement, or a movement of the "radical, angered centre".

The evolution of the League's ideology

In its short life - hardly a decade - the Lombard/Northern League has exhibited a remarkable capacity to adapt its ideology to political necessities. In earlier years, the question could be raised whether its Lombard "ethno-regionalism" would evolve into a small-scale state-nationalism. Subsequent events showed without any doubt that this has not been the case. Early attempts to found Lombard identity on cultural and linguistic commonality (the Lombard People or Nation) failed, because modern Lombardy, as an administrative region, includes provinces with many centuries of separate histories, and speaking very different dialects. The protection and development of local languages and other features of "nationhood" and expressions of "vernacularism" and "folklorism" were thereafter squarely rejected. The situation is different in other Northern regions, such as Veneto, that sport a more consistent unitary history and homogeneous dialects. The several Northern leagues still refer to their constituencies as "nations" but few take it seriously.

The abandonment of the nationalist rethoric is also correlated to the unification of the several regional leagues under Lombard leadership. There is a conspicuous lack of cultural commonality between the several regions of the North. Piedmont, Liguria, Lombardy, Emilia, Veneto and Trentino are the result of at least a thousand years of separate political histories, and this has left its sediments in collective memories and languages (dialects). Several studies have shown that Northern Italy, as a socio-geographical concept, elicits hardly any feeling of attachment or identity (Strassoldo 1992a). Accordingly, the 1992 project to break up Italy into three separate sovereign republics in the North, Centre and South, bound only by a federal-confederate compact, failed to enthuse the League electorate. In more recent times it was described by the League leadership as a mere metaphor.

A more moderate arrangement was then advanced, whereby the concept of sovereign republics was substituted by that of "macro- regions" ("Padania" in the North, "Etruria" in the Centre, and simply "South" for the third one). This model was based on more economic-instrumental arguments (optimal dimensions, efficiency, etc.) than on historic-cultural ones. But this too failed to draw much support.

At the end of 1994 a third model was proposed, in the guise of a constitutional reform project, according to which Italy would stay one, but Federal, Republic; the present twenty regions would be compacted into half as many, endowed with much larger powers and re-christened "states"; Rome would retain its capital status within a "Federal District". This very "American" project, presented on very open terms, clearly goes a long way towards compromise. All other parties have received and even praised it as a serious basis for discussion. The reaction of the representatives of traditional regional identitities remains to be seen.

82

The League's insistence on such projects has brought about an important change in Italian political discourse: the wide acceptance of the concept of federalism. Federalism was the prevalent political doctrine in the early Risorgimento period, but for more than a century after the unification under Piedmont, it was damned as a reactionary device to revive the old statelets and principates and as a threat to national unity. Often praised as good for other countries, like Switzerland and the United States, and as a framework for inter- and supra-national integration, it was considered unsuitable for Italy, for a variety of reasons. Initially, the League's emphasis on federalism was taken by almost all other parties as separatism in disguise; more recently, it has been accepted as a legitimate and positive request for more local autonomy, state decentralization and regional devolution. Almost all Italian political parties now declare themselves federalist - in some sense and to some measure.

A second core-value of League ideology, Europeanism, has been considerably neglected in more recent years, following the decline of anti-Southern polemics. As we have seen, one of the main concerns behind the rise of the League was that the backward South would impede the progressive North to stay in the core countries of the United Europe, and drag it down into the Mediterranean and the Third World. This was the ulgitimate behind the Northerners' separatist temptations, to which other traditional anti-southern motifs and stereotypes undoubtedly accrued. But, as already seen, this strand in the League's political culture immediately became indefensible: it aroused charges of racism, was severly criticised also by the Church, became an embarassment in the face of the growing numbers of Southern immigrants who wanted to joined the League, and blocked its plans to spread in the South. In sum, as the league pursued political respectability and national responsibilities, it had to drop the anti-Southern motive. As it did this its European argument also lost its teeth, because in itself Europe is an uncontentious issue in Italy. For many years, all political parties in Italy have supported European integration; early dissent of the Communists has long since been converted. Many of the leading Italian advocates of the European idea have come from the South. As is well known from many public opinion polls, Italians have always declared themselves more enthusiastically pro-Europe than most other member nations. The reason why the European argument has almost disappeared from recent political discussions in Italy is that everybody agrees on it, and "holier than thou" arguments do not arouse audiences.

More recently, a central place in the League ideology has been taken by the principles of economic individualism, unfettered free enterprise, market economy, deregulation and privatization; which in the 1980s came to be known as Reaganomics and Thatcherism. This correlates with the interests of the original core of the League's constituency - small business - and with some of the macroscopic diseases of Italian society (huge state debt). But the new emphasis on these values is a consequence of the League turning its assaults against the Left. By the end of 1993, the combined effects of Operation Clean

Hand and of the League had been the practical destruction of the centrist government parties - Christian Democracy, Socialists, Liberals, Republicans, Social-democrats. The only traditional political forces left standing were the former opposition parties, at the right and the left. The rightist one seemed too small and irrespectable as a competitor; so the League's wrath turned on the Democratic Party of the Left. The League's campaign against *statalismo* (statism), *assistenzialismo* (welfarism) and public intervention in the economy and so on was aimed specifically against the former Communists. This emphasis however is the less original part of the League's ideology, having been international conventional wisdom of the eighties. It was also reproached (for instance, by the Church) as a symptom of egoistical particularism of the better off groups of Italian society, both territorial and otherwise. In other words, the League's new emphasis on market and business values prompted the inevitable countercharge of lack of social and national "solidarity".

Strategies and tactics

In the course of only five years, the League's strategy and tactics changed remarkably. At the outset it held an uncompromising stance against the established party system (*partitocrazia* or party-cracy). The first goal was to reach absolute majority in the North, and from this power base start negotiations for a radical federalist reform of the Italian state (the "Three Republics" idea). To this goal, a penetration of federalist ideas and movements in the Centre-South was envisaged and attempted, but failed utterly. By 1993 it was clear that the League had insurmountable difficulties in spreading south of the Po river, and that it was losing momentum even in the home bases. The mayoral elections in November 1993, held in the new "majority system", marked the tapering off of the movement's growth curve and an embarassing failure of the much-publicized drive to reach the "openings to the sea", i. e., to capture the city-halls of Genoa, Venice and Trieste. The polls showed that the centrist electorate would not simply turn to the League, but tended to run out in all directions; in larger cities and south of the Po river it tended to turn rather evenly both to the traditional left (ex-Communists and allies) and toward the traditional right (*Movimento Sociale Italiano*). A big surprise came from the South, where it was generally thought that the old centrist parties would be able to hold thanks to the entrenched patronage system; instead, here too the left-right polarization obtained.

At this point it was inevitable for the League leadership to revise its strategy. Unilateral secession, with the inevitable armed confrontation, was not taken as a serious option by anybody; the alternative could only be coalition formation with other parties. This was also imposed by the logic of the new electoral system, introduced by almost unanimous plebiscite in April 1993. After some dallying with the moderate-Catholic splinter group of Mario Segni, in February

1994 the League struck an electoral deal with *Forza Italia*, a brand-new political formation just founded by tycoon Silvio Berlusconi.

The socio-cultural and organizational differences between the two forces were enormous. The League was a spontaneous, genuinely popular movement; *Forza Italia* is the sudden, top-down creation of a single entrepreneur, throwing into the venture all the power of his money, his business organization, and his popular image as a very successful self-made man. This at least is the prevailing view; some plot-theorists think that it had been in the making for many years. The League's early growth was based on grass-roots, personal interactions, with very little, and mostly derisive, exposure in the media. *Forza Italia* was a virtual creation of Berlusconi's media empire. The Leagues' style was aggressive, conflictual, raucous, plebeian; Berlusconi's suave and reassuring. The League poised itself as a revolutionary force, set out to destroy the old party system; *Forza Italia* appeared rather as the anointed heir of the vanished centre parties. The League was inevitably, by the logic of its name, a sectional force; *Forza Italia* appealed, as the name implies, to the whole of the country. Finally, the League appeared bent on breaking up Italy; *Forza Italia* struck all the chords of deep-seated national patriotism.

Against these differences, there were three basic commonalities: both forces were new (one almost, the other wholly) in the political arena, and thus free from the corruption of the old party system; both appealed to basically the same social groups, the productive middle classes (with a more lower-middle and working-class slant for the League, and a more upper-middle class one for *Forza Italia*); and both shared a moderate, "petit-bourgeois" ideology, pitched somewhat artificially in shrill anti-communist tones.

Tentatively, a fourth commonality may be suggested: their roots in the Milan area. The hypothesis may be advanced that the whole of Italy was tired of a political system perceived as dominated by Roman and Southern mores, and was ready to experiment the hegemony of Italy's Moral Capital, as Milan has been known for generations.

However, the Centre South kept some of its differences. While widely accepting Mr. Berlusconi, it lacked the counterpart of a Mr. Bossi. Instead it had a leaning toward the traditional, national, neo- (ex-, post-) Fascist Right. The young leader of the *Movimento Sociale Italiano*, Mr. Gianfranco Fini, was quick to grasp the opportunities opened by the crumbling of the old centrist parties. He managed to tone-down the Fascist heritage, and succeded in presenting his party as a moderate-conservative one, clean and patriotic. At the mayoral elections of November 1993, he enjoyed good success all over the country, and a large one in the Centre-South. In the wake of this, a coalition was formed in this part of Italy between Berlusconi's *Forza Italia* and Fini's party, now re-christened *Alleanza Nazionale*.

Thus a strange situation obtained: in the North, a coalition between Berlusconi and Bossi (*Polo delle libertà*); in the Centre-South, a coalition between Berlusconi and Fini (*Polo del Buon Governo*). But Bossi, with his typical nonchalance for formal logics, negated the transitivity rule, and thundered that he was not, and would never be, allied with "fascists".

The League's campaign for the March 1994 national political elections was likewise paradoxical: the main target for attack - often savage, as usual - was not the opposing left-wing coalition, "The Progressives", but the "fascists", and, to a minor extent, *Forza Italia* itself.

Against most expectations this strange coalition achieved a smashing success: about 43 % of the vote nationwide, gaining a comfortable absolute majority in the House of Representatives. Within it, however, the big winners were Berlusconi and Fini; the League lost almost 15% of its electorate.

The League was now trapped. Having chosen to play national democratic politics and to drive for government positions in Rome, it had inevitably become a minor force (7 % nationwide). Its more moderate supporters spilled over to *Forza Italia*; its more radical ones became increasingly angered over the whole strategy.

The waggling of the League between the temptations of power and the instinct for opposition, between the hope to bring about the "federalist revolution" from the Roman palaces and the desire to take again to the streets calling for the Republic of the North, between sticking to the deals with the other parties and keeping faith to grassroots militants, characterized Italian politics in the following months. While some League representatives have become ministers in Berlusconi's government, Bossi and others kept attacking and threatening to topple it. The tensions between the "ministerial" and the radical souls have already resulted in some desertions to *Forza Italia*. These tensions have provided the groundwork for new elections but most observers think that the League's renovation of Italian politics has already gone as far as it could, and that the Thermidorian restoration has already set in.

Conclusion

The experience of the Lombard/Northern League suggests that the nation-state is still the most powerful level of political organization in Italy. Early proposals that the North secede unilaterally from the rest of the country, or that Italy be broken up into three confederate but separate republics, have not been accepted by the overwhelming majority of citizens, even in the North. Conversely, the force of ethnicity (ethnic regionalism, small nationalism) seems to be very limited in Italy, except for the internationally recognized and protected national minorities (French, German, Slovene) along the Alpine boundary. Regional ethnic patriotism (Venetian, Lombard, Piedmontese, etc.) was important at the beginning of the Leaguist movement, as a radical departure from the dominant political culture of the "Roman" or "Italian" party system; but it proved unviable in practice and of limited political appeal. Due to a very long and complex history, Northern Italy is a patchwork of very small-scale, local cultural identities and dialects. Many earlier studies have shown that Northern Italy is not perceived and felt as an object of positive attachment. None of its local cultures and dialects could aspire to hegemonize it. From the beginning, the Northern League had to use standard Italian in their political communication.

The international level also plays important roles in the development of the League, especially in terms of the European Union. Firstly, it has fueled the North's growing dissatisfaction with the Italian state. The North, bordering with the more advanced parts of Europe, having easier access to them, and having developed strong economic relations with them through the internationalization of the Northern economy, saw in Europe an exemplar of civil development. The central place of Federalism in the League's ideology comes more from the Swiss, German and Austrian examples than from domestic traditions. Thus the international, European level exerted a strong, albeit wholly unintentional, pull in the rise of the Northern League. On the other hand, the international level also discouraged the Northern League's early secessionist tendencies. No known political force, in Europe or in the world, could wish the disintegration of Italy, especially after the Yugoslav precedent.

The role of the border deserves some special discussion in the context of this book. A glance at the Italian electoral map makes it evident that the ethnic (national minority) parties are a border phenomenon, and that the regional Leagues started out from border areas. This is particularly true of the Lombard League, whose cradle and core lies within a handful of kilometers from the border. But this has little to do with the changes in the functions of internal and external boundaries issuing from the process of European integration, since Northern Italy's borders are mostly with non-Union states (Switzerland and, until 1 January 1995, Austria). Rather, it has to do with general aspects of the border situation (proximity, access to cross-border cultures, similiarity of geographical environment and historical experiences) as well as with general features of international relations in this part of the world (such as openness and cooperation) (Gubert 1972; Strassoldo and Delli Zotti 1981).

Ethnic-regional identities were only one component of the set of political resources upon which the Northern Leagues built their early fortunes; the other being economic interests. Their relative importance is hard to assess. Ethnic regional identities seem to have been more important in the earlier, more peripheral leagues (in Friuli, Piedmont, Veneto) and less in the Lombardy case. The Lombard League, and the confederation it hegemonized, the Northern League, seems to be better characterized as a fiscal revolt, a populist or "radical centre" movement than an ethnic-regional one. Its extraordinary success seem to originate from the sheer demographic and economic strength of Lombardy - one of Europe's great industrial regions - and to a constellation of unique historical contingencies: an able leadership, a concomitant set of crises in Italian society (moral, fiscal, financial and economic), the operation "Clean Hand" and the disapperance of the Communist world.

Ethnic-regional claims and the material interests of the productive classes of the North provided only the raw resources for initial political mobilization; they could not be used as such in the political, cultural and moral system of modern Italy. In this regard, the early stern criticisms of the Catholic Church's hierarchies of the League's "particularism" and "lack of social and national solidarity" is significant. So those resources had to be transformed, rationalized and legitimized into the ideologies, respectively, of federalism (including fiscal federalism) and liberalism. Whether, or to what extent, the federalist program can be used to reform the Italian system in such a way as to give some satisfaction to the (rather weak) demands of ethnic-regional movements along the Northern Italian borders remains to be seen. At present the prospects seem dim.

References

Agnew, J. 1987. *Place and politics*. Boston: Allen and Unwin.

Anderson, M. 1983. Frontier regions in western Europe. London: Frank Cass.

Cartocci, R. 1994. *Fra lega e Chiesa: l'Italia in cerca di integrazione*. Bologna: il Mulino.

De Rougemont, D. (ed.) 1968. *Naissance de l'Europe des region*. Geneva: Centre Europeen de Culture.

Diamanti, I. 1993. *La Lega. Geografia, storia e sociologia di un nuovo soggetto politic*. Ronma: Donzelli.

Gottmann, J. (ed.) 1980. *Centre and periphery. Spatial variations in politics*. Beverely Hills-London: Sage.

Gubert, R. 1972. *La situazione confinaria*. Trieste: Lint.

Mannheimer, R. (ed.) 1991. *La Lega Lombarda*. Milano: Feltrinelli.

Poche, B. 1994. *La crise de l'etat territorial: separatismes et federalismes en europoe dans les annes 1990. Les cas belges et italien*. Paper presented at the XIII world Congress of sociology, Bielefeld.

Schmidtke, O. 1993. The populist challenge to the Italian nation state: The lega Lombarda/Nord. *Regional politics & policy*. 3 (3): 140-162.

Shils, E. 1975. *Center and periphery*. Chicago: University of Chicago Press.

Smith, A. 1981. *The ethnic revival*. Cambridge: Cambridge University Press.

Strassoldo, R. (ed.), 1973. *Confini e regioni (Boundaries and Regions)* Trieste: Lint.

____. 1985. The case of Friuli. *International political science review*. 6 (2): 197-215.

____. 1992. Globalism and localism: theoretical reflections and some evidence. In *Globalization and territorial identities*. Z. Mlinar (ed.). Aldershot: Avebury.

Strassoldo, R. and Delli Zotti, G. (eds.) 1981. *Cooperation and conflict in border areas*. Milano: Angeli.

Strassoldo, R. and Tessarin, N. 1992. *Le radici del localismo. Indagine sociologica sull'appartenenza territoriale in Friuli*. Trento: Reverdito.

5　Astride two states: Cross-border co-operation in the Basque Country

Francisco Letamendía, Mikel Gómez Uranga and Goio Etxebarria[1]

Part 1: The political and cultural dimensions

The development of the European Community (EC)/the European Union (EU) regional policy since the early 1970s has allowed regions to take a much more active role in European affairs than previously (De Castro 1992: 41). The Single European Act of February 1986, which came into force in July 1987, decisively transformed EU regional policy. The decision was taken to focus the coordinated action of the three Structural Funds, i.e., the European Regional Development Fund (ERDF), the European Agricultural Guarantee and Guidance Fund (EAGGF) and the European Social Fund (ESF), on priority areas. The Objective 1 areas were the less developed regions where GDP is less than 75% of the EU average; Objective 2 regions were those in industrial decline. Growing regional activism in EU affairs has also led to extensive interregional networking. These networks which have been emerging since the early 1970s, while given momentum by the European Commission, were created from the bottom up. They have been the real driving force in the creation of a third level of influence in the Community, that of sub-state Europe. This has provided a new arena for the Basque country to forge interregional alliances including links across the Spanish-French state border between the Southern and Northern Basque lands.

In 1973, some twenty regions established the Conference of Peripheral and Maritime Regions in the EEC. Since 1989, three large networks have focused on the Mediterranean, the North Sea and the Atlantic. The so-called Atlantic Arc, in which the Basque Country plays an important part, groups together twenty five regions (five from the United Kingdom, one from Ireland, five from France, [among which is Aquitaine] six from Spain [all the Cantabrian "cornice"] and five in Portugal). The Atlantic Arc Network hopes to rebalance

Europe towards the Atlantic fringe given the marginalisation of this extensive area by the London-Milan axis (popularly known as the "big banana"), and the growing strength of the Mediterranean axis.

The Basque Autonomous Community (*Euskadi*) is represented in two other regional alliances. The Association of Regions of Traditional Industry consists of twenty regions with declining industries, among them Euskadi and Cataluña (Catalonia). The aims of this network were taken into account in framing Community regional policy for declining industrial areas. The Pyrenees Working Community, established in 1983, combined the seven Franco-Spanish Pyrenean regions along with Andorra with the joint aim of halting the tilt towards the Mediterranean. Encouraged by the Atlantic Arc Commission, the Congress of South Atlantic European Regions (EAS) met in October 1989; EAS seeks to ease the difficulties brought about in these regions as a result of their peripherality.

The economic logic of the EU, which the Single European Market insured would come to fruition, has led Community institutions to differentiate three overlapping levels of territorial unit, NUTS 1, 2, and 3 (Nomenclature of Territorial Units for Statistics). These set out distinct domains for monitoring EU economic intervention including the least developed regions (Objective 1), regions in industrial decline (Objective 2) and rural regions characterized by lagging development (Objective 5b). The twelve-member EU was divided into 66 NUTS 1, 176 NUTS 2, and 829 NUTS 3. NUTS 1 are the large socio-economic macro-regions which combine various smaller regions and it is at this level that the consequences of processes such as customs union are analysed. NUTS 2 correspond to basic regions such as the Autonomous Communities in Spain, in other words to the units used by member states for their regional policies. NUTS 3 (*provincias* in Spain, *Kreise* in Germany, *departements* in France), facilitate periodic diagnoses for specific regional action. The criteria on which classification are based are purely economic, rather than historic, cultural, juridical or political. These criteria ignore provisions such as Article 149 of the Spanish Constitution, which expressly forbids the federation of Autonomous Communities. The Basque Autonomous Community is part of the *Noroeste* NUTS 1 in the Spanish state along with the Autonomous Communities of Navarra, Rioja and Aragon. The corresponding Sud-Ouest NUTS 1 across the border in France is comprised of Aquitaine, Midi-Pyrénées and Limousin. The cross-border co-operation promoted by the EU has thrown up a broader fourth level of territorial unit which has not been officially recognized, namely the trans-state "Euro-region", which would result from networking across the borders of various NUTS 1 or NUTS 2.

While the Community process of European integration acts as an incentive to cross-border and interregional co-operation, the same cannot be said of the Spanish and French states, which concede only limited participation to sub-state entities in matters external to their own area. The long standing French centralist tradition, cautiously broken with by 1982 laws, insures that international activity on the part of the regions, and more specifically interregional crossborder co-operation, is viewed with suspicion. The Spanish Constitution of 1978, in article 149, attributes exclusive powers in international relations to the state, a situation which, according to Professor Carlos Fernández de Casadevante (1985:194), contradicts article 148, which establishes the exclusive powers of the autonomous communities; since many of these (such as fishing in inland waters, environment, livestock) have an external element to their activity which does not come to a halt at the border lines which separate regions just because they are situated in different states such as France and Spain.

The Basque country in cross-border context

It is necessary to provide a brief description of the border region of the Basque Autonomous Community, along with Navarra (in Spain) and Aquitaine (in France). From east to west, the delimiting areas are: both slopes of the Pyrenean valleys, consisting of parts of Nafarroa (Navarra) in the South and parts of Nafarroa Beherea (Basse-Navarre) and Lapurdi (Labourd) in the North; the "Comarca del Bajo Bidasoa" and the Bahía de Higuer (Higer Bay), between Gipuzkoa (Guipúzcoa) and Lapurdi, which includes both banks of the mouth of the Bidasoa.

In Nafarroa (Navarra), situated within the "Comarcas Pirenaicas del Valle del Ronca" Salazar, Aezkoa and Esteribar-Erro, are the *Municipios* (municipalities) of Isaba, Ustarroz, and Ochagabía; within the *Facerias* are the *Municipios* of Valcarlos, Erro and Burgete. In this part of the Pyrenees the traditional economic base is that of transhumant sheep farming and forestry. These valleys are faced in the North Basque Country (in France) by the Tardets-Sorholus *Canton*, (within the historic territory of Zuberoa-Soule), with its *communes* (municipalities) of Larraun and St Engrace. Remaining in Navarra one finds the *Comarcas* Baztán and Cinco Villas within which are situated the border *Municipios* Urdax, Zugarramurdi, Etxalar and Vera de Bidasoa. These areas are bounded in the North by the *Cantons* of St. Jean de Pied Port, St. Etienne de Baigorry, Ustaritz, and Espelette. The farm economy in these valleys is more diverse: bovine and sheep livestock, forestry and associated varied cultivation (corn, turnip and beans).

When the river Bidasoa leaves Navarra, its last thirteen kilometers form the international boundary which separates the two states. The banks and the riverside of the Higuer bay form the Bajo Bidasoa (Lower Bidasoa) region. In the South this includes the Guipuzcoan *Municipios* of Irún and Fuenterrabía. The former is an urban industrial area and in terms of inhabitants (more than

93

MAP 5. 1
Regionalisation at the NUTS 2 level:
The Autonomous Communities in Spain and the Regions in France. France
does not recognize the Northern Basque Country, included in Aquitaine,
as an institutional entity.

50,000) is the second largest city in Gipúzcoa (Guipúzcoa); up until the present it has survived on customs traffic. In the North Basque Country, on the French side of the interstate borderline, the Hendaye *Canton*, another customs centre, consists of the municipalities of Hendaye, Biriatou and Urrugne.

Until the beginning of modern times the Pyrenean border valleys formed a federation based upon *Facerías*, agreements of alliance and peace about the use of grazing zones and the extent of all external political control. Since the sixteenth century, when the great monarchies of France and Spain were consolidated, the valleys, under the threat of state conflicts of which they were not a part, adapted their old pacts to the new situation, converting them into detailed agreements which determined the limit of grazing zones and the use of water and woods. These agreements sought to provide guarantees against the risks of war. In the Higuer Bay, Fuenterrabía, which possessed a *Carta Puebla* granted by the Spanish king at the beginning of the thirteenth century, used the Bidasoa river as its own, over which it had jurisdiction.

The predominance of the French monarchy over the Castilian monarchy is reflected in the first crossborder agreement of the modern age: the Treaty of the Pyrenees of 1659, following the Hapsburg defeat in the Thirty Years War (Peace of Westphalia). The Treaty of the Pyrenees decided that the Pyrenees should be "taken as a boundary between the Spanish and the Gauls", granting the King of France those territories which he had previously conquered although the frontier remained without an accurate delimitation. The frontier was fixed in the 1785 Treaty of Elizondo and the various delimiting Treaties agreed upon between 1856 and 1866. In accordance with those Treaties France imposed her point of view fixing the boundary in the middle of the Bidasoa river. French hegemony was also shown at the delimitation of the Higuer Bay: the Treaties attributed 257,000 sq. meters of the Higuer Bay waters to Spain, and 1,500,000 sq. meters to France.

The Pyrenean cross-border routes and passes suffered the consequences of lack of trust between the two states. Until the beginning of the eighteenth century a cross-border road did not exist, and by the late nineteenth century there were only eleven such roads. Military considerations were the main obstructions to the opening of trans-Pyrenean roads and these also explain the present day problem of rail links. Fernández de Casadevante (1985: 259) has pointed out that "in relation to the French border, in the same manner as with roads, opposition on the part of military existed to the construction of rail links, as they believed that if opened they could constitute a danger in times of war". These negative opinions triumphed in a way when between 1860-64 the first Spanish trans-Pyrenean railway line was built using a gauge which at that time was not in use in Europe (except in Russia) but which consequentially obliged Portugal to adopt it (presently the change of axles is made in the stations of Irún and Hendaye).

Today, Spanish/French connections are made only at the two extremes of the Pyrenean line: two thirds of the interchanges take place and 51% of goods pass through the juncture which unites Aquitaine and the Basque Country; while industrial products enter at the Basque border (some 80%), agricultural products enter at the Catalan border (some 77%). The Pyrenean cross-border traffic is very limited; there are only six routes, which are the outcome of Spanish/French negotiations. Bordeaux is linked to Donostia (San Sebastián) through Behobia, and to Iruñea (Pamplona) through Dantzarinea. There are only four cross-border train lines, and they are concentrated in the extremes; the most important is Irún-Hendaye. The offices of the *Controles Nacionales Yuxtapuestos* (CNY) are located in Irún and Behobia in the South, and in Hendaye and Biriatou in the North.

There are two intergovernmental border commissions in the Basque Country; however their effectiveness, which is dependent on the Spanish and French states, has been described by Professor Fernández de Casadevante as very poor (1985: 342). They are the International Commission on the Pyrenees, which was founded in 1877, and the later (1978) but equally inefficient *Comisión Técnica Mixta del Bidasoa* (CTMB). Spanish membership of the I.C.P. includes all Ministries of the Central Government as well as the Army, but no regional or local authority is represented. Its bureaucratisation and slowness has made it incapable of finding suitable solutions to such problems as pollution and destruction of some fish species (such as salmon) in the Bidasoa river. The CTMB is alternatively presided over by the Commanders of the French and Spanish Naval Stations. Its operational capacity is almost nil, and the treatment given to local authorities discriminatory.

Cultural cross-border links: The Basque language

The strong position of spoken Basque in the border municipalities, especially in the Western part of Navarra and the whole of the northern part of the Basque Country, should provide for the creation of successful initiatives to conserve and promote the Basque language[2]. Since 1980, the promotion of Basque has been an explicit aim of all the governments within the Basque Autonomous Community, and is included in the text of the *Declaración de Ainhoa*, which was agreed upon in 1993 by the Presidents of the Basque and Navarran Communities and Regional Council of Aquitaine. However, in relation to the northern territories of the Basque Country, cross-border co-operation related to protection of the Basque language is impeded by the following factors: Basque does not have official language status in Aquitaine, and the French State has refused to sign the Social Charter on the Rights of Minority Languages and Cultures. There exists, therefore, a legal vacuum in this state as regards protection of the Basque language.

Thanks to the EU, interregional collaboration between the Basque Autonomous Community and Aquitaine has been able to proceed, beyond the localised nature of cross-border co-operation and the limitations imposed by the two states. This collaboration has increased greatly since 1989, a date which coincides with the reform of the Structural Funds, and the impetus that Community Regional Policy received from the Single European Act.

In October 1989, the Presidents of the Basque Autonomous Community and of Aquitaine, José Antonio Ardanza and Jean Tavernier, signed a protocol on collaboration between the two regions; the protocol was made tripartite after the president of the *Comunidad Foral Navarra* signed a new protocol on collaboration in January 1992. As regards the Basque Autonomous Community, these relations are encapsulated in the construction of an Atlantic Euro-region, and in a similar way to the Catalan case considerations of economic and external representation take precedence over national and ethnic matters.

The region of Aquitaine is made up of five *départements:* Gironde (including Bordeaux) with the largest population (1,400,000 inhabitants); Pyrénées Atlantiques (which includes the northern part of the Basque Country and Béarn, with its capital Pau) with 555,000 inhabitants; Dordogne with 377,000 inhabitants; and Lot-et-Garonne and Landes, each with 300,000 inhabitants. The population of Aquitaine (2,800,000) is not that much greater than that of the Basque Autonomous Community. In 1991 the total population of the three historic territories was 2,159, 000: 1,184,000 in Bizkaia (Vizcaya) with its capital Bilbo (Bilbao), 697,000 in Gipuzkoa (Guipuzcoa),with its capital Donostia (San Sebastián), and 278,000 in Araba (Alava), with its capital Gasteiz (Vitoria). Aquitaine is considerably larger (41,309 sq. kms) than the Basque Autonomous Community (7,261 sq. kms). Nafarroa (Navarra) has a population of 523,000 and covers 10,421 square kilometres; its capital is Iruñea (Pamplona). In the northern part of the Basque Country the population of the three historic territories, Lapurdi (Labourd), Nafarroa Beherea (Basse Navarre) and Zuberoa (Soule) is 250,000; they cover an area of 2,962 sq. kms) (see map 5.2).

The very different financial powers of the Basque Autonomous Community and Navarra (*Comunidad Foral Navarra*) on the one hand and Aquitaine on the other create imbalances for possible collaboration. In 1989 the budget of the Basque Government increased to 380,000 million pesetas, while the budget for the "Consejo General de Aquitania" was 34,395 million pesetas, not reaching a tenth of the value of the former (Gómez & Etxebarria 1993a). With different emphases and levels of enthusiasm, there is agreement on the part of the political forces operating in the three border regions (Basque Autonomous Community, Navarra and Aquitaine) on the need to consolidate an Atlantic

European macro-region which would increase both commercial and cultural exchanges and which would reinforce and complement their economies.

Today, the *Partido Nacionalista Vasco* (PNV, Basque Nationalist Party) shares government in a coalition with the Socialist Party (PSE, *Euskadiko Ezkerra*) and *Eusko Alkartasuna* in the Basque Autonomous Community, Navarra is governed by a coalition of *Unión del Pueblo Navarro* (UPN, Union of Navarrese People) and the *Partido Popular* (PP, Popular Party). In both areas *Herri Batasuna* (HB, United People), a radical nationalist force, is in third place.

MAP 5. 2
The seven historic territories of the Basque Country

In Aquitaine (including Northern Basque Country), in the March 1992 elections for the Regional Council, the conservative alliance UPF (formed by the Gaullist party *Rassamblement pour la Republique* [RPR] and the Christian Democratic party *Union pour la Démocratie Française* [UDF] gained some 32.4% of votes; the Socialist Party 21%. In the northern part of the Basque Country the *Abertzale* movement, consisting mainly of the two left-wing forces *Ezkerreko Mugimendu Abertzalea* (EMA) and *Euskal Batasuna* (EB), and a third centre force which gets votes in both the North and in the South Basque Country, *Eusko Alkartasuna* (EA, Basque Solidarity). Although a minority party, the latter has seen a notable doubling of vote since 1988 (in a process similar to that which has taken place in Corsica).

Since the 1940s the PNV has been a firm defender of European federalism and unreservedly supports the creation of a "Europe of the peoples". The Eusko Alkartasuna representative in the European Parliament is part of the Rainbow Group, the aim of which is to achieve an open Europe of autonomous regions and nations. The radical nationalist HB opposed the entrance of Spain into the Common Market in 1986 and describes the European Community as "the Europe of multinationals and brokers". Even though the PNV and EA support the process of Europe building, and Herri Batasuna does not, the three nationalist forces are supporters, albeit for different reasons, of closer links between the Basque lands across the French-Spanish border.

The Socialist Group in the European Parliament indicated in its 1990 manifesto the need to protect minority languages and cultures, although article 78 of the same manifesto speaks of a "Europe of our States and our citizens". French conservative forces hold differing views on the European Community: the Christian Democrats advocate a federal Europe and call for a sharing of responsibilities between local, regional, national and community levels, while the Gaullists support a Europe of the States, rejecting any type of federal structure for the EU. The UPN of Juan Cruz Alli enthusiastically defends the idea of Navarran regionalism with a European role; the attitude of the PP has evolved, having recently achieved entrance into the Christian Democratic International (much to the displeasure of the PNV).

The September 1992 referendum in France on the Maastricht treaty provided an overview of the various attitudes held by the different political and social forces in Aquitaine (and the northern part of the Basque Country within it) to Europeanism. In Aquitaine the 'No' vote (supported among others by the President of the *Conseil Régional*, Jacques Valade) won with a slight margin at 50.74% (in the north Basque Country the 'Yes' vote dominated with a slight margin with 54% of the vote). The Ecologist, Socialist, and Christian Democrat (UDF) groups advocated a 'Yes' vote, the Communists 'No', and the RPR was shown to be divided with a certain leaning towards 'Yes' but locally elected Basque Gaullists such as Intxauspe in favour of 'No'. The *Abertzale* (Basque nationalist) vote was also shown to be split. So too was the *Abertzale* left which is ideologically close to the postures of its big brother in the South,

Herri Batasuna. PNV and EA defended the 'Yes' vote; on the left, EMA defended a 'No' "against a Europe of the rich", while Euskal Batasuna, closer to HB than to EMA, defended the 'Yes'.

The latter reflects recent developments at the core of radical nationalism in the South. The *Koordinadora Abertzale Sozialista* (KAS), the most left wing nucleus of HB, published an interview with representatives of KAS in which they critically evaluated the opinions that until recently they themselves had held on the building of Europe:

> I don't think that Europe is necessarily going to be an obstacle . . . In our proceedings we have only developed the purely political position, and the economic position very little. Inexcusably, in our analysis we have almost totally forgotten the Atlantic axis, the Mediterranean axis, and the money which is going to come from Europe . . and because we haven't carried out this analysis we haven't been aware of the opportunities, offered to us by this new situation, to play with the new elements (*Bultza* N° 5 1993: 20).

Cross-border co-operation within the ambit of an Atlantic Euro-region has also been supported by the socialists in the Basque and Navarran Communities and in Aquitaine. On the occasion of the signing, in October 1989, of a Basque-Aquitaine protocol on collaboration, representatives of the *Partido Socialista de Euskadi* (PSE, Socialist Party of Euskadi) and the French Socialist Party expressed some criticisms not of co-operation in itself, but rather of the leading role played in it of "the Conservative coalitions and the Basque nationalisms" *(Egin* 4 October 1989). In June 1990 the Basque and Navarran socialists, represented respectively by their leaders Ramón Jauregi and Gabriel Urralburu, expressed their willingness to join forces to create an Atlantic macro-region, which would eventually include Rioja in the South (included at NUTS 1, *Noroeste*) (*El Correo Español* 9 June 1990). Accordingly, this would be the only point of convergence among all the significant political forces (including radical Basque nationalism) on both sides of the border, and it acted as a factor for pacifying the political and national conflicts which exist in the area.

The negative economic repercussions which have resulted from the EU's completion of the internal market and the disappearance of the Irún-Hendaye customs zone are causes for concern for the border municipalities of Irún, Fuenterrabía, and Hendaye. These municipalities are heavily dependent on the tertiary sector given their role in customs, and, in the case of Hendaye, its mercantile character: the tertiary sector accounts for 63% of employment in the South and for 80% in Hendaye. The disappearance of customs barriers looks therefore like a cataclysm with which it will be difficult to deal and which will directly affect 1,275 employees in customs agencies (1,100 in Irún and 175 in Hendaye) and which indirectly could cause unemployment to rise by 20%. As regards Hendaye, one must also take into account the shopping habits of the border population (in 1992 the population in the South had bought goods to the value of 1,700 million pesetas in the North, buyers from the Basque Autonomous Community coming 90% from Gipuzkoa, 8% from Bizkaia, and 2% from Araba) (*Atlántica* Nº 5 1993; Nº 8 1992; Nº11 1993). Without doubt the customs removal will affect the survival of cross-border contraband and small scale illegal dealing (consisting mainly in tobacco, livestock and alcohol smuggling and of some other "limited entrance goods" which are part of the black economy of Irún-Hendaye, and which were a source of income for more than a small number of its inhabitants and of the Pyrenean zone generally). This could be an additional factor in explaining the observation made by Alain Darré regarding the September 1992 referendum on Maastricht, namely that negative voting would increase towards the border areas (reaching 65.5 per cent in areas such as the north border village of Ainhoa). To suspicions of "Southern Imperialism" (i.e., that of the Spanish state), which without doubt exist, and fear of being contaminated by its violence, one would have to add the anguish which the economic repercussions of customs removal has brought about (Darré 1994: 201).

"Fortress Europe" and the foreseeable attempts of immigrants, for the most part from the Maghreb, to enter states at the centre of Europe (such as France and Germany) from Spain, may produce an outcome which is the opposite of that which has been generated by the free movement of goods and services: an increase in the number of police checkpoints on the French/Spanish border, and therefore a further fortification of one of the main zones, that of Irún-Hendaye (see also this volume's chapter by Driessen). The Spanish government set for 1993 an extraordinarily low annual entry quota for immigrants of 20,600; but even this quota has been rejected as being above what was acceptable in terms of the labour market. In Spain this set of circumstances has produced a growing number of immigrants from extra-Community countries who find themselves in an illegal position (in June 1993 a study by SOS Racism estimated that there were around 8,000 foreign residents in the Basque Autonomous Community and that a third of them were not legal). The media has taken as given the existence, in the zone of the river Bidasoa of networks of illegal workers. This situation (which it is very difficult to measure quantitatively) cannot but result in the police checkpoints at the Spanish/French border being strengthened.

Another factor serving to strengthen the Franco-Spanish border was the Spanish pressure on the French government to remove ETA's "sanctuary". Several ETA members were based in the North, some of them possessing the status of refugee. With the Socialists accession to power in Spain in 1982, the Spanish government eventually achieved its aim.

A "Report to the French Senate on Terrorism", produced in the spring of 1984, reveals the logic which is at work: the report, which provides precise figures on the refugee community (it states that there are 11,500 *Spanish* citizens in the Department of the Pirénées Atlantiques; while 850 of them are refugees who have sought political asylum, only eight citizens have been granted it), states that the dual and "brutal outburst of violence (GAL and Iparretarrak[3]) has changed the situation" and that "the Basque refugees should now be seen as a disruptive element" (Letamendía 1994: 27). The report, therefore, supports the ending of French government tolerance towards them and advocates progress in French/Spanish police co-operation. At the end of 1992 forty-four Basques from the southern part were imprisoned in a number of French prisons; to these have to be added the thirteen French citizens linked to them and six prisoners linked to Iparretarrak; to date there have been twenty-one extraditions of Basque citizens to the Spanish state. Also, the reverse situation has occurred with the detention in Spanish territory of citizens from the northern part of the Basque Country who are linked to ETA (in April 1990, Henri Parot was detained and accused of forming part of a "mobile unit" within ETA). There are also French citizens among the Spanish state's current 494 Basque political prisoners.

The implications of this and the preventative measures taken to impede the clandestine cross-border movement of ETA members has produced a concentration of police forces from both states in the border area, which has inevitably led to a strengthening of border control. All of this has also led to fears among the population in the North that closer links with the South might allow them to be contaminated with "terrorism".

The disappearance of armed violence (through integrated and negotiated measures, if possible) would seem to be an essential precondition for extending and making more commonplace cross-border co-operation between the northern and southern parts of the Basque Country, through the process of building a common Europe which looks ahead to a world without borders. In a wider sphere, the cessation of armed violence should enhance collaboration between the Basque Autonomous Community, Navarra, and Aquitaine.

The historic Basque Country stands astride the Franco-Spanish border; the impact of European integration has created a new political and cultural space for cross-border ties to emerge, linking the Basque lands in the French and in the Spanish states. The main political and cultural forces which are aiding the prospects for greater cohesion in the Basque country as a whole are EU regional policy; cultural and language ethnic links; and broad political support for cross-border economic co-operation. However, the conditions and forces which are impeding such co-operation are the history of state formation in France and Spain which strengthened the border and limited crossing points; the different legal and administrative arrangements on either side of the border; the different levels of decentralisation and regionalisation in France and Spain; and the attempts to strengthen the border in response to extra-Community immigrants and to ETA.

How is the new situation affecting the national sovereignty of the French and Spanish states? The evidence is somewhat contradictory at present. In some ways, sovereignty at the border is not much affected, and is even being strengthened by the arrangements to police immigrants and ETA militants (the Maastricht Treaty has explicit provisions which link immigration and "terrorism"). On the other hand, the cross-border economic links between Aquitaine, Navarra and the Basque Autonomous Community, added to the Basque ethnic identity of the population in the border zones, demonstrates the potential for regional cross-border co-operation which might dilute the sovereignty of the French and Spanish states in the long run.

Part 2: The Economic Dimension [4]

The difficulties of designing projects for the future of the Basque economy demonstrates the practical impossibility of reconciling two factors: the legitimate aim of maximising the capacity of the Basque Country to develop its own resources, and the existing economic, social and institutional reality which undermines this capacity. We attempt to analyse below some aspects of this dilemma. We outline the difficulties of reconciling the ideal of national self-government, to the actual trends of economic development shaped by existing institutional frameworks. We concentrate particularly on the development of cross-border physical infrastructure in the context of EU integration. The Basque Country is currently integrated fully into the project of EU economic integration as an economic border zone. The latter is not a privilege, however, at least at present, because national states play the crucial role in configuring EU economic policy.

The analysis of the relations between various border regions is becoming more important insofar as Europe is moving towards greater integration. In the first place we shall try to discover the possibilities which the current project of the EU offers for a major integration of the Basque economy and society *as a whole*. It should be remembered that, as indicated in part 1 of this chapter, the *entire* Basque Country is comprised of its northern and southern parts, belonging to the French and Spanish states respectively. Our study will be focused on certain communication infrastructures which are considered to be of strategic value in the achievement of the greater European economic integration. The EU recognises that border areas have suffered as a result of their location (Commission of the European Communities 1991: 169). Firstly, they are often located at the periphery of their states and are frequently isolated from the core areas of economic activity and decision-making. Secondly, their commercial centres are often cut off from their natural hinterlands, affecting trade patterns and the provision of services. Thirdly, they often lack a developed infrastructure because they are located at the extremities of national transport and communication networks. Fourthly, peripheral frontier regions are often poorly endowed with natural resources and have less developed social and business services. There are notable exceptions, such as the nature parks on the French and Spanish sides of the Pyrenees. Finally, border areas often have different legal, administrative and social welfare systems, languages and cultural traditions from adjoining areas which hinder communications and co-operation.

Infrastructure and cross-border co-operation

The policies to promote infrastructure are one of the strategic variables of regional politics of the EU. The development of cross-border co-operation aims at harmonising communication infrastructure networks in the first place. In the context of an internationalisation of networks the following question has to be asked: what are the regional effects of this new planning of infrastructures? Trans-European networks are more geared to linking important economic centres than to providing for balanced regional development. Therefore, some of the regions are simply crossed by networks which connect centres that sometimes belong to other regions. But what we would like to underline is the associated tendency that can be observed: the trend towards a reinforcement of international and local elements. In the field of infrastructure this trend emerges in the tendency towards networks linking metropolitan centres.

The creation of important infrastructures mainly intensifies the relations between metropolitan centres with a certain level of endogenous potential, making more difficult balanced, coherent and homogeneous regional development. The diffusion and reinforcement of extensive networks of infrastructures within a macro-region would require the development of intraregional networks. The internationalisation of major infrastructures, however, does not guarantee a more integrated regional development at all, but reinforces the more consolidated centres. At best new inter-metropolitan relations might appear as a consequence of major investments in external networks, consolidating relations almost non-existent at present. An example of the latter is the inter-metropolitan connection between Bordeaux and Bilbao in the Atlantic arc. The consolidation of powerful relations between intraregional centres - such as the links between Bilbao - Pamplona - San Sebastian in the Basque Country - seems to be much more difficult in the context of diffusion of European networks. Without strong intra-regional links, it is impossible to achieve balanced development in regions such as the Basque Country.

An improvement in the position of the less developed areas on the southern and western periphery of the EU will depend to a major extent on investment in basic infrastructure and productive capacity, to be undertaken by the EU and by national, regional and local authorities in the 1990s. Much will depend on whether these border regions can achieve economies of scale and improved efficiency through the joint planning and provision of public services, the organization of common transport and communication systems and the joint promotion of industry and services. Border areas are particularly important for

104

the EU because they represent both a potential impediment to, and a potential model for, the integrated development of the economic and physical space of the EU as a whole. It seems likely that measures to improve the economic infrastructure of border areas will be maintained at a significant level during the 1990s. "National, regional and local authorities as well as the Community . . . have already indicated major plans for investment in border areas in transport and communications (in Spain, Portugal, France, Ireland), industry (in France / Belgium / Luxembourg and Lille), tourism (in Ireland, France / Spain and France / Italy) and environmental protection and waste disposal (France / Spain and Ireland / N. Ireland)" (Commission of the European Communities 1991: 171/172).

The configuration of large metropolitan areas

The aim of achieving a better integration of the northern and southern part of the Basque Country does not fit in any way the current central trends of development in the EU. The configuration of large metropolitan centres and the consideration that infrastructure follows development rather than vice versa are factors which do not favour a deeper integration of Basque economy and society. The hinterland of the "French" Basque Country is undergoing a process of depopulation; industry is not being promoted there and is in a situation of profound dependence (for instance, Dassault's aeronautics factory in Angelu (Anglet) is a division that depends on the headquarters in Bordeaux). On the other hand, tourist and real estate activities are expanding in ways which hardly encourage the indigenous development of the area. These activities have few multiplication effects on other economic sectors and do not favour further economic or social cohesion either.

But what causes development to especially concentrate on metropolitan agglomerations? In modern, more flexible forms of production the activities which are not directly productive, and which require very high levels of skill (e.g., in the fields of research and development, management, quality control, customer relations and marketing) displace the productive activities themselves (manufacturing and assembly) to more peripheral spaces. This process of displacement results in a division of labour in which the most advanced activities and services are concentrated in major metropolitan areas. In these metropolitan cores, external economies emerge which are derived from demographic concentration, and from the availability of infrastructure and services (transport communications, financing, training and research) to enterprises at more competitive prices.

Trends towards the concentration of development are redrawing the map of the cross-border region with the following characteristics: it is dependent on two large poles (Madrid and Paris), and in the medium- and long-term there is a further polarisation of the Aquitaine/Basque Autonomous

Community/Navarra Region between the two metropolitan centres, Bordeaux and Bilbao. As the President of Aquitaine's Economic and Social Council put it: "It is obvious that the competition between the regions of the Community will become tougher as the construction of Europe advances. Every region will back certain poles in order to defend its position not only in a unified European but also on the world market." (*Atlántica* no. 9: 14).

Public projects in the Basque Country favour the development of the metropolitan area of Bilbao, but in order to guarantee its consolidation, it is necessary to overcome obstacles of a political nature. It would mean, for instance, reinforcing certain local spaces as against others by means of the budget of the entire Basque Autonomous Community. This problem does not arise in the same fashion in the French region for two reasons: firstly, Aquitaine's political autonomy is more limited and it is more dependent on the plans of the state; and secondly, the northern part of the Basque Country has almost been annihilated politically within Aquitaine

Analysis of the main infrastructure networks

Railway lines

Without any doubt, the construction of a high-speed railway line constitutes the most significant venture among all the projects of collaboration between the regional institutions of the Basque Autonomous Community, Navarra and Aquitaine. At present, there are major differences between the Spanish and French railway systems insofar as technology, network extension, quality and service are concerned. Moreover, France is a developer of high-speed trains, which are often portrayed as a matter of "national prestige". The plans of the railway routes in the Pyrenees, designed by the governments in Madrid and Paris, are to be co-ordinated.

In this context we have to point out the considerable economic and ecological costs of these high speed lines. The promotion of "high speed" sometimes involves a marginalisation of other means of transport, including conventional railways, because of its cost and it function - a fact which might have important repercussions for the regions concerned. The Basque railway network is at present very deficient, not only with regard to its contribution to internal cohesion, but also because of the difficulty of connecting with interregional and international railway junctions. Suffice it to say that it takes almost four hours to get from Bilbao to San Sebastian [distance: 100 km (ca. 60 miles)].

The Railway Plan[5] of the Basque Autonomous Community envisages a high speed connection between the three major towns of that Community (the so-called "Y-link"). After that the Ministry of Transport in Madrid - according to a project draft - connects this triangular network with the Ebro-valley and

Pamplona. This way a higher level of integration between all four major towns of the southern part of the Basque Country could be reached, although always in dependence on other more important centres, mainly Madrid.

Airports

From the perspective of economic development airports constitute one of the principal expressions of the processes of spatial concentration and centralization. The economies of agglomeration and of urbanization play such an important part in this field in that they make it impossible to build and expand important airports in those areas below a minimum size. With regard to flight frequency and international lines the Basque airports are in a position of dependence on others of superior category (Madrid), or do not even reach a minimum size, as in the cases of Pamplona and San Sebastian.

The different amounts to be invested in Basque airports clearly show the trends towards concentration in large metropolitan areas. Although the Spanish government has introduced major cutbacks in its airport investment projects, the clear preference for the airport of Bilbao over other Basque airports remains. The marginalisation of the airport of Vitoria is not due to technical reasons (the technical equipment is in fact better than Bilbao), but to the centripetal tendencies of Basque development. At the same time other objectives, such as the ones that aim at a major internal cohesion of the macro-region of the Basque Country, are abandoned. A different redistribution of the loads among the various Basque airports would reinforce the external networks so as to achieve major intraregional cohesion. In this sense the airport of Vitoria could be promoted for international flights. The time that would be required to reach this airport from other major Basque towns is absolutely identical to the time commonly needed to get to large international airports.

In Europe the train is used more than the aeroplane for distances under 1000 km (600 miles); it is seldom used for distances under 200 km (125 miles) (Pavaux 1991: 29). In the case of small regions like the Basque Country, however intra-regional connections are made only by means of train or road. The train might be an alternative to the aeroplane in the case of inter-regional connections including Madrid or Bordeaux. We can infer from the above that railway connections are of great importance not only for inter-regional but also for intra-regional cohesion; they might even counteract an excessive trend of metropolitan Bilbao towards centrality.

Roads and motorways

Without pretending to be exhaustive we now outline the main functions fulfilled by the different road connections in the southern Basque Country (see map 5.3):

1. Primary international routes: these include the connection between the A8 and A 68 motorways, and the conversion of the N1 into a dual carriageway over the Etxegarate pass. The latter would be relegated in its function by the Deba route (the so-called Urbina-Maltzaga), a project which has been started to link Gasteiz (Vitoria) with Elgoibar. The N1 and the Deba route may eventually compete with each other. The outcome of this competition depends on the tolls which will be charged on the Urbina-Maltzaga carriageway and the A8 motorway, if the N1 is free of tolls, At present, the toll issue has not been settled.

2. Major inter-regional roads: the construction works at Ugaldebieta (on the border of Bizkaia and Cantabria), which would establish a link with the Atlantic Arc regions, are nevertheless subject to the decisions of our Atlantic partners Cantabria, Asturias and Galicia. These decisions are also largely a matter for the Spanish Government.

3. Major intra-regional roads: the Deba connection will link a group of valleys, where we can also find the basic productive nucleus of the co-operatives of Mondragon; the dual carriageway that goes through the Leitzaran valley (Irurtzun - Tolosa) (creating a major political and ecological issue) will constitute a link between Pamplona and San Sebastian; the construction of the connection Pamplona - Vitoria which has been somewhat deferred, and the transverse link, which would link various inland valleys (Beasain - Durango), and which has been shelved. These developments show how projects are designed and later postponed in order to adapt to the dominant logic of centrality. In brief, those projects which would foster major internal cohesion of the inland zones of the Basque countries are reduced in significance.

4. Finally, of those projects which favour certain forms of development in metropolitan areas, the Txoriherri carriageway and its extension to the coast is of particular significance. This carriageway to the east of Bilbao is meant to provide a link between the A8 motorway and major residential areas on the coast. The importance of the Txoriherri connection lies in fact that the following facilities will be situated in its vicinity: the airport of Bilbao, the technology park, and various estates which will be the destination of most relevant foreign investments. The latter will form a central axis within the residential zones of the wealthy middle-class. These carriageways, situated in areas to the north of Bilbao, are directly related not only to the future expansion of the internal networks in this area but also to a restructuring and an improvement of Bilbao's arterial roads. In this sense, Bilbao's new metropolitan transport network will reinforce the internal cohesion of the city and contribute to a major rationalisation of road transport.

If any European road has truly intercontinental character, it is the road which connects Paris with Algeciras and Lisbon (via Baiona-San Sebastian-Vitoria). The region formed by Aquitaine and the Basque Country is merely transit territory in this link, although this through road would also improve the internal cohesion of the Basque Coast to some extent. Over the last five years the French government and the EU have given preferential financial treatment to the extension of this international connection. It is the projects which mainly aim at unifying France's metropolitan areas that stand out from all Aquitaine projects as in the connections between Bordeaux - Toulouse and Bordeaux - Lyon. These projects are also supposed to function as an international link, e.g., the motorway between Baiona, Pau and Toulouse.

In the context of cross-border co-operation Aquitaine's prime interest lies in the improvement of the connection with the metropolitan area of Zaragoza via Pau and the Pyrenean tunnel of Somport. This connection with the Spanish Aragón region is in line with the declared interest of Aquitaine's regional government to diversify its external relations, thereby avoiding restricting these relations to the "Atlantic Pact" signed with the Communities of the southern part of the Basque Country. When signing an agreement on technological co-operation with Aquitaine, Aragón had a reciprocal interest in improving the supply of manufactured goods in general and in gaining access to markets.

Aquitaine's preference for infrastructure projects that facilitate the link between its central nuclei - above all Bordeaux - and other metropolitan agglomerations has two major effects: on the one hand, Aquitaine improves the conditions for the international transit traffic, but on the other it abandons or considerably cuts back on those projects of communication routes that would improve the internal connections between the different sub-regions of the macro-region Aquitaine and augment the internal structure and cohesion of these areas. In the case of the northern part of the Basque Country, for instance, it would be possible to modernize the transverse roads which link Baiona with Maule, even extending it to Pau.

Adopting criteria which are very different from the above philosophy of improving the "regional competitiveness" we would like to refer to another option not mentioned so far: a higher level of internal cohesion between the northern and southern parts of the Basque Country might be obtained by updating and extending cross-border communication routes across the Pyrenees. Some connections would require the construction of tunnels, as, for instance, in the case of the link between Pamplona and Donapaleu (Nafarroa Beherea). We furthermore maintain that the reinforcement of the axis Bordeaux–Zaragoza could marginalize other links with a higher cohesion potential, such as the connection Pau - Pamplona. In the same way as in the southern part of the Basque Country, a significant part of the French road construction budgets is spent on by-passes and metropolitan feeder roads, rather than on intra-regional routes. Bordeaux illustrates this in the case of Aquitaine.

The sharp increase in the potential demand for services and markets in metropolitan areas requires a continually improved organisation and planning of infrastructure networks. As a result, joint action plans have to be carried out in various fields of infrastructures. In the area of transport we would like to mention by-passes and major interchange terminals with access to various means of transport. Additional measures have to be taken in the area of urban planning, housing and the environment. Those action plans would regulate and rationalise existing networks thereby reducing social costs in the long term. But as this also implies large investments, which would increase the centrality of Bilbao, it will be necessary for those action plans to be accompanied by decentralising measures. These measures will have to counterbalance the effects caused by the above action plans.

The application of a comprehensive transport plan in metropolitan Bilbao is of utmost importance. Among five major metropolitan areas on the Peninsula it is Bilbao which has the greatest difficulties in the field of urban transport. In this sense the construction of an underground line is a logical measure to overcome at least some of the difficulties mentioned above. However, the discussion about a reduction of private transport ought to be accompanied by further measures to promote public transport. A major part of these infrastructure works will be financed by the Basque Autonomous Community and the Provincial Council (*Diputación*) of Bizkaia.

Regional competencies, national governments and EU priorities

At present the regions are endowed with different areas of competence and form multi-functional entities. These functions can be classified in three groups: (1). lobbying capacity: i.e., the potential to exert political pressure on the central governments in fields under their respective authority; (2) assistance to promote economic activity based on private initiative, i.e., the creation of conditions to improve the competitiveness of those companies presently or in future located in the region; and (3) decision-making powers in economic matters in general and in infrastructure projects affecting the region in particular. With regard to these functions we advance the following hypothesis: the more dependent or the less autonomous a region is (i.e., where its decision-making powers are virtually non-existent), the more important and the weaker is its lobbying capacity and, to a lesser extent, its potential to give assistance to economic activity. Aquitaine, for example, with limited decision-making powers, is principally dedicated to its lobbying function. The Basque government has a greater potential to promote economic activity while its freedom to take decisions (e.g., about transport infrastructures) which are of major concern to the Basque economy and society is very limited.

Our analysis of the regional administrative systems has shown that the provinces which form the southern part of the Basque Country are endowed with more competence than Aquitaine to assist various economic agents. They

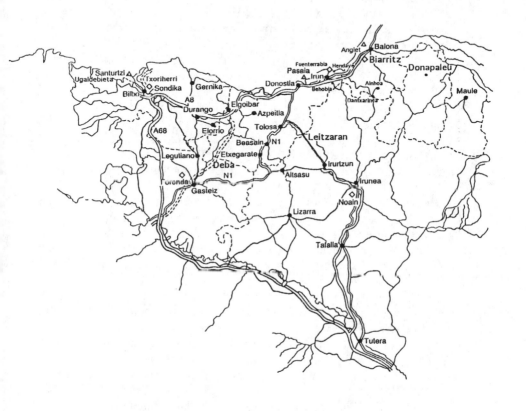

Map 5.3
Infrastructure in the Basque Country

can also contribute to a wider extent to the development and implementation of infrastructure projects. We also observe, on the other hand, that the lobbying function of each region is all the more powerful if various regions get together to exert pressure on the EU. Hence, cross-border association and co-operation is fruitful as it allows more influence to be exerted on the real decision-poles, mainly Paris, Madrid and Brussels.

At times, the plans and policies which are designed by national governments and receive the approval of the EU have a negative effect on local development. In the case of Liverpool, for instance, the regional necessity to develop a modern transport network for the freight traffic in the area has to face stiff opposition from "the policy of the national Government towards rail transport with its emphasis on rail privatisation and its proposals for British Rail to withdraw from railfreight operations" (Meegan 1993: 12).

The regions do not take part in the elaboration of EU economic policy. For example, the EU fails to take into account the urgent necessity of the Basque Country to modernize its steel industries when it is deciding on the restructuring of this sector at European level. The attempt to reach a consensus between various Atlantic regions in order to modernize certain industrial sectors, for instance, or the demand to place certain European investments in those areas which are losing a large number jobs but which have a high regenerative capacity because of skilled labour, have no chances of success within the present organisation of the EU. On the contrary, the decisions of the EU contribute to dismantling regional industries. The subsidies are mainly used to cushion the social effects of this process of deindustrialisation (Meegan 1993: 17).

In this chapter we have analysed types of communication infrastructure. We have not dealt, however, with the areas of technology transfer, technological infrastructures, research and development, and professional training. The Autonomous Communities of the southern Basque Country as well as the Aquitaine region dedicate a part of their budget to these fields. They have designed some aspects of regional technology plans and developed the first, and still insignificant, initiatives of co-operation, for example, between the universities of Bordeaux and the Basque Country. The first steps towards closer collaboration between Bordeaux and Zaragoza have also been taken.

The Basque Country as an economic border region

The capacity which the cross-border projects of communication infrastructure may have for the development of a cohesive Basque territory and economic space has to be analysed in the light of two tendencies related to capital flow and the localisation of resources in the EU.

The first is the trend towards centralization or concentration of resources, investments and population in metropolitan areas. In this respect, all available evidence indicates that the intensification of interregional cross-border relations clearly favours the links and communications between the metropolitan areas of Bordeaux and Bilbao. Although we do not consider this to be previously determined, we do not believe that the current supra-municipal district of Baiona - Anglet - Biarritz, the so-called BAB, will go beyond the dimension of a local project. In any case it will be subordinate to the urban centres, Bilbao and Bordeaux.

The second is the localisation of capital which tends to take place in spaces which offer better short-term conditions for developing new markets. An increased number of links between various metropolitan areas corresponds with this trend. Therefore the diversification of Aquitaine's co-operation with other metropolises and regions is a good example of the intensification of inter-metropolitan relations in the quest for new markets. Aquitaine's regional government does not limit its co-operation agreements to those with the Autonomous Communities of the Basque Country and Navarre, but expands those cross-border pacts by signing protocols of agreement with Aragón in order to improve existing or create new routes of communication. The link between Bordeaux and Zaragoza is an example for this.

In the context of the tendencies described above, the present communication infrastructure projects do not appear to contribute to a more balanced integration of the different historical regions on both sides of the Pyrenees. Neither do they reinforce the internal cohesion of the regions nor help to define economic development schemes which structure the territory and the Basque economy. On the contrary, the processes of metropolisation seem to be closely linked with the polarisation of productive economic activities. In this process the historical regions and nations without a state gradually lose economic attraction and fail to be interesting projects for capitalist development.

The project of EU economic integration is not in itself conducive to forging links across the border between the Northern and Southern Basque lands. It may, however, focus more economic activity in the metropoles of both Aquitaine and the Basque Autonomous Community while encouraging links between them. In encouraging inter-metropolitan relationships, the form taken by EU economic integration makes it easier to facilitate co-operation between European states rather than between regions located in different states. Thus, the national sovereignty of France and Spain is not modified significantly. On the other hand, border regions like the Basque territories become transit zones traversed by roads and railways leading to external Euro-centres.

While the dominant project of capitalist development on an EU scale does not favour the construction of cross-border links between the Northern and Southern Basque lands, this does not preclude the development of closer cross-border relationships, in part as a response to marginalisation. It is here that the political and cultural space for such relationships within the EU becomes important, and it is here that local, regional and state relations may redefine sovereignty in Spain and France.

Notes

Our special thanks go to our translators Tim Moore (part 1) and Karl M. Adler (part 2). We thank them for their painstaking work and patience.

1. Part I of this essay, on the political and cultural dimensions, was written by Francisco Letamendía. Part II of this essay, on the economic dimension, was written by Mikel Gómez Uranga and Goio Etxebarria.
2. In 1990 and 1991, the percentage of Basque speakers in the combined areas of the northern part of the Basque Country, Navarra and the Basque Autonomous Community, was 22.4%. In Navarra the figure was 10%, and in Guipúzcoa it was 44%. In the three demarcations (historic, not administrative) in the North, the percentages are notably higher. In Labourd 26% are Basque speakers, in Basse Navarre the figure is 64.5%, and in Soule 54.7% (*Egin* "Euskadi 1977-1982", 1982: 248). Navarra, in linguistic matters, is divided into three zones, Basque speaking, Mixed, and Non Basque Speaking. The Western Pyrenees Valleys are included in the Mixed zone, whilst the rest of the border area of Navarra is in the Basque speaking zone. The percentage of Basque speakers in all the municipalities included in the border areas of both states are listed below (the figures are taken from a study carried out in 1970 and which should be brought up to date): in Guipúzcoa - Fuenterrabía 65%, Irún 16%; in Navarra (from West to East) - Vera de Bidasoa 65%, Etxalar 90%, Zugarramurdi 94%, Urdax 87%, Burgete 13%, Erro 18%, Valcarlos 83%, Ochagabía 12%, Uztarroz 0%, and Isaba 0% (the percentages are high in the areas of Cinco Villas and Baztán and decline in the Pyrenean valleys towards the East until they reach zero at the border with Aragón). In the Northern part of the Basque Country the figures are as follows: St. Engrace 95%, Larraun 93%, Lekunberri 92%, Esterencuby 97%, St Michel 96%, Arneguy 99%, Lasse 100%, Banca 100%, Urepel 100%, Aldudes 96%, St Etienne de Baigorry 98%, Bidarrai 97%, St Pée-Sur-Nivelle 85%, Ixassou 80%, Ainhoa 65%, Sare 96%, Biriatou 47%, Urrugne 75%, and Hendaye 19% (*Egin*, Euskadi 1992, 1992: 182) (It should be noted that the Eastern Pyrenean valleys located on the Northern slopes have maintained the Basque language, and that in the Northern zone the only border municipality which is not predominantly Basque-speaking is the border settlement of Hendaye).
3. IPARRETARRAK (those from the North) is an armed Basque nationalist group formed in the North Basque Country in 1975. Their activities were intensified after 1982 as a consequence of the failure by the French Socialist Government to fulfil the promise made in 1981 to create a separate Départment for the Basque Country. GAL (Armed Liberation Groups) is an

organization using violence against Southern Basque political refugees in the North Basque Country. This group replaced previous similar groups that had used violence with the same purposes between 1975 and 1981: ATE (Anti-Terrorism ETA), BVE (Basque-Spanish Battalion). GAL has been responsible for more than twenty five murders, some of the victims having been kidnapped first. Between autumn 1983 and the beginning of 1987, many of the victims were French subjects. In 1991 two Spanish policemen, Mr. José Amedo and Mr. Michel Domínguez, were found guilty of organising these crimes. In 1995, court proceedings were opened, followed by several imprisonments, against some high ranking officials at the Spanish Ministry of Interior during those years.

4. The second part of this chapter is based in part on "Networks and Spatial Dynamics: The Case of the Basque Country", European Planning Studies, Vol. 1, No. 3, 1993, pp. 299 - 318 and "*Concentraciones Metropolitanas e inversiones en comunicaciones: El caso vasco-aquitano*" (Metropolitan Concentrations and Investments in Communications: The case of the Basque Country and Aquitaine), presented by Mikel Gómez Uranga at the "Conference on Cross-Border Cooperation Basque Country - Aquitaine: Political, Economic and International Aspects", Leioa, University of the Basque Country, 26/27 November 1993.

5. The Railway Plan of the Basque Autonomous Community has to respect the guidelines of the Spanish Government and therefore can be considered as a Government-approved plan, although the Basque Autonomous Community finances a considerable part. This is why we might call it a mixed "state-regional" plan. On the other hand, it has to be pointed out that the co-ordination of the Basque Railway Plan with its French counterparts does not go beyond the stage of good intentions at present. This is so because there exists no real co-ordination in spite of the occasional declarations from different regional Basque and Aquitaine entities.

References

Anuarios de Egin 1982 and 1992 *Egin 1977-1982* and *Egin 1992*. San Sebastián: Orain S.A.

Atlántica, Euromagazine, various numbers.

Bultza 1993.

Commission of the European Communities. 1991. *Europe 2000 - Outlook for the development of the Community's territory.* Brussels / Luxembourg: European Commission.

Darré, A. 1994. Los Países Vascos frente a Maastricht y el difícil borrado de una frontera. In F.Letamendía (ed.). *Cooperación transfronteriza Euskadi-Aquitania (aspectos políticos, económicos y de Relaciones Internacionales).* Leioa, Bizkaia: UPV/EHU (University of the Basque Country),

De Castro, J. L. 1992. *La emergente participación política de las regiones en el proceso de construcción de la Unión Europea,* doctoral thesis. Leioa , Bizkaia: UPV/EHU (University of the Basque Country),

Fernández de Casadevante, C. 1985. *La frontera hispano-francesa y las relaciones de vecindad: especial referencia al sector fronterizo del País Vasco.* Leioa, Bizkaia: UPV/EHU (University of the Basque Country),

Gómez Uranga, M. 1993. Concentraciones metropolitanas e inversiones en comunicaciones: El caso vasco-aquitano. Paper presented at Conference on Cross-Border Co-operation: Basque Country - Aquitaine, Political, Economic and International Aspects. Leioa: University of the Basque Country (UPV/EHU), 26/27 November.

Gómez Uranga, M. and Etxebarria, G. 1993a. Communication infrastructure: cross-border cooperation and cohesion of the Basque economy. Unpublished paper, The Queen's University of Belfast, April.

_____. 1993b. Networks and spatial dynamics: The case of the Basque Country. In *European Planning Studies* 1 (3) 299 - 318.

Letamendía, F. 1994. ETA y el Gobierno del PSOE. In *Historia del nacionalismo vasco y de ETA,* (3 volumes). San Sebastián: R&B Ediciones.

Meegan, R. 1993. A Europe of the regions? A view from Liverpool on the Atlantic Arc periphery. Paper presented at a Conference on The European Periphery Facing the New Century. Universidad de Santiago de Compostela. 30 September - 2 October.

Pavaux, J. 1991. L'Europe du transport aérien. In *Réalités Industrielles,* Avril: 27-30.

6 Securing the Irish border in a Europe without frontiers

Liam O'Dowd and James Corrigan

For a quarter of a century before August 1994, the British-Irish border was the most violently contested boundary in western Europe. Like Yugoslavia, Lebanon, the allocation of Nagorno Karabakh to Azerbaijan, and the division of the Middle East into several Arab states, the Irish border was a product of the first major wave of state and border reconstruction this century - after World War I (Fisk 1993). Like them it has remained a source of an unresolved conflict over national sovereignty.

This chapter focuses on the struggle over the physical fortification of the British-Irish border in the two years prior to the ceasefires of 1994. In so doing it illustrates three interrelated dimensions which are of wider relevance to the study of borders and national sovereignty in Europe. Firstly, it illuminates some of the meanings and practical manifestations of contested national sovereignty in the context of European integration. Secondly, it provides an example of the response of EU states to ethnonational pressures to change national boundaries. Thirdly, it demonstrates the tendency of states to follow "political objectives and priorities, rather than economic rationality, in the administration and development of border regions" (Suarez-Villa et al. 1992: 97; see also Hansen 1983: 256).

Since its creation in 1920, the Irish border has been central to the ethnic-national conflict in Northern Ireland in that it represents the territorial demarcation between Irish and British national sovereignty. Indeed, once Northern Ireland was established, electoral politics quickly became a recurring communal referendum on the border (Buckland 1981). The outbreak of the longest period of violent conflict in Northern Ireland since 1921 almost coincided with the accession of both British and Irish states to the European Community in 1973. Violence was to persist until recently despite the border becoming an internal EU frontier subject to the permeating effects of European economic and political integration.

The conflict, which had its origins in the Northern Ireland Civil Rights Movement of the 1960s, quickly became a major issue in the international relations between the

United Kingdom (UK) and the Republic of Ireland. It also led to the gradual militarisation of the border between the two countries, a process which seems to contradict the movement to abolish internal border controls within the Single European Market and the Maastricht Treaty. The militarisation of the border reflected one of the oldest attributes of state sovereignty, i.e., the claim to monopolise the means of legitimate violence within fixed territorial boundaries (Weber 1978: 56). The IRA campaign (1970-95) was the latest, and most sustained, in a series since 1921 aimed at contesting Britain's claim to sovereignty over any part of Ireland.

The British-Irish case poses the question to what extent, and under what conditions, the coercive, security, or barrier functions of borders remain significant in an environment where European integration is increasing the permeability of national borders in a variety of ways. The answer to this question can contribute to a wider debate outlined in the introduction to this volume over the future of national sovereignty and national borders in Europe. On one side of this debate, writers such as Hobsbawm (1990), Lash and Urry (1994) and Mlinar (1995) stress the permeability and diminished significance of borders as the sovereign power of the nation state becomes diffused upwards to transnational agencies and downwards to sub-state groups. On the other side, Giddens (1985), Mann (1993) and Milward (1992) argue that the EU may actually sustain the national state and its sovereignty within fixed territorial limits.

In order to specify the merits of the Irish border as a case study, it is necessary to outline the conditions under which the border was initially created and the form it took prior to the outbreak of the current conflict. The Irish settlement of 1920-21 was unusual in that it marked the partition of one of the Great War's victorious states. Irish nationalists were refused the right to present their case to the Versailles conference and the precise delimitation of the border was decided by the British parliament in 1920 without input from the new Irish Parliament in Dublin or from the remaining Irish M.P.s in the House of Commons. The confirmation of the partition of Ireland by the Anglo-Irish Treaty of 1921 reflected the balance of coercion in the country between the Ulster unionists supported by the British army and the guerrilla forces of the IRA under the control of the secessionist Parliament in Dublin. While unionists were given the right to opt out of the all-Ireland parliament created (which they duly did), the 1920 border was to be subject to the recommendations of a Boundary Commission. Article 12 of the Anglo-Irish Treaty stated that the Commission "shall determine in accordance with the wishes of the inhabitants, so far as may be compatible with economic and geographic conditions, the boundaries between Northern Ireland and the rest of Ireland" (Hand 1969: xiii).[1]

Irish nationalists pressed for a plebiscite along the lines of those carried out in Upper Silesia, Schleswig-Holstein and other border areas of Germany (North Eastern Boundary Bureau 1923). In the event, the Boundary Commission proved to be a fiasco. It interpreted its terms of reference narrowly, inferring that it had no powers to hold a plebiscite. It published a plan for minor rectification which was suppressed by agreement of the Northern Ireland, Irish Free State and British governments in 1925.

The result was a straggling and erratic boundary line of 240 miles which followed existing local authority boundaries, running through a largely agricultural area of dispersed settlement. When established, the border cut across 1400 agricultural holdings, 180 roads and bisected several villages and even individual houses (Douglas 1976; Laffan 1983; Busteed 1992). For example, the town of Clones in Co. Monaghan became an enclave, and the village of Pettigo in Co. Donegal was split in two down the middle of its bridge. Its political and historical rationale rested heavily on the seventeenth century plantation of Ulster by the British state which had settled Protestants from Scotland and England on land confiscated from rebellious Gaelic chieftains. Even so, the border did not include all the "planted" counties; it divided Ulster as well as Ireland. Its effect was to further disorganise anti-unionist forces (Phoenix 1994) and cede to Ulster Unionists the maximum area in which they felt they could retain a permanent pro-British majority. This meant excluding 70,000 unionists in the three Ulster counties left to the Free State, and enclosing in Northern Ireland over half a million Catholics and nationalists who rejected the legitimacy of partition from the outset.

Perhaps even more significantly, the British state devolved responsibility for law and order to one ethnic group in Northern Ireland, which led to the installation of one-party government between 1921-1972. The built-in unionist (or Protestant) majority was decisive but not overwhelming. In much of the Northern Ireland border region unionists were locally in a minority and had to suspend nationalist councils, gerrymander constituency boundaries and manipulate the franchise and the election system to ensure control of these areas. This political and administrative control was supported by an exclusively Protestant militia, the B-Specials, and an overwhelmingly Protestant police force. Northern nationalists, for their part, were rendered powerless and continued to reject a state from which they were excluded. A series of electoral campaigns and spasmodic IRA campaigns challenged the 1921 settlement culminating in the prolonged struggle since the late 1960s and the re-imposition of Direct Rule by the British government in 1972.

The British government had a strategic interest in retaining a foothold in Ireland, which proved important in 1939-45 when the Irish government remained neutral in the war and the border separated belligerent and non-belligerent states (Fisk 1993). However, it seems likely that few, if any, of the protagonists of the early 1920s envisaged the border turning into a fully fledged international boundary. British government preference was probably for a united Ireland closely tied to Britain. However in the interests of restoring stability and marginalising the disruptive potential of the "Irish Question" in British politics, it supported in practice the position of the Ulster unionists. With the growth of the infrastructural power (see Mann 1984) of both the British and Irish states and the creation of separate policy agendas and priorities (even after jointly joining the European Community), the border hardened into an international frontier (O'Dowd et al. 1995). For this reason, the early attempts of the British government to treat the Northern Ireland conflict as

119

a purely "internal" matter were doomed to failure. Instead, the conflict has become gradually more internationalised, creating the conditions for a formalised inter-governmental strategy involving both the British and Irish governments aimed at managing the conflict and bringing forward a solution.

Unlike many other national borders in Europe, the Irish border remained relatively open and in places quite invisible. At partition dense networks of roads and railways criss-crossed the region. The border cut across the existing railway system at fifteen points, traversing some lines more than once (North Eastern Boundary Bureau 1923). By the late 1950s, the decline of the railways had resulted in the closure, bar one (Dublin-Belfast), of all the cross-border railway lines. In the absence of the railways, the road network assumed greater importance for the economic and social development of the border region.

From the creation of the border, the matrix of cross-border roads presented administrative and political difficulties for both governments. In the first instance, separate revenue systems had necessitated a separation of customs and excise and the imposition of border controls - 1 April 1923 saw the birth of the customs land boundary. As a result, sixteen roads were approved for cross-border traffic, each having a boundary post and a customs station on both sides of the border. The remaining routes (numbering on some estimates 180) were designated "unapproved" and prohibited for wheeled or commercial traffic. Concession passes were granted to those persons who needed to cross the border as part of their work (e.g., clergymen, doctors etc.) and to border residents (within five miles of the boundary) who needed to cross the border for business purposes. "The use of a concession pass for social purposes was strictly forbidden and if a pass was used for this purpose it would be treated as an offence" (Denton and Fahy 1993: 23). Nevertheless, state regulation of the cross-border road network for economic purposes remained limited and the "unapproved" roads remained relatively open. Indeed, the road network facilitated the emergence of a flourishing informal smuggling economy which operated within the official economies of both states and which saw the development of a specific border culture.

It was in the area of politics and security policy that the Northern Ireland state focused its greatest attention on the network of cross-border roads. The confirmation of the border in 1925 did not remove the widespread opposition to its creation. Nationalists' opposition to the state and their exclusion from participation were mutually reinforcing, especially in the border regions. For the Unionist government, the borderlands were regarded as both the "frontier" against the nationalist Free State and as an area of questionable allegiance and loyalty. The combination of these factors ensured that the border region had a high security presence especially during periods of ethnic-national violence.

The periods of communal violence in Northern Ireland were always centred on the urban ghettos of Belfast and throughout the border regions. The main incidents occurred during the communal violence of the 1920s which attended the creation of Northern Ireland, the IRA "border campaign" of 1956-62 and the recent conflict

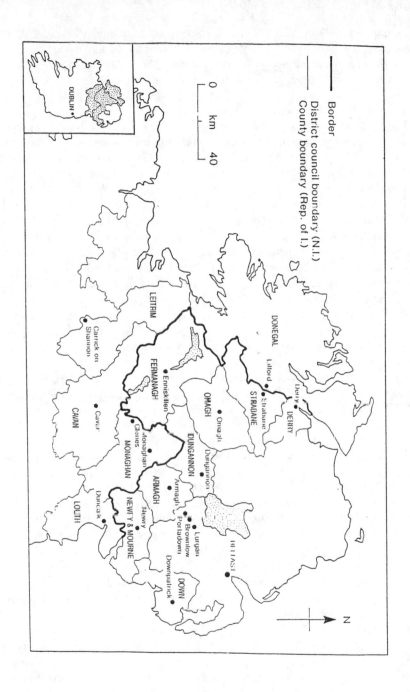

Map 6.1
The Irish Border Region

121

beginning in the 1960s. In all cases, the response of the Northern Ireland state was the increased fortification of the border through security force mobilisation and at times the closing of selected cross-border roads. For example, "Lackey bridge, connecting Counties Monaghan and Fermanagh was first closed in 1922, reopened in 1925, spiked again in the 1950s, re-opened in the 1960s and closed again in the early 1970s" (*Sunday Tribune* 10 January 1993).

The escalation of the conflict in the early 1970s resulted in the proroguing of the Northern Ireland parliament at Stormont by the British government. This meant the replacement of indirect rule through the unionist controlled devolved administration by Direct Rule from London. This course of action was influenced by the increasing involvement of British soldiers in the conflict. Initially, the role of the British army was the protection of Catholics in the face of sectarian attacks, but its role changed as it was increasingly portrayed as an "occupying force" and became more involved in the war against a revitalised IRA. Indeed, local commanders of the British army stated that "the IRA has done us a favour, it gave us the best training ground we could ask for" (BBC, 2 November 1995). Increasingly, the border became a main theatre of the war as the rugged terrain and access to the Republic of Ireland facilitated guerrilla warfare. As before, but this time through the direct involvement of the British army, cross-border roads were blocked and elaborate security fortifications built to control the border and its surrounding region. This policy was supported, with varying degrees of reluctance, by the Irish government as it policed its side of the border.

The huge scale of the border fortification policy can be attributed to a combination of factors such as the intensity and duration of the violence, the greater capabilities of the IRA and the direct involvement of the British army, with its massive resources, in the conflict. However, a single fortification policy was not applied throughout the whole region. It could be argued that border fortifications were adapted to local conditions along the frontier. In the east border region of South Down and South Armagh, border security took the form of heavily fortified army bases augmented by a chain of surveillance towers. This is the region where the IRA was most active and where the security forces were under the greatest threat. The region is predominantly Catholic and nationalist. The major local controversies centre around the activities of the British army and "high incidences of cancer" found in the area which locals allege is linked to the use of electronic surveillance equipment (*Irish News* 9 April 1992; Porter 1993).

In the west border region of Derry and Tyrone, security policy has concentrated on a combination of fortified check-points and the closing of minor cross-border roads. The region is mainly nationalist but has a significant Protestant minority on both sides of the frontier. The fortified check-points have come under severe criticism from nationalists on both sides of the border. Paddy Harte T.D. (Irish Member of Parliament) for Donegal described the checkpoints as "warlike intimidating monstrosities" (*Donegal Democrat* 21 May 1992), while Neil Blaney MEP likened them to "wild west stockades" (*Donegal Democrat* 16 July 1992). John Hume MP MEP (leader of the Social Democratic and Labour Party, the main nationalist party in Northern Ireland) stated that they served little or no security purpose and were merely targets for paramilitary gunmen and bombers. He remarked in the context of the Single European Market, that it was "ironic that the only place in Europe where there will be any sign of a border will be the checkpoints on the Irish border. And those check-points are only there to deal with people who want to get rid of the border" (*Derry Journal* 30 June 1992).

In the mid-border region of Fermanagh and South Tyrone, security policy concentrated on heavily fortified army bases and the systematic closure of most cross-border roads. For example, all of the cross-border crossings between counties Leitrim and Fermanagh were closed, and according to Jimmy Leonard T.D. "in County Monaghan 41 of the 131 [crossings] are blocked" (*Northern Standard* 20 February 1992). This mid-border region of scattered settlements, ethnically mixed population with a nationalist majority, and a relatively poor farming economy, provoked the most intense conflict. More complaints were lodged with the Northern Ireland Office from this region than any other.[2] Unionists were insisting on protection against an IRA campaign of assassination of locally recruited and resident security forces. Nationalists, on the other hand, deeply resented the disruption of cross-border communication and contacts.

Security policy vis-à-vis economic development

The issue of border fortification and cross-border road closures in particular, is a visual and physical expression of the conflict between political and security expressions of national sovereignty, on the one hand, and economic rationality on the other (Corrigan and O'Dowd 1993; O'Dowd et al. 1995; Tomlinson 1993). The British government and the unionists have accorded primacy to issues of territorial sovereignty over the economic development of the region. This policy was a clear contradiction of economic rationality and the process of European integration. Much of the official rationale for border fortifications was based on the perception that the Republic of Ireland was a "safe haven" for the IRA and thus acted as a base for the IRA. Indeed, the Unionist M.P. for Fermanagh-South Tyrone regarded increased border security as "crucial for the overall security in the whole of the province" and went on to state that the RUC Chief Constable "is now convinced that only when the border is effectively sealed will the flow of arms and explosives to the IRA, throughout Northern Ireland dry up" (*Impartial Reporter* 23 January 1992). This view was endorsed by the leading unionist politicians and some even called for the border to be "sealed and mined" (See O'Dowd et al. 1995).

Results from our survey of elected councillors on either side of the border indicate the scale of the divide between unionists and nationalists. It is clear from Table 6.1 that a majority of border councillors (59%) were opposed to road closures for security reasons. The divide is between unionist councillors who accept that road closures are necessary for security reasons and nationalist councillors who disagree.

123

The two poles are represented by the Democratic Unionist Party (DUP) (100% in agreement) and Sinn Fein (87% in opposition).

Table 6.1
Road closures are necessary for security reasons

Political Party	Agree %	Disagree %	Neither %
Fianna Fail	25	75	0
Fine Gael	19	74	7
Others RoI	28	68	4
Ulster Unionist	89	8	3
Democratic Unionist	100	0	0
SDLP	15	71	14
Sinn Fein	13	87	0
Others NI	50	50	0
Total	36	59	5

When asked whether "road closures hinder economic contact across the border", both main Republic of Ireland (RoI) parties (90%) and the Northern Ireland SDLP (84%) were strongly in agreement. Sinn Fein councillors were unanimous. The majority of Ulster Unionist Party (UUP) councillors (64%) and DUP councillors (63%) disagreed, although about one third accepted that economic contact was hindered by the closures (Table 6.2).

Table 6.2
Road closures hinder economic contact

Political Party	Agree %	Disagree %	Neither %
Fianna Fail	90	5	5
Fine Gael	90	7	3
Others RoI	76	20	4
Ulster Unionist	28	64	8
Democratic Unionist	37	63	0
SDLP	84	11	5
Sinn Fein	100	0	0
Others NI	46	54	0
Total	74	21	5

Unionists who felt that security strategy should take the economy of the area into account were clearly in a minority, however. This minority unionist view was expressed by Raymond Ferguson of Fermanagh District Council:

> We would be against any further closing of roads. We want the present roads kept open as more road closures would affect the economics of this area. We have a tourist industry to maintain here and we also do quite a bit of cross-border trade (*Impartial Reporter* 16 January 1992).

The majority of border residents interviewed by us believed that British government/unionist security considerations were really part of a political agenda to accord primacy to British territorial sovereignty and thus maintain the monopoly of state power in the region. Claims were made that the roads were "closed for political rather than military reasons" (*Irish Times* 14 April 1992). A recent report arising from a non-governmental commission [3] dealing with freedom of movement stated that "security concerns are not sufficient to justify the restrictions placed on movement within and between communities here by the closure of border roads" (*Fermanagh Herald* 17 July 1993). Indeed, elements within the British army questioned the rationale of static border fortifications as an effective security policy as too many troops are deployed in operating such check-points. Brigadier Peter Morton, described such fortifications as "Crusader Castles" that sapped the strength of the British security forces (*Ulster Herald* 9 May 1992). This view was supported in a recent documentary on the British army on the border demonstrating that some of the local commanders doubted the policy on the grounds that it exposed soldiers to excessive risk in order to ensure a token presence of police in some border areas (BBC 19 October 1995). This was a result of the British government's policy of restoring the primacy of the police in order to "normalise" security in Northern Ireland.

The Irish government, while recognising the security aspects, felt that the road closures were seriously disadvantaging the region. The dilemma was expressed by the Minister for Foreign Affairs when he stated that "there are serious security considerations arising from the continuing campaign of violence...these considerations must be weighed carefully against the negative economic and social effects of the crossings remaining closed" (David Andrews T.D. in response to Irish Parliamentary question by Gerry Reynolds T.D. in *Leitrim Observer* 4 March 1992). The Irish government advocated the reopening of some key roads "in conjunction with adequate security measures being put in place to guarantee the protection of life and property" (David Andrews T.D. in *Anglo-Celt* 16 February 1992).

Effects of border fortification

The impact of the fortifications for cross-border contacts was reflected in the responses to our survey of border councillors:

Table 6.3
Army checkpoints restrict cross-border contacts

Political Party	Agree %	Disagree %	Neither %
Fianna Fail	83	15	2
Fine Gael	81	13	6
Others RoI	68	24	8
Ulster Unionist	16	76	8
Democratic Unionist	0	75	25
SDLP	83	8	8
Sinn Fein	100	0	0
Others NI	50	50	0
Total	67	26	7

It is clear from Table 6.3 that a majority of border councillors (67%) felt that army checkpoints restricted cross-border contacts, but once again there is a clear divide between unionist and nationalist opinion. Nationalists councillors such as those in Fianna Fail (83%) and the SDLP (83%) strongly agree as opposed to unionist councillors in the UUP (76%) and DUP (75%) who strongly disagree. Of course, it seems likely that nationalists in general have more cross-border contacts than unionists.

Border fortifications and in particular the closing of the roads in the mid-border region directly impinged on the economic, social and cultural lives of the border communities. The region is heavily dependent on tourism and has obtained government and EU funding for a number of tourism projects. The contradiction in policies prompted one local public representative to comment on "how can cross-border tourism develop if the infrastructure on which it depends is being systematically closed down?" (*Leitrim Observer* 14 July 1993). In a debate on the issue at the SDLP annual conference, Councillor Tommy Gallagher of Fermanagh stated:

at least 5,000 people were affected by road closures in Fermanagh and as a result were suffering a serious loss of income, and that in the worst affected areas turnover in the local shops was down by 40%, or as much as £3,000 per week. Singling out Roslea as one of the most affected areas, eight cross-border roads remained closed and to date, the village had lost a chemist's shop, with extra expense and inconvenience been caused to workers and local farmers (*Fermanagh Herald* 30 November 1991).

The town of Clones in County Monaghan suffered particular economic and social disruption because of closed border roads. Historically, the town's economic and social hinterland lies in south Fermanagh. The parish of Clones is split by the border and the road closures prevented sections of the community from participating in parish activities. According to one local resident, Clones became "a little island on its own cut off from all the rest" *(Northern Standard* 5 March 1992).

Border militarisation: the internationalisation of the conflict

By the late 1980s increasing border fortification seemed increasingly anomalous in the context of plans to abolish border controls within the European Community. It began to attract growing international attention. Nationalist politicians on both sides of the border raised the issue in the national and European Parliaments.

At grassroots level, a number of local community groups in the border region were highlighting the problems of conducting economic development across a "closed" border. However, their impact at the national and international level was minimal. As a result, an umbrella community organisation was formed which represented a range of cross-border community associations. The main aim of the combined cross-border community association committee was the re-opening of all closed cross-border roads and the dismantling of the fortifications. The campaign was led by a number of community associations and supported by the Irish National Congress.[4]

At a local level, the campaign claimed to have cross-community support for its objectives, although activists tended to be exclusively nationalist. There was also the perception that the campaign had a strong Sinn Fein influence which alienated many unionist and some nationalists. While supporting the aim of re-opening the roads, some nationalists refrained from participating in direct action:

the tension has increased significantly and many local people have condemned what they describe as a sinister element which have entered the campaign since the IRA fired shots at the British army after a road was reopened by local people (Local development activist in interview with authors, 12 February 1992).

The perceived involvement of Sinn Fein in the local campaign added to unionist opposition and led one DUP MP to call on the security forces to "deal with the law-breakers now" *(Irish News* 25 November 1991).

The campaign was based on "days of action" where local communities organised the re-opening of closed cross border roads. The largest "day of action" took place on January 1 1993 to coincide with the start of the Single European Market. The movement was soon engaged in direct confrontation with the security forces. As one Northern Ireland police constable commented "it's a tit-for-tat job, they open them and we close them again" *(Leitrim Observer* 6 May 1992). In areas hostile to the security forces, the re-closing of border roads was a major logistical undertaking in bringing in heavy machinery and the careful staking out of the area by the army while the work was in progress. The protests also became highly mechanised with the use of heavy earth-moving equipment which was likely to be confiscated by the Northern Ireland security forces if discovered on their side of the border.

The campaign was focused on two levels. Firstly, it represented a co-ordinated local response to the negative implications of the road closures. Secondly, the campaign was structured around set-piece confrontations with the security forces in order to appeal to the international media. American and British politicians were invited to see the road closures and their effects were publicised internationally.[5] The rhetoric of the campaign was internationalist and it drew parallels with other international conflicts. The campaign made much of the fact that as borders were coming down within the EU, road closures had created "a Berlin type wall on our doorsteps" *(Fermanagh-Monaghan Community Association* 1991; 9).

Secondly, the policies of the British security forces were compared to contemporary international conflict situations. For example, local residents stated how the security forces used them as "human shields" by locating their bases besides dwelling houses and, and in one case, beside a school. This was compared to the actions of Iraq during the Gulf War and more recently to the hostages held by the Bosnian Serbs. Overall the campaign against road closures and bases was driven by opposition to their disruptive effect on everyday life, by a rejection of the presence and activities of the securities forces. Fortifications and road closures symbolised the government's determination to protect border unionists and were a means of convincing them that it was serious about asserting British sovereignty. Nationalist opposition, on the other hand, was effective in portraying them as symbols of oppression which were anachronistic in a Europe where border controls were being abolished. Against this symbolic and propaganda battleground, it difficult to assess what real effect they had on the military campaign between the IRA and the security forces.

The peace process

At another level, however, the gradual development of inter-governmental links which developed between both sovereign governments from the early 1970s onwards reflected a commitment on both sides to ensure that the Northern Ireland did not escalate into an inter-state conflict. The British government, between periods of negotiations on new governmental structures, sought to mobilise acquiescence, if not active consent, from both communities in Northern Ireland. The government of the Irish Republic had a part to play in delivering nationalist acquiescence.

The Anglo-Irish Agreement of 1985 reflected a type of inter-governmental networking familiar in the European Community to which both states belonged. This was taken a stage further by the Joint Declaration of 1994 which provided a framework for the present ceasefires and possible negotiations arising from it. Both governments retained their different agendas and priorities but the border question raised no pressing strategic questions, nor did the area contain any valuable economic resources which might provoke a clash of interests. On the contrary, the availability of development funds from the US and elsewhere (to support the Anglo-Irish Agreement) and of various structural funds from the EU encouraged co-operation between both governments to combat common economic problems of unemployment and weak economic infrastructure in the region (O'Dowd et al. 1995).

Since late 1994, the ceasefires have resulted in a gradual decrease of the security presence in Northern Ireland and most of the cross-border roads have been re-opened. The process of de-militarisation is much slower in the border regions than in the main urban trouble-spots. Both governments and a range of political parties are keen to take praise for the peace process and its advantages to areas like the border. In line with these sentiments, Sinn Fein have paid tribute to the cross-border community associations which were "the real force behind the current re-opening of the closed border roads" (*Northern Standard* 24 November 1994). However, they point out that the border continues to be the most militarised internal frontier of the European Union with its fortifications and watchtowers still intact. The campaign has now shifted its objective to a total demilitarisation of the border with the army checkpoints as the main target. Demonstrations have been held at all the checkpoints and "eviction notices" have been served on the occupants. In addition, "mock auctions" have been conducted where the checkpoint is sold at knock-down prices.

The re-opening of the cross-border roads is conditional on the continuation of the peace process. The warning from the British state is quite clear: it retains the monopoly on the means of violence, and any challenge to that monopoly will result in the reassertion of territorial sovereignty through an increased fortification of the border. At the same time, the Single European Market has had a visible effect on the border. The disappearance of the borders customs' posts marks the end of an era which began in 1923 when such posts first marked a border between both parts of the island. On the other hand, two fully separate educational, health and welfare, and administrative systems have created new and invisible barriers which differentiate social life on either side of the boundary.

Conclusion

The consolidation of the Irish border through its fortification and militarisation has re-emphasised the importance of national territorial sovereignty to the British state. The struggle over the roads is an important indicator that territorial boundaries retain their significance for nation-states and for ethnic-national groups within the EU. The British government and to a lesser extent the Irish government, have accorded primacy to security issues over economic development. The planning of border security has been much more elaborate and systematic than any planning to revitalise the economic base of the region, despite the availability of external funds (O'Dowd 1994; O'Dowd and Corrigan 1995). Here, as noted by Baker elsewhere in this volume, mismatched administrative structures as well as the highly centralised form of both the British and Irish states have ensured a rather localised and fragmented approach to local cross-border cooperation.

The road closure issue has also provided a sharp illustration of what can occur when moves towards European integration come face to face with deep-rooted ethnic-national conflict. It demonstrates that, even where the border region is of little strategic value, and even where the region concerned has been accorded the right (in principle at least) to secede from the state, the British government asserted its territorial sovereignty with the consequences outlined above. In reasserting territorial control, the state has continued, in practice, its long tradition of drawing on one ethnic group to police the other in a deeply divided society. In conjunction with the IRA campaign, this policy underlines the coercive basis of the Irish border and its capacity to reproduce ethno-national division. But the policy is also bound up with the primary aim of the state in maintaining law and order within fixed boundaries - as such it takes priority over the stated aim of British policy in Northern Ireland which is to encourage agreement and reconciliation between Irish nationalists and unionists.

As in border regions elsewhere, the assertion of territorial sovereignty and administrative integrity is given higher priority in the Irish border region than coherent cross-border economic planning (Hansen 1983: 256). The British-Irish border lends support to Christaller's "socio-political separation principle" despite the favourable conditions for cross-border cooperation within the EU generally. Here too, however, the British Conservatives' preoccupation with protecting national sovereignty against the encroachment of Brussels contrasts with the Irish government's more enthusiastic commitment to use the EU to minimise the real effects of the border in Ireland.

The European Union and Anglo-American relationships however have influenced the methods by which territorial sovereignty has been maintained in Northern Ireland. It has facilitated the internationalising of the issue and created a framework which makes it more difficult for the stronger state to impose a solution as it did, in conjunction with Northern unionists, in 1920-21. New intergovernmental frameworks have also made it possible for local groups and Northern nationalists generally to use the border as a means of overcoming the isolation and powerlessness of their position within the Northern statelet in the first fifty years of its existence.

Notes

The research project on which this chapter is based was funded by the Economic and Social Research Council (Grant No. R000233053). Entitled "Negotiating the British/Irish border: transfrontier cooperation on the European periphery" data collection was carried out between 1991 and 1994. This included a survey of all elected councillors in the border region (N=238); a sample survey of border residents

(N=400), interviews with key officials and local development activists and systematic analysis of local newspapers in the border region over a two-year period.

1. The British Prime Minister Lloyd-George wrote to the Ulster Unionist leader Craig on 5 December 1921 with a copy of the Anglo-Irish Treaty, outlining the options for Northern Ireland of joining the Irish Free State or remaining with Great Britain. He stated:

> In the latter case, however, we should feel unable to defend the existing boundary, which must be subject to revision on one side and the other by a Boundary Commission under the terms of the Instrument' (North Eastern Boundary Bureau 1923: 35).

In the event, Craig refused to co-operate with the Boundary Commission and concentrated on consolidating Unionist military and political control of the six county area of Northern Ireland. Conservatives in Britain began to urge a highly restrictive interpretation of the Commission's remit, while Irish nationalists hoped for an outcome which would so reduce the size of Northern Ireland as to make it a non-viable entity eventually (Hand 1969; Phoenix 1994).

2. Personal communication from Northern Ireland civil servant to O'Dowd.

3. The commission formed part of the Convention on Human Rights in Northern Ireland held in London in April 1992. It dealt with "freedom of movement" and was chaired by Professor Richard Falk. A contrary view was put to one of the authors by a Northern Ireland Office official who claimed that the border policy had reduced the killings of the locally recruited Ulster Defence Regiment and the police in border districts by making it more difficult to escape into the Irish Republic (personal communication).

4. The Irish National Congress seeks an end to partition and supports the claim that Ireland has rightful jurisdiction over Northern Ireland as stated in Articles 2 and 3 of the Irish constitution. (Article 2 states that the national territory is the whole of Ireland, its islands and the territorial seas; Article 3 asserts the right of the Irish parliament and government to exercise jurisdiction over the North, but says that until they do so in reality, their actual jurisdiction is confined to the 26 counties). The chairman of the INC is the Dublin artist, Robert Ballagh, a fact which may have influenced the highly magnetic and visually striking nature of many INC demonstrations.

5. For example, the Fermanagh-Tyrone Community Association submitted a report on the effects of the road closures to the Convention on Human Rights in Northern Ireland in London, April 1992.

References

BBC 1995. *In the company of men.* (Television documentary on British army [Welsh Guards] on the Irish border) BBC 2, 19, 26 October, 2 November.

Buckland, P. 1981. *A history of Northern Ireland.* Dublin: Gill and Macmillan.

Busteed, M. 1992. The Irish border - from partition and confrontation to cooperation? *Boundary Bulletin* 4: 13-17.

Corrigan, J. and L. O'Dowd 1993. Dragon's teeth on the Irish border. *Boundary and Security Bulletin* 1(1): 45-48.

Denton, G and T. Fahy 1993. *The Northern Ireland land boundary 1923-1992.* Belfast: H.M. Customs and Excise.

Douglas, J. N. H. 1976. The irreconcilable border. *Geographical Magazine* XLIX 3: 162-168.

Fermanagh - Monaghan Community Association 1991. *Freedom of movement - submission to Northern Ireland human rights assembly.*

Fisk, R. 1993. Will anyone be satisfied at the bargain? *Fortnight* Supplement, December 323: i-vii.

Giddens, A. 1985. *The nation state and violence.* Cambridge: Polity Press.

Hand, G. 1969. (ed.) *Report of the Irish Boundary Commission 1925.* Shannon: Irish University Press.

Hansen, N. 1983. International co-operation in border regions: an overview and research agenda. *International Regional Science Review* 8(3): 255-70.

Hobsbawm, E. J. 1990. *Nations and nationalism since 1780.* Cambridge, Cambridge University Press.

Laffan, M. 1983. *The partition of Ireland 1911-1925.* Dundalk: Dundalgan Press.

Lash, S. and Urry, J. 1994. *Economies of signs and space.* London: Sage.

Mann, M. 1984. The autonomous power of the state: its origins, mechanisms and results. *European Journal of Sociology* 25 (2): 185-213.

_____. 1993. Nation states in Europe and other continents: diversifying, developing, not dying. *Daedalus* 122: 115-40.

Milward, A. 1992. *The European rescue of the nation-state.* London: Routledge.

Mlinar, Z. 1995. Territorial dehierarchization in the emerging new Europe. In J. Langer and W. Pollauer (eds.) *Small states in the emerging new Europe.* Klagenfurt: Verlag fur Soziologie und Humanethologie, Eisenstadt.

North Eastern Border Bureau 1923. *Handbook of the Ulster question.* Dublin: Stationery Office.

O'Dowd, L. 1994. *Whither the Irish border? sovereignty, democracy and economic integration.* Belfast: Centre for Research and Documentation.

O'Dowd, L. and Corrigan, J. 1995. Buffer zone or bridge: local responses to cross-border economic cooperation in the Irish border region. *Administration* 42 (4): 335-351.

O'Dowd, L.; Corrigan, J. and Moore, T. 1995. Borders, national sovereignty and European integration. *International Journal of Urban and Regional Research* 19 (2): 272-285.

Phoenix, E. 1994. *Northern Nationalism: nationalist politics and the Catholic minority in Northern Ireland 1890-1940.* Belfast: Ulster Historical Foundation.

Porter, S. 1993. Unhealthy surveillance: investigating public health in south Armagh. *Critical Public Health* 4 (2): 9-16.

Suarez-Villa, L., M. Giaoutzi and A. Stratigea 1992. Territorial and border barriers in information and communication networks: a conceptual exploration. *Tijdschrift voor Econ. en Soc. Geografie* 83 (2): 93-104.

Tomlinson, M. 1993. Policing the new Europe: the Northern Ireland factor. In T. Bunyan (ed.) *Statewatching the New Europe.* London: Statewatch.

Weber, M. 1978. *Economy and Society.* G. Roth and C. Wittich (eds.) London: University of California Press.

7   New states and open borders: Slovenia between the Balkans and the European Union

Zdravko Mlinar

The Slovenian daily *Delo* reported on 26 April 1989 that a military border patrol had prevented a group of eleven Romanians illegally crossing the Yugoslav-Austrian border near Šentilj, between Maribor and Graz. It added that "as regulations require, our border guards first stopped the group and then one of the soldiers fired a warning shot in the air. The fugitives then began to scatter into the night. However two bullets from one guard's gun stopped the mother of five children and their 56 year-old father". This fragment reminds us that even in Yugoslavia, which had been the most open of the "socialist" states, the state border was more important than human lives. The collapse of the socialist states and exclusionist ideology, which had maintained internal unity by stressing the threat of external foes, offered the prospect of the opening up of state borders. The European Union (EU) and its "Europe without borders" programme provided a model for this. But the course of change in the former Yugoslavia, Soviet Union and Czechoslovakia has not followed that pattern; their disintegration has been accompanied by the erection of borders where there were none before. Bosnia-Herzegovina, Serbia and Croatia are embroiled in war due precisely to the drawing of new borders.

This parallel dismantling and erection of borders has often been described as a paradox which has not been adequately explained sociologically. The perplexity arises from the simultaneous presence and intermixing of elements of two essentially different types of territorial-social organisation. In one, the "territorial community" is based on proximity, contiguity, internal homogeneity and frontal territorial separation (demarcation) and an *a priori* exclusiveness towards the outside world. The other is marked by deliberate, selective and dispersed interconnections across increasingly permeable (open)

135

borders which thus become irrelevant. In sociology the transition from the one to the other type has been given different denotations, such as the shift from a "cumulative community" towards an "aggregate divided into functional associations" (Sorokin 1930), from a "space of places to a space of flows" (Castells 1985), from "identity as an island to identity as a cross-roads" (Williams 1992), or from "the old to the new localism" (Strassoldo 1992).

Underlying these transformations is "the unity of the opposites", the processes of the autonomisation of subsystems (actors) and their cross-border interlinking. The autonomisation of the smallest ethno-nations, such as the Slovene, Croatian, Slovakian and Macedonian nations, is the most belated because they had the least opportunity to resist the logic of "power politics". Although they are only now establishing the borders of their newly-attained national states these borders are a component of the full constituting of their national identities. At the same time there is an asymmetry. The new demarcations are defined primarily in relation to the formerly dominant state core (such as Belgrade, Serbia) while programs are pursued to open up the borders to European integration processes at the other end. This raises the question whether the barely-won national sovereignty is not being lost as the new state relinquishes control of, or is unable to control, the cross-border flows of people, goods and ideas in the broader European space.

Possibly more than any other state in Europe, Slovenia is an example of maximal time and space compression of the dynamics and contradictions of the two developmental stages in the territorial organisation of European societies. Using empirical data from Slovenia I shall try to show how borders spring up and disappear in the mutual conflict and interweaving of the long-term processes of autonomisation (diversification) and integration (homogenisation), a groundwork which is essential to an understanding of both Balkanisation and the "new Europe" without frontiers.

Borders and national identity

Conflict situations have been operative in the formation of Slovenia's territorial identity, and were particularly dramatic four times: at the break-up of the Austro-Hungarian Empire in 1918; at the end of the Second World War in 1945; in 1953, when an armed clash loomed between Yugoslavia and Italy; and upon Slovenia's declaration of independence and the disintegration of the Yugoslav federation in 1991. In each instance the border was at issue, whether there was a bid to change it or to take control of it as in 1991.

In their centuries-long subjection to the Hapsburg monarchy, up to 1918, the Slovenes had not shaped their own national identity to the point of its territorial and political demarcation from other nations. There had been a drive for a "united" Slovenia within the empire, but not for an autonomous Slovene state.[1] The defeat of Austria in the First World War allowed the numerically small Slovene nation to form a new state together with the Croats and the Serbs. Its delineation from the former hegemon was fraught with difficulties.

The battle for the northern border of Slovenia (Yugoslavia), against the powerful economic, cultural and political predominance of the German-speaking populace, resulted - notwithstanding the referendum amongst Slovenes in Carinthia (Koroska) 1920 - in a Slovene minority being left on the Austrian side and henceforth rapidly assimilated in the following decades. Unfortunately for the Slovenes in Carinthia, they were not given enough time before the referendum, held straight after the war was over, to make their choice in an autonomous way. They had to choose between joining Serbia, which was ethnically closer to Slovenia but was a socially relatively backward Balkan state which had warred with Austria, or of remaining an integral part of Central Europe, which promised greater democratisation and ethnic tolerance.

As its reward for switching to the winning side during the First World War Italy was given Slovene ethnic territory. It annexed not only nationally-mixed territory, but also purely Slovene-inhabited areas. Consequently, at the end of the Second World War, the border between Yugoslavia (Slovenia) and Italy was sharply disputed. Since it was tantamount to a demarcation between East and West (at least until the Tito-Stalin confrontation in 1948) the "power politics" were again brought to bear on this border. In 1953 there was even the danger of a military confrontation over the Trieste area. Only in 1975 was the question finally resolved consensually with the Osimo Accord. But some nationalistic groups in Italy have never recognised this agreement as definitive and have kept raising the border issue. With the break-up of Yugoslavia and the emergence of new, relatively weak neighbours such as Slovenia and Croatia in 1991 these pressures have resurfaced. Attempts are even made to find support amongst chauvinist groups in Serbia and the Serb "Krajina" in Croatia.

The disintegration of the former Yugoslavia in 1991 has also opened up new border disputes. They still continue to create tensions between Slovenia and Croatia,[2] although neither side shows any propensity to use force and in the worst case they will probably seek international arbitration. The core problem is the demarcation of the respective territorial waters.

Thus, Slovenia's territorial identity has been shaped by conflicting border aspirations between itself and its neighbours. Paradoxically, it could be said that a premodern chapter is being closed for Slovenia at the very time West Europe is opening up and transcending state borders and territorial exclusivity (Ceccini 1988; Duroselle 1988). In this sense, Slovenia may share the fate of small states that have emerged belatedly and are in danger of losing their hard-won sovereignty and national identity (Mlinar 1993).

Some writers depict Slovenia as some kind of initiator of the process of Yugoslavia's disintegration (see for example *The Federalist* 1993: 2). They ignore, however, the fact that Slovenia's political platform was not secession but was greater openness and easier interlinking in all directions, particularly towards West Europe. For some time Slovenia had staunchly advocated opening Yugoslavia's borders and its accelerated inclusion into European integrative processes. It pursued this in two ways: by putting pressures on the federal government in Belgrade and by taking the initiative and establishing direct cross-border links (e.g., through the Alps-Adria Working Community, small-border co-operation projects, etc.). But it failed to win satisfactory support in Belgrade. While Slovenia stressed the need to open the borders, the central government countered with proposals for additional border control measures, such as a special border zone with a tight regime of control by the Yugoslav Peoples' Army. Slovene proposals for cross-border regional co-operation were particularly opposed in Serbia where they were lampooned in the media, or even admonished for "disloyalty".

Map 7.1
Slovenia and bordering states

Pursuing its own interests, Slovenia proceeded to try to increase its autonomy by reducing uni-directional links to the federal centre. But it had no interest in breaking off its very favourable economic and other ties within Yugoslavia. Although the growing aspirations for autonomy resulted in some connections being severed and the disintegration of several federal organisations that had their seats in Belgrade, the most dramatic break was effected by Serbia which imposed a full trade embargo on Slovenia in retaliation for its political support for the Albanians in Kosovo when Serbia abolished their autonomy.

Yugoslavia had had the most open borders of all the "socialist" states, and as its most developed federal unit Slovenia had the most intensive cross-border traffic. "In 1989 Slovenia had 8.2% of the population of Yugoslavia (1,948,000 out of the total 23,690,000). Its share of the Social Product (roughly comparable to GDP) that year was about 16%. Its share of exports amounted to 22.2% of total Yugoslav merchandise exports" (Trošt 1993). A more detailed account of Yugoslavia's various policy swings, such as the considerable liberalism of the 1960s, or the internal ideological strains over "foreign" and "hostile" influences in the 1970s, or the gradual relaxation and opening up of the borders in the 1980s, is beyond our scope here.

In Slovenia today there are two contrary tendencies. While the borders to Western and Central Europe are opening, the border with Croatia is just being erected (and is not yet quite definite). While it is setting up free trade zones with the Višegrad Group, new barriers are cropping up in trade with Croatia. Croatia's war situation, and the occupation of part of its territory these past few years, must be borne in mind, together with the fact that Croatia rejected a Slovenian offer of a free trade zone and introduced protective customs duties instead (which brought retaliatory, though somewhat milder, measures from Slovenia).

These asymmetrical tendencies actually represent a kind of correction of the lop-sided direction of links and dependencies in the past. The easing of the mobility of people, goods and ideas inside Yugoslavia had for almost three-quarters of a century been accompanied by separation from the West. Many other factors were also involved. Just as the Southern Railway line had once symbolised Slovenia's connections to the capital of the Austrian Empire up until its disintegration, Slovenia's principal transportation routes and connections in Yugoslavia were uniformly directed towards Belgrade. Ljubljana had several daily connections to Belgrade but no direct air connection to nearby Vienna, Budapest, Munich and Milan. Similarly, immigration into Slovenia was almost exclusively from other parts of Yugoslavia, with virtually none from other European countries.

Yugoslavia declared its willingness to open up and join the world market but clung to numerous restrictive mechanisms that in fact prevented economic actors (subject to government interventions) from entering it autonomously.

The extremely firm ideological option, which was characterised by its exclusion of all others (whether communist, socialist or liberal conservative), clashed with the declared reorientation towards a market economy and the world market. Yugoslavia's openness to Europe and the world was differentiated widely from sector to sector. There were mass flows of tourists from West Europe. Similarly, there was mass employment of workers from Yugoslavia (though few were from Slovenia) in West Germany and elsewhere. At the same time there were numerous restrictions in various politically sensitive areas. Claims that Yugoslavia's borders were the most open in Europe are based on indicators such as tourism, or shopping *en masse* in neighbouring countries, especially in Italy and Austria. However, borders can also be hidden. Limited openness is evident from immediate control measures at border crossings, as well as indirect measures like penalties for expression of ideologically alien ideas.

In Slovenia today it is argued that the country belongs to Central Europe by virtue of both its geographical location and its cultural traditions. The seventy or more years spent as a part of Yugoslavia now represent an encumbrance that is slowing down its reintegration back into Central Europe, where it had always been for centuries. Other East European countries might overtake it in this because Slovenia is now immersed in the former-Yugoslavia's problems.[3] As a result its decades' long market experience cannot come fully into play, particularly in defining its status in relation to the European Union and other organisations, like the OECD.

State and ethnic delineation

Slovenia borders on the European Union to its west and north, with Austria and Italy respectively. As with Hungary, Slovenia's state borders are not congruent with ethnic lines of division. There are Slovene minorities in all three countries, and there are Italian and Hungarian minorities in Slovenia. However all three of these minorities are in numerical decline. In the case of the Italian minority this came with emigration from the Slovenian Littoral to Italy after the Second World War. The Slovene minorities in Italy, Austria and Hungary, by contrast, are undergoing rapid assimilation. Inside Slovenia assimilation is the least marked in the mixed Slovene-Hungarian area near the Hungarian border. An unusually high level of minority protection (e.g., with bilingual instruction at all educational institutions) is provided both there and for the Italian minority on the coast. Slovene children also attend bilingual programmes in the same classrooms. This has produced its first fruits:

in the ethnically-mixed area near the Slovenian-Hungarian border more than 80% of Slovenes speak or understand Hungarian and more than 90% of

Hungarians speak or understand Slovene. A similar level of bilingualism is found with the Slovene majority and the Italian minority in the ethnically-mixed area of Koper . . . This system of bilingual education enables further study at secondary and tertiary schools in either Slovenia or Hungary, or Italy (Klemencic 1992: 34).[4]

Although the government took these measures to promote coexistence in ethnically-mixed areas, there is another process at work. While the borders were tightly closed, minorities in the border areas were being rapidly assimilated. But when they began to be opened, the minorities acquired a new role, namely that of being a mediating link between two language areas. Expanding cross-border trade has increased the need for Slovene-Italian and Slovene-German communication (the border areas with Hungary are more rural and trading is less intensive). Thus the roles of minority languages are strengthened as borders are opened. It may also be noted that besides the minority's mediating role, the business interests of traders and others incline them to not just tolerate but even learn the language of their neighbours. This is seen amongst small traders and private business-people in Gorizia, Italy, even though border officials and others often show disinterest or even objection to acquiring or displaying knowledge of the neighbouring language.

Sometimes there is a latent congruence of interests sustaining non-co-operation, although for different reasons. The Austrian authorities were not interested in helping Slovenian TV programmes reach over the Karavanke Mountains because it might slow down the assimilation of minority Slovenes. On their part, the Yugoslav authorities were eager to prevent the spread of "alien influences". As a small ethno-nation within the relatively less-developed country of Yugoslavia, the Slovenes have always nursed a fear of dominating influences from abroad. Thus opening the borders of Slovenia is an agonising issue because it could lead to a loss of identity (e.g., the Slovene language) in the border areas. Hence Slovenia is concerned that more and more students from its border areas are welcomed to enrol *gratis* in Italian secondary schools in Gorizia or Trieste.

With the formation of the state of Croatia and its new state borders there has been a radical break in the movement and settlement (mainly by building holiday homes) of Slovenes in Istria. In earlier decades this area had been accessible as part of the single Yugoslav space. On its part, sensitive to possible changes in the national composition in Istria - where regionalist interests are already at odds with Zagreb - Croatia has curbed the flow of Slovenes seeking out the nearest holiday area on the Adriatic. There is a third party involved as well. Italy is now demanding greater access to both the Croatian and the Slovene part of Istria (in terms of property purchases), and is banking on "Europe without borders" reaching into Istria sooner or later. In place of the "single Yugoslav space" and its familiar ramifications, it is now possible to anticipate a single European space with all its consequences.

Openness for access and transit

With regard to the changing role of state borders consideration may be given in particular to the distinction between: inward or outward openness of the national borders and transit flows, including Slovenia's transit function. The ongoing war in Bosnia-Herzegovina and Croatia has substantially curbed the transit function of Slovenia's territory which used to be very marked along the West Europe-Southeast Europe-Near East trajectory. This is very apparent on the border between Austria and Slovenia where the Karavanke tunnel was built precisely because of the heavy traffic in this direction. Since the 1991 war, traffic has dropped substantially and is not covering costs. By contrast, the function of the Barcelona-Milan-Budapest-Moscow transversal has grown greatly in precisely these past four years. The invigoration of international trade in the East European countries has already led to critical overloading of the infrastructures of these connections, particularly border crossings with Hungary, especially with regard to freight transport where lines of trucks sometimes wait to cross for days.

Much discussion in Slovenia focuses on the danger of the country's transportation isolation due to the shift in European and Balkan political geography (Mušic 1992: 39), and its ending up just a corridor for transit traffic and all its harmful ecological impacts (Klemencic 1992: 37). It is already evident, for example, that Italy is linking up with Hungary around Slovenia, travelling from Udine, Villach, Wien and then taking the fork to Budapest, rather than going along the route of the one-time "Southern Railway" from Vienna to Trieste. Ecological problems in Slovenia's becoming a corridor are raised by proposals to activate the comparative advantages of its geographical location, which offers the shortest land route from the Mediterranean (the port of Koper) to Central Europe - and especially to Austria, Hungary, the Czech Republic and Slovakia.

Another issue is the potential function of becoming either a channel or a buffer zone for immigrants from Southeastern Europe and Asia who seek illegal entry into Western Europe. Sometimes comparisons are even drawn here with Slovenia's past role as a military frontier, when it acted as Central Europe's bulwark against the Ottoman Turks.

One practical dilemma is whether Slovenia should impose selective restrictions on the kinds of commodities shipped through it in order to limit ecological impacts. Although this would resolve only a small part of the problem. But even here the question arises of how autonomous Slovenia could be in regulating international flows if it becomes more closely integrated in European processes.

Control of the border was a direct cause of the armed conflict of 1991. But in the long run will Slovenia lose this control if it has to bow to the general standards of the European Union? This brings us back to the general problem of preserving and transforming territorial identity: identity as an island, or identity as a cross-road? (Mlinar 1992a)

Open borders and national autonomy

Realising the vision of "Europe without borders" poses the challenge of preserving national autonomy and historical-cultural distinctiveness. This is a central issue in the processes of European integration, not only for Slovenia but all European countries. We may leave aside the general question - is the nation state going to lose its sovereignty (autonomy) or is it only a question of pooling sovereignties at a "higher" level? It is clear that the capacity and need to control trans-border flows of people, goods and ideas tends to decline with the advancement of these integration processes. For example, the 300 technical homogenisation measures, and the increasing autonomy (diversity) of subnational actors, both tend to weaken the nation state's control (Ceccini 1988; Wistrich 1989; Mlinar 1992b).

We cannot assume without qualification that having more open borders automatically implies less autonomy. The latent issue here is "whose autonomy"? While the nation state as a territorial unit may be losing it, it is being gained by subnational units and individuals (Mlinar 1994). Empirical data on how people relate to these two political options is relevant here. Survey data based on a national sample for Slovenia (*Slovensko Javno Mnenje* [SJM] 1993) shows the following:

Table 7.1
Open borders and the autonomy of Slovenia

	Agree %
my first priority is Slovenia's autonomy	33
my preference is opening up to the world and doing away with state borders	30
I advocate practical case by case solutions	25
do not know, undecided	12

N=1050

The responses fall into three categories of approximately the same weight (adding 3+4). The balance is striking between those opting primarily for autonomy and those opting for opening up Slovenia ("do away with the borders"). This split reflects a deadlock with a real or apparent incompatibility of two important social values. Neither autonomy with closure nor openness without autonomy are acceptable for a majority of the respondents.

Preference for open borders increases relatively with level of education. The strongest support for autonomy (in the above sense) comes from respondents with lower levels of education. Some regional differences were also found. Respondents from the Coastal-Karst and the Karst region show the relatively greatest preference for openness. These are border regions whose development is strongly dependent on an open border with Italy.

Additional information is provided by the responses to the statement: "There is an increasing number of problems which cannot be solved by Slovenes alone, but only together with other European nations" (SJM 1993). This implies rejection of self-sufficiency (autarchy). 63.5% of respondents (fully or mainly) agreed, 14.6% (mainly or completely) disagreed, the others were undecided or did not know. This shows a high awareness that in today's circumstances autonomy with isolation is no longer a realistic option. But co-operation, clearly, is a different issue than say choosing a country in which to live. Given a choice (SJM 1993) 89% chose (certainly or probably) Slovenia, 8% (probably or certainly) some other country; the others did not know.

Cross-border mobility of people

In contrast to general expectations, actual changes do not manifest a uniform trend toward increasing cross-border mobility of people in all geographical directions. Despite the commitment to a "Europe without borders", there are two qualifications: firstly, the introduction of new barriers, especially to inflows of people from the Southeast (i.e. from the rest of former Yugoslavia); and secondly, mobility of people is considered less acceptable (and should be more restricted) than the mobility of goods and ideas.

Public opinion surveys in Slovenia (SJM 1991, 1992, 1993, 1994) clearly show a trend of declining acceptability of immigrants from former-Yugoslav republics. Contrary to expectations that as time passed after the 1991 war the ratio between negative and positive attitudes would change in favour of the latter, the survey data shows the opposite (and a similar tendency is seen in attitudes towards refugees from Bosnia-Herzegovina). This may reflect the political changes and a deteriorating image of the Balkans. It is also related to the fact that the immigration wave of the 1970s brought mostly low-skilled workers who found jobs in industry, construction works, mining, municipal services, and the military especially. Regarding future immigration, 28.6% of respondents would stop all immigration into Slovenia, 44.4% would limit it, 9.1% would allow in only family members, 8.3% would allow the immigration of professionals and entrepreneurs, while 9.6% are undecided. For attitudes to immigrants from the rest of Yugoslavia see table 7.2.

Table 7.2
Attitudes to immigrants from the "South"
(the rest of former-Yugoslavia)

attitudes:	negative or very negative %	positive or very positive %	neutral or do not know %
1991	30	22	46
1992	42	14	43
1993	43	13	33
1994	53	9	38

(Source: SJM annual reports)

Such an exclusionist tendency (see also Klinar 1994) may be a reaction to the geographically one-sided openness toward the Southeast of the past, although it must be noted that the Slovenian government did exercise some indirect control over immigration at the time through employment policy.

It may be hypothesised that the expected increase in immigration from other European countries will heighten negative attitudes, although for different reasons. While immigrants thus far entered the lowest strata of Slovene society, future trends may be very different. The inflow of foreign capital and foreign company management may be indicative. These managers enter as bosses rather than as workers, and assume leading positions in society.

Liberal or exclusionist policy on Slovene citizenship

After a decade of an "extensive employment" policy the resulting wave of immigration came under attack in the 1980s. During the time of uncertainty about Slovenia's future, whether inside or outside Yugoslavia, and especially before the independence plebiscite (December 1990), care was taken by most politicians to avoid this issue so as not to provoke opposition to the proposed independence of Slovenia. This was reflected in the rather liberal definition of requirements for Slovenian citizenship.[5] Once the future status of Slovenia was clear and the new state was internationally recognised, demands for a more exclusive citizenship policy surfaced in parliament and the media. Since then, political parties have been strongly divided on this issue.

145

The Public Opinion Survey of Slovenia (April 1994) shows attitudes towards citizenship requirements. Six possible requirements were ranked as follows:

Table 7.3
Attitudes towards Slovene citizenship requirements

	%
knowledge of Slovene language	91
long residence in Slovenia	86
knowledge of Slovene culture	72
Slovene descent (Slovene father/mother)	52
born in Slovenia	42
Christian faith	27

N=1050

On the long-term view the concept of citizenship itself corresponds more to the metaphor "space of places" - which implies the existence of closed territorial systems - rather than to the emerging "space of flows" (Mlinar 1992a). Nonetheless, the first three requirements listed above do not belong to the category of "ascribed characteristics" (independent of the will and action of the individual himself). "Slovene descent" and "birth in Slovenia" on the contrary do belong there. Some substantive specification of the negative attitudes toward immigration is disclosed by answers to the question about the probable effects of mass immigration.

Table 7.4
Probable negative effects of mass immigration
(certainly or probably)

	%
crime rate will increase greatly	85
conflicts between native born and immigrants will increase	83
unemployment of native residents will worsen	83
worsening of housing situation (availability, price)	82
wages, working conditions will worsen	76
streets and railway stations will be dirty	65
gradually it will not feel like home	46
Slovene language will gradually be ousted	39

N=1050

Although the question referred to mass immigration in general the table clearly shows a preoccupation with immigration from the South. As the borders open to the North and West the relative rankings may change with some concerns declining and others rising in importance (e.g., the threat to the Slovene language) and completely new ones appearing (e.g., foreigners taking a position of dominance in business, ousting native firms from prime locations in towns).

Native minorities and aliens/immigrants

There are strong tendencies towards establishing two different sets of normative and institutional provisions for native minorities, like the Italians and Hungarians, and recent immigrants. The status of native minorities is enshrined in the Constitution, which guarantees them special protection and rights. However, the long-term prospect of transformation from a "space of places" into a "space of flows" implies a melding of the native and immigrant populations. In a context of open borders and high mobility it will become unrealistic to expect all foreigners to assimilate, i.e.,. adopt the language and culture of the native population. (For an opposing viewpoint, see Toporišic 1991). At present opinions are polarised over the proposal that "immigrants from the former-Yugoslavia should have the same rights as members of the Italian and Hungarian minorities". Only 45% of respondents (April 1994) agreed, while 55% disagreed with the above statement. This may be explained by the predominance of a conservative rather than a liberal understanding of national identity, which clashes with multiculturalism and interculturalism (Tarver 1989).

What is being underestimated here are the dynamics of spatial mobility ("flows"), which tend to spill widely over the more traditional concepts of immigration, and emigration. Changes of location in space involve an increasing variety of moves of varying duration and distances. This is especially true for professionals, managers and artists, as well as sportsmen and others. The logical consequence is what we find in Slovenia today: the paradox that 3064 native Italians and 8503 Hungarians enjoy many special rights while the largest part of non-Slovenes, namely 227,341 immigrants from the South (census data: *Statisticni letopis Republike Slovenije* 1991), are granted only the "right" to assimilation.

Cross-border mobility and the boundedness of the "life-world"

The question of open/closed borders and the inflow of people may also be examined in terms of the ease of cross-border mobility (which does not necessarily involve change of permanent residence). The changes in the political system are perceived as having brought (in addition to more freedom of expression, joining political parties and other organisations) improvement in the sense that "everybody can travel wherever he/she wishes". For example 58.3% of respondents consider that conditions in this regard have "improved" or "essentially improved" and only 5.3% that conditions have worsened or "essentially worsened" (30.3% that they are the same, 6.1% do not know).

Some insight into the actual extent of cross-border mobility is allowed by the question (April 1994) "Have you been abroad (outside Slovenia) during the last two years?" 71% of respondents answered yes, 29% no. Another question was: "Have you ever been in another country for more than one month?" and nearly 80% answered yes and 20% no. Their reasons for going abroad are ranked as follows (by frequencies):

1. shopping trips
2. visits to relatives, friends
3. vacation, holidays
4. business trips, fairs
5. cultural events, expositions
6. sports events
7. pilgrimage, religious events
8. others

More open borders do not automatically mean greater cross-border mobility of people. Thus we observe a recent decline in shopping trips to border areas in Italy and Austria because the range and quality of goods and services available at home have increased and price differences have decreased. The lifting of import restrictions has made travel across the border to places like Trieste, Gorizia, Klagenfurt, and Graz unnecessary.

The insularity of a state is not defined only by restrictions and control of border crossings but also by the inertia of the boundedness of the "life-world". This point was addressed by the following question: "Have you ever considered living outside Slovenia for some time". A positive reply was given by 28 % and a negative by 72 % of the respondents. In evaluating this it may be noted that the response pattern was nearly the same with regard to living for some time in another place in Slovenia (30% yes, 70% no). This may mean that local embeddedness is more fundamental and the state border in the broader sense should not be considered solely as an imposition from above.

Who needs borders?

The idea of abolishing borders has the general connotation of an emancipation from different forms of territorial confines upon social life and thinking. A border is often considered to be a limitation imposed upon people by the state, "from above". Thus it comes as a surprise to find out who actually needs borders: it is we rather than them! At present in Slovenia uncompetitive enterprises, farmers, wine-growers and others are demanding protection, and higher tariffs on imported goods.

The period of rapprochement with the EU is characterised by asymmetrical relationships: the Slovene economy has more protective tariffs on imported goods from EU countries than the other way around. This arrangement is supposed to enable a smooth transition to a fully open market economy. It has been complemented by free trade agreements with the Czech Republic, Slovakia and Hungary and shortly with Poland. Paradoxically, no such arrangement has been achieved with Croatia, an incomparably more important trading partner, or Macedonia. Croatia was the first to introduce tariffs after the break-up of Yugoslavia, in line with the prevalent view then that the more-developed federal units exploited the less-developed. Slovenia retaliated to a limited extent. Yet this is at odds with developments within the EU, which both states wish to join.

Public opinion of Slovenia is split over the general dilemma whether to reduce tariffs on imports or protect domestic enterprises. But the specific question (SJM, 1993): "What to do with domestic enterprises, that cannot compete efficiently on the international market, but provide many jobs?" elicited a surprisingly clear message: two thirds (65.7%) favoured the option that only competitive and efficient enterprises should survive; only 14.2% favoured protecting the enterprises if this entailed higher taxes and more expensive products (20.1% did not know).

This indicates public support for open borders and international competition, which implies a commitment to the principle of "survival of the fittest" regardless, or perhaps because, of the high protectionism in the former "socialist" state. This general attitude does not preclude strong demands for protection by those directly affected by the increasing competition from abroad (such as those unemployed because of factory closings).

Slovenia's opening up is especially sensitive for small, private farmers. Farming based on highly fragmented plots, mainly in hilly areas, cannot compete with modern and subsidised agriculture in EU countries. At the same time it is becoming more and more clear that agriculture's importance does not stem solely from its economic function. Sustainable development, conservation of the cultural landscape, environmental protection, and national defence and security, among other things, have to be considered as well. Understandably the protection of domestic agriculture has much more public support than protection of other economic sectors. Several *ad hoc* demands by farmers have won protective measures (e.g., tariffs on imported wine from Macedonia, which caused retaliatory measures by Macedonia, and the restricted import of peaches in the high season. Two thirds of respondents (April 1994) agreed that: "Farmers have to be protected from foreign competition, even if we have to pay more for food".

149

Similarly, a highly sensitive issue is the right to land purchases by foreigners. As a small country in Europe's "sun belt" (tourist slogan: "on the sunny side of the Alps") Slovenia is potentially highly attractive to foreigners. But selling land to foreigners is generally seen as losing territory and a threat to national identity. This is even more so in the coastal region bordering with Italy (and Croatia) with its small Italian minority. In view of the territorial pretensions of some Italian nationalist groups demands for revision of the Osimo agreement between Italy and Yugoslavia and for the right of Italians to own land in Slovenia, this is one of the most delicate border issues in Slovenia today, and one that has long-term consequences for the survival of the national identity. Article 68 of the Constitution says: "Foreigners cannot obtain property rights to land except by inheritance on condition of reciprocity". But as shown in the case of Greece, which had to revoke similar bans for the 50 km border zone for nationals of other EC countries, this conflicts with the conditions for entering the EU. On one opinion survey (SJM 1993) 71.5 % of respondents agreed that purchases of land by foreigners should be banned (11.9% disagreed, 16.5% undecided). Quite the opposite was the case with foreign investments. Only 21.2% of the respondents agreed with a ban on foreign investments (52.0% disagreed, 25.8 undecided or did not know). This indicates that inflow of foreign capital (in general) is perceived as less threatening if it does not involve immigration and "losing" land.

The borders are thus perceived to be less a matter of direct confrontation between neighbouring states than the representation of certain universal principles. These require greater constraints on a powerful neighbour (restricting discretionary power and the use of force) and the small state's restraint from any discriminatory measures based on nationality. Small nations, which face the greatest threat of losing their identity in a "space of flows", are thus losing regulatory capacity. Fully aware that staying out of integration processes is a non-choice, they strive to join the "new Europe" even though its order is incompatible with their newly-promulgated national constitutions.

Prospects for the future

In spite of the complexity of the present changes in the role of the nation state's borders some general trends can be discerned. The perplexity of the empirical evidence on borders in Slovenia is largely due to the coexistence of two different stages of socio-spatial development in the country. The first, characteristic of West Europe, can be seen in the processes of transnational integration; the other, which is present in the Balkans, manifests itself in the inertia of traditional territorial exclusivism and confrontations.

The belated emergence of small ethno-nations is introducing new borders. In Slovenia's case these new borders are directed at the previous Yugoslav core. The dissociation from the previous hegemonic centre allows a richer association with the wider space of Europe. The multiplication of linkages provides a basis for a gradual decrease in the importance of bilateral relations (delimitation or confrontation) with neighbouring states. The solution to problems concerning borders with neighbours is increasingly determined by the EU and general norms. These preclude territorial expansionism and changing borders by force (the Balkans are clearly an exception) and provide the basis for economic and cultural interpenetration rather than territorial confrontation. Thus, on the one hand, European integration offers small nations higher security from frontal territorial expansionism (change of borders at the expense of the weaker unit); yet at the same time it makes borders increasingly porous and penetrable, thus creating a new threat to ethno-national identities. This in turn provokes new waves of ethnocentric responses. Over the long run however, the difference between domestic and alien has been declining and borders are gradually becoming less consequential.

Bids to keep out "aliens" and to exclusively restrict certain rights to the autochtonous population can only work in the short term. Inasmuch as it is becoming increasingly anachronistic, the nation state itself cannot in the long-term act as a guardian and controller of the national border. The strong desire for free access to "others", while maintaining control over others' access to one's own territory, is an inconsistency which cannot be sustained. The long term prospect can be only a balanced openness by which internal differentiation and autonomisation become a condition for transnational European integration.

What today appears as a decisive choice to open up Slovenia's borders and join the EU, or not, may in the long run turn out to not be an option. An open or closed nation state are not realistic alternatives. The question is really only one of the dynamics involved in opening nation state borders. The smallest states, although latecomers, will be the first to face the reality of interpenetration. This may prove an advantage and a threat. More than ever before their borders will be protected from the territorial expansionism of their more powerful neighbours. But at the same time these small nations will be those most exposed to the erosion of their traditional identities.

Notes

1. The Illyrian Province approached this in Napoleon's time, although it had not been created on an ethnic principle and it was not an independent state.

2. Opinion surveys in Slovenia show that while earlier it had been the conduct of Serbia that generated feelings of threat, in 1993 and 1994 it was instead Croatia's conduct that threatened Slovenians.
3. It may be noted here that the arms embargo still applies to Slovenia although it is not involved in the war in Bosnia and Croatia. The economic and political differences between Slovenia and the other parts of former-Yugoslavia are too little known and appreciated internationally. Some companies estimate that this is costing them fully a fifth of potential revenue.
4. Yet this creates a new problem: departure from the border region in the course of study tends to end in employment outside too, so that the best-educated part of the minorities is dispersed widely through the country and is predisposed to mixed marriages and, hence, are sooner or later lost to the minority that remains in the border area.
5. The Citizenship Act was accepted on 5 June 1991, shortly before the declaration of independence of Slovenia on 25 June. It enabled Slovene citizenship to be acquired by 170,000 applicants mostly originating from other federal units of Yugoslavia. This provoked a negative reaction, and led to further government measures, such as to reduce the number of dual citizens.

References:

Castells, M. 1985. *High technology, space and society.* London: Sage.
Ceccini, P. 1988. *The European challenge 1992.* Aldershot: Wildwood House.
Duroselle, J. 1988. Western Europe and the impossible war. *Journal of international affairs* 41 (2): 345-361.
Federalist, The 1993. Europe and the crisis in Yugoslavia. 35 (2): 1-10.
Klemencic, V. 1992. *Geopoliticni polozaj Slovenije in njena odprtost v Evropo* (Geopolitical position of Slovenia and its openness to Europe). 12. Zveza društev urbanistov Slovenije: Sedlarjevo srecanje.
Klinar, P. 1994. O nacionalni identiteti in etnonacionalizmih (On national identity and ethno-nationalisms). *Teorija in praksa* 5-6: 421-437
Mlinar, Z. (ed.). 1992a. *Globalization and territorial identities.* Aldershot: Avebury.
_____. 1992b. European integration and socio-spatial restructuring. *International journal of sociology and social policy* 12 (8) 33-58.
_____. 1993. Small nations and European integration. In Devetak, S., Flere, S., and Seewann, G. (eds.). *Small nations and ethnic minorities in an emerging Europe.* München: Slavica Verlag, dr. Anton Kovac.
_____. 1994. *Individuacija in globalizacija v prostoru* (Individuation and globalization in space). Ljubljana: SAZU.

Mušic, V. B. 1992. *Evropski izzivi prostorski integraciji Slovenije* (European challenges to spatial integration of Slovenia). 12. Zveza društev urbanistov Slovenije: Sedlarjevo srecanje.

Slovensko Javno Mnenje (SJM, Slovenian public opinion research reports*)* 1991-1994. Ljubljana: Faculty of Social Sciences.

Sorokin, P. (ed.). 1930. *Systematic source book in rural sociology.* Minneapolis: The University of Minnesota.

Statisticni letopis Republike Slovenije 1993. Ljubljana.

Strassoldo, R. 1992. Globalism and localism: Theoretical reflections and some evidence. In Mlinar, Z. (ed.). *Globalization and territorial identities.* Aldershot: Avebury.

Tarver, H. 1989. Language and politics in the 1980's. *Politics and society* 17 (2): 225-245.

Toporišic, J. 1991. *Dru`benost slovenskega jezika* (Social character of the Slovene language). Ljubljana: DZS.

Trošt, F. 1993. Problemi mednarodnega gospodarskega sodelovanja Slovenije po osamosvojitvi (Problems of international economic co-operation of Slovenia after independence). *Slovenska ekonomska revija* 44: 1-2.

Williams, C. H. 1992. Identity, autonomy and the ambiguity of technological development. In Mlinar, Z. (ed.). *Globalization and territorial identities* Aldershot: Avebury.

Wistrich, E. 1989. *After 1992, the United States of Europe.* London: Routledge.

8 The recomposition of identity and political space in Europe: The case of Upper Silesia

Wanda Dressler Holohan and Maria Ciechocinska

Silesia is the site of one of the largest coal deposits in Europe and also contains significant deposits of zinc and iron ore. For these and other reasons since the eleventh century, it has been a bone of contention between the Poles, the Germans and the Czechs. Silesia covers the basin of both the upper and middle Oder river whence the region is divided into an Upper and Lower part. By the middle of the nineteenth century, Lower Silesia had become almost wholly German, while Upper Silesia retained a mixed German-Polish population. This chapter deals mainly with Upper Silesia which is divided into three provinces, Katowice, Czestochowa and Opole, with two major urban centres in Opole and Katowice. Since the redrawing of Poland's borders in 1945, this region is no longer situated near the German border but lies 200 kilometres away at the Czech border. In all but geography, however, it remains a German-Polish frontier zone.

Situated throughout the centuries at the cross-roads of differing political and cultural influences, Upper Silesia, nevertheless, has never become entirely German or Polish but has generated a mixed identity which is more regional than national (Michalczyk and Zagorny 1993: 113). Intra-regional differences remain significant, however, with a greater concentration of German speakers in the Opole region for historical reasons. Due to its great economic significance and its fluid regional auto-definition, the "minority problem" has presented a persistent border question for Polish rulers and intellectuals. The issue today is whether the recently redefined and politically re-mobilised German minority is loyal or irredentist, whether it is simply forced to defend its rights or property or whether it is actively undermining Polish interests (Waskiewicz 1994: 73). A clear answer to this question is hindered by the definitions of national character accorded to the Silesians by historians. In periods of rising nationalism, Silesia has been presented more as a zone of confrontation than as a region of inter-penetrating cultures. Such a representation fails to take into account the Silesians' self-perception as inhabitants of adjacent state territories with a population of mixed national and ethnic genealogies. In Silesia, the so-called "pro-German option" can be seen as a reminder of the character of nation-formation in every borderland where there is uneven economic development and a juxtaposition of different attitudes of life and social values (Chlebowczyk 1980: 26-7). Silesia nowadays demonstrates a borderland consciousness which is indigenous rather than imposed and which reflects the interaction of the economic, cultural, linguistic and political influences of Germany with those of Poland.

Yet, it is worth asking why so many Silesians today identify themselves as Germans after having resisted Germanisation for centuries? One of the aims of this chapter is to outline the reasons for the reconstructed German minority consciousness in Silesia. Historically the western Polish borderlands were German until after the Second World War, when they were re-populated by a majority of Poles and included in the redefined Polish state. Some Germans remained in Silesia despite their massive expulsion from the new Poland. In the new Polish state which was far more ethnically homogeneous than its pre-Second World War predecessor, national minorities were concentrated in the new border zones - the remaining Germans in the west and the Lithuanians and Belorussians in the east.

In Upper Silesia, two elements have come together in the 1990s: the modernisation of political and administrative structures in Poland in the wake of the collapse of state socialism and the attempt to bring about closer links between Poland and the European Union. This chapter explores the changing nature of national sovereignty and international relations by analysing the recent political evolution of Upper Silesia. The process of European economic integration, considered as a regional aspect of the globalisation process (itself greatly responsible for the implosion of the Communist system and the dismantling of the Cold War's borders) has led to the increased salience of the Upper Silesian borderland and encouraged political and cultural mobilisation among the German minority. The latter has gained two new functions, first in preserving the existing national boundaries and the political stability which they express, and second, in contributing to the redefinition of the sovereignty of the centralised Polish state so as to accord more autonomy to Upper Silesia as a peripheral border region.

There are many facets to Silesia's role as a frontier between Germany and Poland. This chapter will show how Silesia has played an active role in redefining, in a more pluralist direction, the symbolic foundation of the Polish state, and in reshaping the latter's international relationships with Germany in particular. Upper Silesia is a reminder of the old civilisational border between German and Slavic culture and retains an old border culture itself. Its difficult cultural and economic situation in the 1980s has played a central role in the German-Polish treaties of good neighbourliness and friendship signed in 1990-

91. The aims of these treaties were to reassure the Polish state by the stabilisation of borders established after 1945. They were also aimed at reassuring the Silesians, including the "German minority militants" who chose not to migrate, by encouraging the protection of minority rights and measures to counteract economic decline.

The possibility of Upper Silesia "becoming a hotbed" for nationalist activists from both sides in the early 1990s required an urgent response from the Polish and German governments in order to prevent a rapid destabilisation of the 1945 borders. It seemed clear that failure to manage Upper Silesia would pre-empt cross-border co-operation in other areas on the actual geographical border between Poland and Germany. This account of Upper Silesia gives an important place to the resolution of minority problems at the national and the regional level. It suggests that recognition of a borderland minority is a preliminary step towards the normalisation of relationships between the two countries and between them and the international community which imposes itself as the main arbiter.

This chapter is divided into three sections: the first begins with an analysis of the complexity of the cultural identities in Upper Silesia, seen as a consequence of its turbulent history. This provides a starting point for understanding strategies of cultural and political mobilisation essential to the rebuilding of regional identity in a new Poland, aiming for European Union (EU) membership. The second section describes how the democratised Polish government and the changing framework of international relations has impacted on diverse Upper Silesian claims for regional autonomy and cultural expression. Here, it is recognised that government policy has had to contend with the heavy heritage of the nineteenth century nationalist revival which aimed for a unified Polish state under the Catholic banner. The failure to manage the conflicts in the multi-national Polish state in 1935 and the subsequent post-1945 policies of the Communist regime have been influenced by the historical ideology of a homogeneous, unified state. The third section explores in more detail the strategies of mobilisation employed by diverse cultural and political groups in the Upper Silesia borderland between the start of the democratisation process and 1993.

The main argument developed here, and in the conclusion, highlights the forces which encourage the Polish state to resist, or alternatively to accommodate, the new pressures for pluralism and regional autonomy in Upper Silesia. Resistance is linked to the old fears about powerful German and Russian neighbours and to rejection of the shock economic therapy advocated by western experts. Polish-German accommodation is facilitated by the stability of the institutional and political compromises reflected in the treaties signed with Germany and in international pressure to respect the Helsinki principles in order to maintain Poland's chances of entering the EU. In this context, the prospect of EU membership may be seen as limiting the assertion of national sovereignty in the face of growing regional demands.

Evolution of Silesian border identity

The origin of the jig-saw puzzle of communities of Upper Silesia is to be found deeply embedded in the region's history. In the Middle Ages, Silesia was an important part of the Polish Kingdom; in the 14th century, it became part of Bohemia, when Poland had dynastic unions with it and Hungary. Silesia was then incorporated into Austria and colonised by Czechs and Germans and so did not belong to the Kingdom of Poland (1500) or to the Grand Duchy of Lithuania-Poland. The German and Czech colons left a lasting cultural imprint on Silesia. In the second half of the 18th century, the early stages of industrialisation attracted many Prussian migrants. At the end of the 18th century, Poland was divided into three parts: the region of Krakow came under the control of the Austro-Hungarian Empire, the eastern portion of the country went to Russia and Silesia became Prussian.

From 1792 to 1918 the enforced Germanisation penetrated the upper classes of the province and changed its political culture. As a result, many local Silesian elites were often absorbed into the wider German culture. The peasants and lower classes thus found themselves ruled by a "foreign" nobility. Polish by culture, the peasants and workers were submitted to the pressure of Germanic cultural influence which they resisted. Economic migrations, such as that of peasants in Galicia, started as a seasonal migration between localities and industrial towns in the course of the 19th century (Davies 1984: 255). The impetus behind this migration was the poverty of the Polish countryside where there were few sources of employment other than subsistence farming. The most industrially developed regions of south and western Poland, included in Prussia and Austria at that time, were the first to be affected by peasant emancipation. Generally, most of the urban centres were distinctly German in character, while many agricultural districts were clearly Polish, even if a sizeable portion of the miners and unskilled industrial workers were Poles. During this period, rural Silesians were incorporated into German work forces, hastening the disintegration of feudal bonds in Silesia, and through the greater mobility of labour, helping to integrate Silesia into Western Europe.

Unlike what was happening in the rest of Germany, which saw a massive shift toward the Ruhr valley, Upper Silesia became an alternative magnet for immigration from the economically stronger regions of Germany. The privileged economic position of the region gave it a major strategic importance after the cessation of hostilities in Europe in 1918. The task of redefining and allocating Upper Silesia lasted nearly three years (1918-21) and marks one of the most complicated episodes in boundary settlement in modern European history. After a controversial plebiscite procedure and two Polish uprisings which were violently repressed (Wozniak 1994), the redefined region was given to the Polish state. The inhabitants from the agricultural region of Opole voted in favour of inclusion in Poland by a narrow margin of 480, 000 for and

310,000 against. About 150,000 emigrated subsequently to Germany. The part of the region most favourable to the national movements for the rebirth of Poland was the industrial area of Katowice. Those Germans who did not wish to become Polish left this region of Silesia. In the ten years after 1918, about 600,000 Germans (more than half the Polish-Germans) left Poland. According to Brubaker (1993), this was the biggest German emigration since the end of the Austro-Hungarian empire.

In June 1919, Poland signed, under pressure from the Allies and to the discontent of a majority of Poles, the Minority Protection Treaty which guaranteed political and legal rights to non-Polish minorities. This legal guarantee did not remove the distrustful atmosphere, however, which was aggravated further by Polish elites advancing chauvinistic institutional and political measures which denied any real autonomy to minorities and encouraged deeper hostility. The areas with large German populations were targeted for sub-division. The government pacified the situation for a while only. In 1934, the Polish government abrogated unilaterally the Minority Protection Treaty. Nazi propaganda and the rise of German power strengthened the position of those of German origins at Poland's Western borders (Simoncini 1994: 22), rendering difficult the integration and accommodation of minorities within the Polish state.

Although Silesia was once again occupied by the Germans during the war (1939-45) the victory of the Red Army in 1945 with Polish assistance shifted the Polish borders westwards once more, resulting in the repatriation of seven million Germans between 1945 and 1947. The waves of German emigration did not end there. Between 1957 and 1985, about 700,000 more Germans left Communist Poland. Subjected to forced assimilation by the Communists and in despair because of the disastrous regional effects of the regime's economic policy, those who remained started to look again towards Germany, especially West Germany. The latter's immigration policy of extending German citizenship to all of German origin encouraged immigration. When Polish travel and emigration restrictions were liberalised, the pace of migration picked up even more. More than a million Germans settled in West Germany from 1988 to 1991 as a result of advantages granted to Germans displaced after the war (*Biuletyn Biura* 1994).

In Upper Silesia, however, a very strong regional sentiment of cultural belonging had emerged with inter-mixed Polish and German elements. The Silesians' priority was to defend their religious and cultural freedom and to maintain their political and economic position. Realism, pragmatism and rationalism characterised the patriotism of the Polish and German Silesians. Under the influence of the movement for Polish political and cultural emancipation in the second half of the 19th century, the first Polish-language newspapers appeared along with a quasi-national awareness of identity. In Opole, there was a clearer process of local syncretism through the use of a Silesian language mixing German and Polish. This created more intra-community bonds of solidarity than national ones. Silesians began to distinguish themselves by the care they took in using the Polish language. When opposing pressures built up with the rise of Nazism, Silesians once again became bilingual and developed mechanisms to preserve the independence of their community values and to escape national rivalries vying for conquest of Silesia.

A situation such as theirs, however, led to unstable feelings of cultural belonging in some portions of the population and in the experience of a number of individuals. Silesians often felt there was a gap between their nationality and their ethnic origin. Rituals such as placing some identifying symbol in a new-born baby's cradle show a desire to mark the regional group as the main purveyor of identity (Berlinska and Frystacki 1991). Community values seem to have strengthened further since the Second World War through a combination of number of factors: the Polish-Silesian dialect (called "Wasserpolish" by the Germans), the Catholic religion, intra-Silesian solidarity, recognition of past German influence, and attachment to the Silesian fatherland, to the work ethic and to the family. Knowledge of the German language is often seen as a sign of adherence to Silesia's past and is generally considered to be desirable. The fact that "Silesian" is used as a noun and "Polish" and "German" as adjectives illustrates where cultural priorities lie and is also a reminder that national identity is acquired and founded upon criteria that can be objectivized (the Polish language, for instance, or the rejection of the German language as a means of denying ethnic origin).

Regional consciousness diminished, however, after the Second World War, when Silesians were re-incorporated into Polish territory and submitted to the repression of the Communist regime. One outcome was the loss of their rights of decision-making within the region. Many stayed on, nonetheless, because of their strong ties to the family house or agricultural property. Some fled and then returned to find their homes occupied by newcomers from the Eastern border regions of Poland. Many people lived in fear. People daring to speak out concerning their German roots risked being placed in a camp in the occupied zones devastated by the war.

The experience of Communist re-Polonisation after 1945 has determined in large part the attitude of Silesians since the democratisation of 1989. It shaped not only Polish-German Silesian relationships but also those with immigrants and settlers from central Poland and the eastern borderlands. The imposed Communist regime attempted to stamp out regional differences and squeeze everyone together under a popular national banner which was modified to suit its own purposes. In order to legitimise this project historically, the regime sought to "construct" the Polish People's Republic as the heir to the Piast dynasty which presided over the first four hundred years of the "Polish state" between 966 and 1400. After several centuries of expansion, contraction, and even obliteration, the post-1945 borders could be claimed to approximate those of the Piast dynasty. Piast Poland could also be presented as an ethnically homogenous state with a history of struggle with its German neighbours in the west (Kubik 1994: 64-5).[1] The Communist anti-German mythology was dominated by the idea of co-operation with fellow Slavs against Aryan supremacy (Skurnowicz 1994: 102). When the Communists started to lose their power, they focused on the denunciation of Zionism allied with American imperialism and west German revanchism. This served to create the image of a beleaguered Poland threatened from within and without - an image which appealed to deeply rooted popular emotions in Poland (Schatz 1994). The Silesians did not fit easily into this version of an ethnically homogenous anti-German Poland or with an ideology which considered all inhabitants of the region to be native Poles (Silesian Poles). They rapidly lost confidence in the ability of the Polish state to protect their interests. Discrimination against Silesians increased, creating a sense of insecurity which led to the massive emigration mentioned above and to a general withdrawing into tighter groups. As a virtually closed mostly rural community Silesians became more endogamous, in part as resistance to the newly arrived immigrants from the East who were ignorant of the region's customs.

Minority identity in Upper Silesia

Today, Upper Silesia manifests a patchwork of cultural identities. The concentration of German speakers is greater in the Opole *voivodship* (administrative unit), in the Southern part of the Czestochowa *voivodship* and in the Western part of Katowice *voivodship*. This higher density is due to the fact that the native inhabitants have undergone linguistic shifts and resisted the massive waves of emigration their compatriots have taken part in at various times in history. These German Silesians, who had the highest standard of living in all Poland between the two wars, do not constitute a powerful group today, but they are in a comparatively favourable economic position, largely due to the attractive investment opportunities in the local food industry. The region is also relatively independent and dynamic compared to that of Katowice, which is more heavily industrialised and heterogeneous. The industrial population has always been less deeply rooted and more mobile with greater social mixing as migrants have come to Katowice from all regions of Poland. However, the region which long produced 1/3 of Poland's GNP and inspired successive surges of re-industrialisation (the latest from 1970 to 1975) is now in a steep economic decline. Katowice is today a region of emigration despite its vast programme to offset job losses. The reigning atmosphere is one of catastrophic decline causing a large number of immigrants to move back to their areas of origin (Wodz 1990).

The question of collective identification seems to be posed in quite different terms in these two regions and dictates different strategies. Today, the natives from Opole are more active in creating bonds with Germany. Yet, when we look back to the 1930s, we see that the Opole region contained a continuum of regional and national sensibilities despite the success of Germanisation before 1921. The same was true of the Polish Katowice area under Nazi occupation (Berlinska and Frysztacki 1991). In the census of 1931 a relatively common response to the question about mother tongue was "Silesian", even if the Silesian language was not recognised as a language. Poles, Germans and Czechs tried to define themselves as Silesians in a regional example of ethnogenesis (Simoncini 1994: 19).

Many causes can be adduced for the re-awakening of the German minority in Silesia today: the socio-economic crisis of the 1980s in Poland, the attraction of a much more prosperous Germany, German immigration policy which favoured those of ethnic German origin, the ambivalence of the Polish authorities towards Germans (Michalczyk and Zagorny 1993: 114), the new awakening of cultural minorities in centralised states all over central and eastern Europe since the 1970s and the increased recognition of such groups by international law. When the socio-economic crisis of the 1980s gave a new impetus to mass migration, some of the older and middle-aged generation of native people, and even some post-1945 settlers from Central Poland, began to form local pro-German associations. They also began to organise youth organisations for the revival of popular culture (Michaczyk and Zagorny 1993:114).

Toward the end of the 1970s and early 1980s, central control over national minorities lessened somewhat leading to a political awakening among minorities. The Communist government became more preoccupied with *Solidarnosc* and its underground activities. This period was marked by the beginning of an intense cultural and spiritual renaissance set in motion by the *Solidarnosc* movement. This context facilitated the sudden emergence of German minority associations in the wake of the reunification of the German state. Almost overnight, activists emerged in local communities in Upper Silesia taking advantage of the new democratic rights and freedoms accorded in April 1989. A network of regional branches embraced almost the whole territory of Poland where there were German minorities, with Silesia as an important focal point. All this was a great shock to Poles who thought that the integration of ethnic Germans had been achieved.

The cultural mobilisation of the German minority movement received a further boost when the Provincial Court refused to register the Sociocultural Association of the German Minority in Silesia and decided not to give formal recognition to the existence of a "German minority" in Poland. This refusal seemed to go contrary to the right to form associations conceded in April 1989. In this case international law prevailed over the local law on associations. After further Polish High Court proceedings and legislation in parliament, the Association was registered. This success was accompanied by the action organised by the leader of this movement to collect a list of signatures of people declaring their German origin. The resulting 200,000 signatures surprised the organisers. A further boost for the movement was the success of a campaign to allow Masses to be said in German (a return to pre-1939 arrangements) despite opposition from the non-Silesian clergy, notably the primate of the Katowice region.

Rykiel (1993: 75) has suggested that Polish-German cultural polarisation threatens the destruction of a regional Silesian identity. Others, however, argue that a regional identity is being re-forged in Upper Silesia by a complex social process involving mutual contacts and interchange of certain cultural elements. In this view the post-1945 settlers have adopted some indigenous Silesian habits and given some of theirs to Silesians, creating a new Silesian symbiosis (Dulczewski 1970: 165) of national awareness and local and regional identity. This process is mainly visible among the youth who try to build a Silesian identity for and by themselves (Michalczcyk and Zagorny 1993: 120-121). In this view, identification with Germany is a pragmatic choice made by Silesians which is aimed at securing the future and avoiding the social degradation and poverty they see around them. Older migrants to the region from the East (Belorussians, Ukrainians and Poles) tend to identify with Poland, seeing themselves as liberated pioneers resettling the old Piast lands. Whatever the precise meaning of cultural mobilisation in Upper Silesia, a series of major changes at national and international level began to give a political shape to regional identity after 1989. These changes encouraged a newly organised and powerful association of German Poles which underlined Upper Silesia's historical role as a borderland between Germany and Poland.

Early moves towards the democratisation of the Polish state, such as The Round Table held in 1988, encouraged a new approach to state structures, civil society and cultural minorities. After the first elected parliament in June 1989, there was a strong will to breathe new life into institutions which could contribute to a democratic renaissance. At the same time, the privatisation of the economy was getting underway as a first step towards the market economy. European integration and the Helsinki process were beginning to transform international relations in the wake of the collapse of communism. Respect for human and minority rights came to be regarded not just as matters internal to particular states but as the responsibility of the international community. These new principles cut across existing rules of international relations which emphasise the maintenance of borders, territorial integrity and non-intervention in the internal affairs of national states. The challenge for states throughout Europe has become to accommodate these new constraints on their national sovereignty while not endangering their own internal cohesion. The challenge was particularly critical for Poland given its long history of attempting to preserve its integrity as a state.

Since 1945, Poland's international relations were dominated by the Soviet Union and Germany, and also by the new fear of potentially heavy demands that displaced populations might make if given the opportunity. Thus a policy of cultural repression dominated and weakened minorities' links to their ethnic origins while it aimed at stabilising the newly established borders through the integration of displaced groups. By the late 1980s, the Polish government was being forced to revise its symbolic structures. The legitimacy of the "monoethnic nation-state" was now being undermined from outside by international pressure and from inside by the emergence of the national minorities as factors in both national and international politics. However, for the Polish state the problem of national minorities (who are only 4% of the population) remains secondary to the problems of general economic and political organisation.[2]

Yet, the minority issue was important enough to lead to the creation, in 1988, of a Commission for National and Ethnic Minorities within the first post-Communist government. As a consultative body, its task was to implement measures to ensure protection of minorities' rights and to give administrative impetus to the development and co-ordination of cultural initiatives in the regions. The change of direction was further symbolised by the transference of the Commission from the Ministry of the Interior (ex-KGB) in 1990 to the Ministry of Culture and Art. In 1992, the latter created a Bureau of National Minorities with its own budget.

Educational reforms in 1991 and 1992 authorised the preservation of the national and ethnic identities of minorities in the school system. As a result bilingual instruction was set up in nursery and technical schools. Simultaneously, new laws were passed which encouraged moves to a multi-cultural state. In elections, changes in the number of signatures required to put forward candidates to Parliament favoured the more concentrated minority groups. Following these provisions, six Germans and one Belorussian won Parliamentary seats in 1991. However, at the national level, initial enthusiasm for settling minority grievances soon gave way to apathy and passivity. The main reason was local-national tensions in Poland. The past is far from forgotten and mutual suspicion runs high, particularly in border regions. The nationalistic Catholic Church also contributed to blocking reforms. Within the second democratic parliament, partisans of reform seemed to lose interest in the minority problem. In the third democratic parliament, the problem remains unresolved. The government Commission for National and Ethnic Minorities was terminated in 1991 without having carried out its programme, although its existence was mentioned in the bilateral treaty signed by Germany and Poland in June 1991.[3] This treaty, the 1991 German-Polish Treaty on Good-neighbourly Relations and Friendly Co-operation based on the Conference for Security Co-operation in Europe (CSCE) standards promised a new framework for addressing the issues raised by Poland's German minorities. The two governments recognised the importance of increased co-operation and peaceful co-existence. Accordingly, Polish authorities allowed the members of the German minority and their associations to receive financial aid from the Government of the Federal Republic of Germany. The latter has supported the German minority in Poland since 1990 by assigning teachers to Polish schools, financing German language programmes, providing medical equipment, and generally supporting community development, meeting centres, clubs and associations, culture, and the media.

The authors of the Helsinki Human Rights Foundation report on the protection of minorities' rights (Kazanecki 1993; Wierzycka and Holuszko 1993) underscore, however, the lack of any authoritative body in Poland at the national level responsible for policy towards national minorities. They point out that this is a major obstacle since, without such an authority, negotiations cannot take place. As a result minority problems have been handled in a somewhat haphazard fashion by the Polish departments of Culture, Education, Foreign Affairs or the Interior, depending on the degree of activism among local minority associations and the policy of provincial authorities. A risk of incoherence exists in the relationship between local and central authorities. The former often block more liberal central initiatives because of local tensions that are frequently aggravated by local officials. After a series of conflicts between the local administration and the German minority of Opole, a plenipotentiary was appointed in 1992 in the district to apply the provisions of the German-Polish treaty. As this was the only case of this kind, it indicates both the potential for conflict in Silesia and the existence of a political will to overcome it.

Poland is now seen once again as an important hub between Eastern and Western Europe and also as a vital east-west civilisational link. The CSCE has no doubt been instrumental in this process as it has transformed position papers into bilateral international treaties between Poland and its mostly ex-Soviet post Communist neighbours.[4] Nawrocki (1993: 105) suggests that the recognition of people seeing themselves as German became necessary for the normalisation of social relations in the whole region. Nevertheless, there are many important consequences for the conception of the state and the nation: the German minority must accept that they belong to Polish society (as constituted by the state), if not to the Polish nation (in the Herderian sense of the ethnic nation). The Poles must accept that state and nation are not co-terminous, thus giving up the idea of a homogeneous Polish nation-state. Instead, they must consider the Polish nation as constitutive of most, but not all, of Polish society.

On the one hand, it was essential for the Poles to regain an attractive image in the eyes of Silesians and to check the sort of population movements that occurred just after the fall of the Communist regime. On the other hand, they were anxious to maintain control at national level at a time when Polish society was being transformed. The new liberalism had swept away most of the prestigious institutions of cultural integration and economic re-organisation leading regional inhabitants to re-imagine their futures in more autonomous and more individualistic ways. Regional and ethnic pressure combined to force the Polish state to reform the structures in the direction of looser control of the border regions.

The politics of border identity in Upper Silesia, 1989-1993

Upper Silesians now had the opportunity to develop their regional identities on a new basis guaranteed by the international treaties and the good will of the newly elected Polish authorities. The regional population responded with a variety of strategies. For many, migration was the main strategy because of the appeal of the higher living standards in West Germany. So, they quickly became known in Germany as "Volkswagendeutsche" or "Markowicz" because of their admiration of the German currency. The approximately two million people in Germany who have family connections with Poland have served as a first contact for immigrants. With Poland's opening to the world, Polish Germans were able to help their relatives in Upper Silesia by facilitating the flow of investment and goods. Some of them, visiting Poland on business, started to set up branches of commercial enterprises and to use existing cultural infrastructures. A big role was also played by people who had spent their childhood in what are now Polish lands and who wished to see the landscapes they remembered as children and to trace family roots. The flow of population and goods intensified across the border. A new political and economic dynamic emerged from this cross-border phenomenon. Given the inadequacies of the party system, social movements of a regional and national character played the major role in structuring the regional political scene (Nawrocki 1993: 99).

Three strategies of identity politics presented themselves to Silesians: "pro Polish", "pro German" and "regional". In 1989, Otto de Habsbourg, a member of the European Parliament, made a proposal to organise a new plebiscite to make Upper Silesia an independent European enclave. His declaration set off heated political discussion in Silesia and subsequently led to the break-up of the German minority into many groups and movements (Szczepanski 1993). In Katowice, two kinds of groups emerged (Nawrocki 1993 :98). The first was based on German minority groups, such as the movement of the German workers' community called Reconciliation and Future (with its origins in the Upper Silesian Charity Society), and German socio-cultural societies. The second type of group was more regionalist than ethnic; here The Union of Upper Silesia and The Liberal Democratic Congress are representative, and are mostly based in the Katowice region. The movement for the autonomy of Silesia is more radical. Among those favouring the "pro-Polish" option, the Movement for a Polish Silesia is a regional branch of the Union of the Western Poles developed from the Confederation for Independent Poland.

In the Opole region, the Socio-Cultural Society of the German Minority is dominant. The main socio-political options are: "Europeanisation" (de facto Germanisation of Upper Silesia, favoured by part of the German minority); autonomy for the Opole region (a bi-cultural option); the unification of historical Upper Silesia, favoured by the Union of Upper Silesia; the defence of the territorial status quo (supported by most of the post-war newcomers); and the Union of Western Poles policy that the region should be culturally integrated with the rest of Poland (Rykiel 1993: 74).

In the Katowice region, Reconciliation and Future includes in its ranks regionalists with Christian Democratic leanings who emphasise German national identity. Their movement is based on the working class and a few members of the intelligentsia who have tried to lay the ideological and doctrinal groundwork for Silesian regionalism (Silesia treated as a *Heimat*). Their central goal is to reconstruct regional imagery in people's minds through socio-cultural actions, according to the principles of the Organisation for Security and Co-operation in Europe (OSCE, the renamed CSCE) and the European Commission for Human Rights. Their main guidelines were mostly formulated by the militants from the Union of Compatriots of Germany *(BdV, Bund der Vertriebenen)*. One example is the demand for the autonomy of Silesia and for a Silesian Euroregion (Nawrocki 1993: 107) which is aimed at limiting the sovereignty of the Polish State and putting Upper Silesia under the protection of Europe. Operating mainly in the Katowice *voivodship*, it strongly emphasises its aim of a non-conflictual co-existence with the Polish majority: "to build a bridge between the Polish and the German nation" (Joint Polish-German report on the implementation of the Bilateral Treaty 1991).

In Opole, the Socio-Cultural Society effectively promoted a highly diversified range of cultural activities such as running libraries, orchestras, choirs, saying Masses in German and teaching the language. The goal of bringing back community use of the German language (practically lost in the Opole region) was the first objective of the Society. In particular, demands were made to get German taught in schools again, where it had been replaced by Russian under the Communist regime, and also to organise adult education so they too could learn or practice the language.

Publication of a bi-monthly Upper Silesian journal by the association *Gazeta Gornoslaska*, financed by the Ministry of Art and Culture, and of the bi-weekly *Upper Silesian Gazette* (in Polish and German since 1990), added to the two previously existing German newspapers and ensured the regular presence of German-language news in Upper Silesia. Work began on a television programme called *Oberschlesien Aktuel* in 1992. A Polish radio network in Opole and Katowice now broadcasts a weekly programme in German. The main stumbling block they have encountered in their effort to further the German language in schools has been the lack of textbooks and trained teachers. The German Republic has recently lent a hand in this respect.

Another goal of the socio-cultural societies has been to raise the social and economic status of the community within the Polish nation and to gain more representation in local affairs. They have actively supported municipalities and, in elections, managed to win some key positions in local government and in liaison organisations with the central administration charged with rebuilding local groups. German minority mayors organised clubs in order to

167

present their economic and cultural initiatives to the public under the motto: "Let's take our affairs in hand" (Kazanecki 1993: 3).

The Union of Upper Silesia was initially created by the Silesian intelligentsia in the Katowice region in 1989, more as a movement than a political party. It was ideologically close to the more liberal wing of the Catholic church and *Solidarnosc* and wanted to promote the cultural values of Upper Silesia within the Polish nationality. It became, in two years, a mass movement with 6,000 members and 62 organisations all over Upper Silesia. It became the main political force in Katowice by its representation in most of the organs of the *voivodship*s, in the main cities and in the Polish Parliament (which at present contains seven German deputies, one Ukrainian, one Gypsy and one Belorussian, as well as one German senator). Its strategy is one of social integration of minorities in a core culture enriched by new cultural values. It favours the creation of a Silesian Euroregion which would include the territory of Novel Slank, of Cieszyn (an Austrian area near Galicia), the part conquered by Prussia and the part near the Polish border. The Union argues that more investment, from German capital in particular, is necessary to restore the productive potential of the region and ensure its future economic prosperity.

During 1990, the Union of Upper Silesia opted for self-governing Polish regions rather than autonomous regions, even though they entered an electoral alliance for the 1991 Parliamentary election with the Liberal-Democratic Congress which favoured autonomy (Rykiel 1993: 74). The leader of the Liberal Democratic Congress believes that Silesia should be preserved within its ethnic borders (the Opole region, a part of Czestochowa and a part of Katowice) and that it should be organised along the lines of the German Länder thus avoiding the centralised French model. He argued that the region should keep up good relations with Poland and avoid all forms of separatism, thus going against the grain of German minority organisations in Opole. The leader of the Congress is convinced, on the other hand, that Silesia's future must include co-operation with Germany.

At variance with the Union of Upper Silesia, the Silesian Autonomy Movement, set up in 1990, is bi-cultural, includes former Communists, is critical of the regional elites in power and is not open to newcomers. The movement would like to see a fully autonomous region but within the framework of the second pre-war Polish Republic. Its aim is to achieve the degree of autonomy officially acquired after the plebiscite in Silesia but which was not implemented. The key issue for this increasingly important movement is financial independence, the freedom to collect its own taxes and construct its own budget. It also aims to recover some of the resources the region contributes to the Polish economy.

The initial priorities of the socio-cultural societies, as well as of other movements such as the Union of Upper Silesia, was to consolidate intra-Silesian relations. The most eminent figures in the German minority, in struggling against the isolationist tendencies in Silesia, encouraged internal integration and co-operation especially through education. However, the developments which gave back freedom of expression to disenchanted Silesians also left them free to express xenophobic tendencies. These tended to become manifest through the verbal violence of an anti-Polish rhetoric, used by most groups when they started the concrete work of rebuilding a Polish-German historical community with a positive Silesian identity. The fracture lines, which were noticeable between Slavic and Germanic culture under the totalitarian system, and the resulting feelings of inferiority thrust upon Silesian culture, have provoked a move to embrace German identity in oppositional terms - reasserting the "organisational superiority" of Germans and old stereotypes of that kind.

Silesians availed themselves of the opportunity to air their opinions at all levels of society. This included some of the elderly who had been through it all and who see little difference between democratisation and confiscation of their Silesian identity under the Nazi regime. A mutual lack of confidence came to light and fears arose that abuse of the new democratic freedom might threaten the territorial integrity of Poland. The flames were fanned after the first municipal elections when the tone and content of Silesian demands changed and there was talk of economic and financial (if not political) autonomy. Some of the demands put forward included the granting of dual nationality, more co-operation with exiles' associations, changed place names, the recognition of two official languages and direct participation in international treaty negotiations.

New problems emerged which were difficult to resolve, such as the matter of place names which set off heated local debate. After 1921, the Poles had wiped all the German names off the map. More than a thousand were changed back during the 1930s in the Opole region alone. Today, old people still demand that those names be brought back in the formerly Silesian regions occupied by the Poles since the Second World War because they remain the only reference points of their collective identity. These demands usually meet with refusal from a majority of Poles for whom the names are too closely associated with the Third Reich but some agreements have been reached on this issue.

Likewise, on All Soul's Day in 1993 it was difficult to reconcile commemoration of those who died in the last war with the aim of inter-community co-operation. Hard words and strong demands were heard coming from both sides. In particular, the Germans demanded that grave sites be repaired in Poland (including Silesia) using the German cross. This was refused by the Poles. At the end of 1992, a public argument arose about graves erected in memory of the Wehrmacht soldiers. At the end of 1992, the pressure from below increased. A commission constituted by representatives of the German minorities, the Catholic church and the central government decided that war memorials will be bilingual and that the German cross will be replaced by the Christian crosses. The normalisation of inter-community relationships was full of such events. Despite the generation of a certain amount of tension, in most instances solutions were reached by the regulating institutions created by the government and the minority associations.

In 1991, groups of Silesians went to the Federal Republic of Germany in order to make increasingly vehement and nostalgic statements about the "lost Fatherland". These were supported by Silesian extremists in Germany and Austria. However, such moves were quickly neutralised by the Polish government through its negotiation of bilateral treaties with Germany and with the Czech Republic, itself worried about the possibility of Moravian separatists linking up with this sort of movement. The bilateral treaties acted as international regulators, controlling the way in which borderland identity is being rebuilt in popular discourse.

The debate between the various regional political movements on these matters was just beginning, however. The conflicts unavoidably generated anxiety among Polish residents and emigrants from other regions of Poland. The newcomers were worried that German influence might become predominant in Upper Silesia. National identities tend to polarise in this sort of situation, pointing to the need to work out new forms of "Silesian" community life so as to maintain peace and solve the problems of coexistence within borders recently confirmed in treaties. Difficult choices have come to the fore again given the need for both individuals and groups to negotiate the new and uncertain pressures of ethnic and national divisions in Upper Silesia.

For Polish authorities, a new framework for co-operation had to be defined. A new form of civic association was aimed both at solving local problems and promoting mutual respect of cultural differences. City governments took on this task as they tried to involve the whole population in limiting conflict and solving problems by setting up cultural groups for people with different cultural origins. The territorial bond was also supposed to cement unity around the shared idea of regional development. The debate on development linked the reform of regional structures to the question of how best to promote economic development in Upper Silesia. The Euroregion idea promoted by the Union of Upper Silesia led to considerable controversy. The strategy of Euroregion formation originated in Germany, before reunification. In the 1980s and 1990s, it became a means of getting money from Brussels for development programmes and for offsetting the inefficiency of central states by micro-level co-operation with foreign partners. But before 1993 the European Community did not finance transborder co-operation with non-EC members. The Madrid Convention (signed by Poland in 1993) created the possibility of getting EU funds for co-operation between the two sides of the Oder-Neisse line. New proposals were brought forward for a number of Euroregions along the western borders of Poland and along the borders of several other countries such as the Czech Republic, Slovakia, Ukraine and Hungary. Other forms of co-operation, such as the German-Polish Intergovernmental Commission, organised investment in building cross-border infrastructures to facilitate co-operation in 1991. It is no wonder that the leaders of Upper Silesia, not directly involved in

170

transborder collaboration, wanted to benefit from such opportunities in trying to build a Euroregion to include neighbouring regions across the border.

The idea of a Euroregion was apparently taken seriously by almost everyone. Broad public opinion and many intellectuals considered it to be the first step toward autonomy in the lands acquired after the Second World War. In particular, such plans put to the test the very nature of bonds linking the region to Poland and led some to believe in the gradual incorporation of the cross-border regions into the German state. Some were convinced that entrance into the European fold could be achieved only through alliance with the Germans and by transforming Silesia into an autonomous zone. Many saw in the Euroregions a possibility for some countries to extend their influence beyond their borders and to fulfil long-standing territorial claims. In this context, the debate quickly took on dramatic and emotional overtones.

Firstly, militants in the Union of Upper Silesia had to reassert their loyalty to Polish national unity and to constitutional principles to avoid being branded as separatists. Even though all agreed that the framework of state institutions needed to be changed, a climate of suspicion began to spread and was all the more difficult to uproot as some had gone so far as to set up unofficial Upper Silesian structures for cross-border co-operation. Militants of the Union of Upper Silesia justified their Euroregion project by referring to the process of regionalisation now unfolding in Western Europe and to the logic behind it. They provided symbolic quotations to support their views:

The region of the 21st century must contribute to the development of citizenship and be a place where people can fulfil themselves, not where they are invisible individuals outside of their cultural, ethnic and political groups (J. Buszman cited in Szczepanski 1993: 10).

The setting up of the Union of Upper Silesian and northern Moravian communes was seen as a dangerous step toward a Greater Silesia by its detractors and as an important step toward decentralisation by its initiators:

In keeping with our cross-border position, what we have to do is develop different forms of co-operation between neighbours: this union of communes foreshadowed the creation of a cross-border Silesian/Moravian region (J. Paczocha cited in Szczepanski 1993: 12).

Secondly, movements were created from the top to counterbalance such regionalist movements and autonomous initiatives at the local level. The Union of Western Poles, through its regional branch the Movement for Polish Silesia (a secular and moderately nationalist group) opposed any form of regional autonomy. It was politically associated with the Confederation for Independent Poland (a rather radical pro-Solidarity, anti-Communist party) and saw the

German minorities' visions of the future for Silesia as xenophobic and disloyal to the Polish state.

The Movement for Polish Silesia based its views of administrative reform on the results of social research studies. One example of the latter was a pilot survey carried out in 1992 in the Tichy region, situated at the south of Katowice (Szczepanski 1993). Here the Silesian organisations mentioned above were well represented and only 30% of the inhabitants are Silesian. The results suggested that the region of Upper Silesia was not as clearly defined in people's minds as the political parties tended to argue, and that the main sources of antagonism were linked to the different regional origins of the inhabitants. The survey indicated that weakened national bonds with Poland have been replaced by horizontal ones favouring emancipation and citizenship. Though a minority might seek to develop in tight symbiosis with Germany, according to the survey the majority, in this kind of mixed region, wished to refashion its identity by means other than by polarising national identities. The majority of the inhabitants shared with the native Silesians an opposition to the diminished socio-economic status of the region from a self-centred regionalist perspective. They differ on the strategy to be adopted to overcome the decline.

So, demands for the economic autonomy of Upper Silesia (i.e., keeping a large part of local finances in the region to self-finance economic development) were supported by one-third of the people in the Tichy survey. Twenty-five per cent of those questioned opposed this economic independence as they felt that Upper Silesia's financial problems were being under-estimated and they also feared that political autonomy would reinforce separatist actions. Many believed that the region needed emergency aid from the Polish government to deal with serious problems concerning the environment, social disorganisation, health and employment.

The economic situation of Opole was quite different. Local associations have tended to look less to the Polish State than to the promotion of increasingly successful commercial business with German partners. The Parliamentary elections of 1991 showed clearly the differences of political attitudes between Katowice and Opole regions. Opole, which constitutes a separate electoral region, returned three seats for the German minority, one for the Confederation of Independent Poland and one for the Liberal-Democratic Congress (i.e., five of the ten elected representatives had either regionalist or ethnic labels). Katowice, on the other hand, is divided into three electoral regions, one of which has a majority which is ethnically non-Silesian. German minority candidates gained two seats, the Liberal-Democratic Congress four, the Movement for Silesian Autonomy two, the Confederation for an Independent Poland four and the Union of Western Poles two. Regionalist and ethnic candidates won only fourteen of the forty seats available in Katowice.

Whereas the German minority candidates performed well in Opole, the nationally based Democratic Union won in Katowice as it did at national level. Strict regionalist movements gained only one seat in each of the two centrally located electoral regions of Katowice. In the Senate by-election of 1990, in Opole *voivodship*, a Polish Upper Silesia candidate won the elections in the second round, beating a German Upper Silesian (Rykiel 1993: 76). Thus, a half of the elected candidates in the Opole region and about one third in Katowice ensured a regionalist and ethnic voice in the Polish Parliament elected in 1991 but the centralist political parties still clearly dominated, even in Upper Silesia.

Preparations to officially establish Euroregions have begun in most of the Polish borderlands but not in Silesia. A number of regional reform proposals to revise the size and structures of the *voivodships* have been mooted in order to prepare Poland for European integration but none was implemented because of the politicians' reluctance to change the political map. Moreover, in the 1993 elections, the ex-Communists returned to power and were given the role of managing the social crisis brought on by the economic shock therapy administered under the influence of western experts by Lech Walesa and his pro-European supporters.

In the country as a whole, the results of the 1993 parliamentary elections were strikingly different from those of 1989 when the great enthusiasm for change and quick prosperity gave victory to the anti-Communists. In 1993, in regions where a national minority was present, voter turn-out was 10% higher than the national average. Poland was clearly divided in two by the results of the 1993 election, which proved a big success for the two pro-Communist parties, the SLD and the SLP. Warsaw and Lodz voted SLD, as did a majority in the Eastern part of the country. The West voted more as it had in preceding elections: Upper Silesia confirmed its more westward-leaning orientation. Its German minority candidates tried to draw the Polish population to them with the motto: "Together for Europe". The German minorities from the Opole *voivodship* got as many votes locally as the SLD (three each), but they got only one seat in Katowice to the SLD's three.

The new members of national parliament wasted no time in showing their penchant for centralised decision-making and their hostility to change in relation to minority problems. The Parliament set about re-installing the state-model that their predecessors were in the process of liquidating, and it resisted the segmentation brought about by European integration and by those that helped it along (e.g., multi-national companies and the World Bank). A country which, not long before, was in the vanguard of anti-communism, now produced a centrifugal movement which advocated re-centralisation in the name of national cohesion in order to limit the social costs of socio-economic transition. The German minority in Poland, since it favoured decentralisation and recognition of cultural differences, had less room to manoeuvre in the new context of reaffirmation of national sovereignty.

Regional reform projects were stopped, the minority's budget was cut by half, and the troublesome debate on the subject was halted. It is not easy to assess the consequences of this change in Silesia. Certain news items and several

173

conflicts would seem to indicate that the situation is still very fragile with growing intolerance emerging often from radicalised fringe groups or other Polish organisations. However, even if the pro-Europeans are losing influence and credit among the important nationalistic fringe, the Polish government still wishes to join the EU and is unwilling to risk undermining the spirit of the German-Polish treaty of 1991. Against this background, the German minorities in general, and in Upper Silesia in particular, have chosen to reassert their loyalty to the Polish government in order to have the freedom to develop further their impressive economic and cultural revival.

New discourses on national and local identity are essential to creating new German-Polish partnerships. The Goethe Institute of Warsaw and its Krakow branch have rapidly earned an elite reputation thanks to the high level of cultural events and language courses organised by them. The efforts of the relatively affluent German minority compare favourably with those of other minorities. Stimulated by the economic investment drive, a university was opened recently in Opole with a Belorussian Institute, aimed at facilitating the penetration of new markets beyond the Opole region. It confirms the good relationship Bonn has developed with Poland today, making it easier for Polish workers to work in Germany. The dual citizenship, now given to a majority of Silesians (initially proposed by the more radical minority organisations), has helped reinforce German-Polish links. But, it will certainly limit the sovereignty of the Polish state in Upper Silesia to a certain extent, allowing greater strategic possibilities to the German minorities.

Conclusion

Poland's national unity has always depended on vigilance against danger from outsiders, mostly Russia and Germany. The liberalisation of the Communist regime re-opened old fears which lie deep in Polish history while obliging the Polish state to find means of keeping its unity other than through nationalistic discourse and ideology. Upper Silesia finds itself at the epicentre of these fears and of the new ideological constraints. With democratisation, demands for economic and cultural reparation and political autonomy have developed among the native Silesian population of German origin who lost much of their culture and economic wealth under the Communist regime.

Upper Silesia could have become a bone of contention between Germany and Poland if the global context had been different. The potential conflicts threatened by pressure from below and the implosion of the state socialist regime have been regulated by new international law, the supranational organisations and their local and national representatives. The Polish state has been obliged to bring in democratic reforms on minority rights. These reforms have also reshaped centralised and authoritarian structures and state-region and inter-state relationships between two traditional enemies, Poland and

174

Germany. The emergent relationships are analogous to the French-German agreements since 1945. International law has favoured the constitution of German minority in Upper Silesia with cultural rights acceptable to Poland. This marks some limitation of the sovereignty of the Polish state with respect to its internal affairs. The new situation encourages the economic and cultural standing of the Silesian natives with German financial help. Such help will inevitably modify, in the future, regional socio-economic structures (hitherto benefiting the Poles), while running the risk of a new national polarisation of identity inside the region.

The prospect of polarisation, raised by the process of democratisation, has been somewhat controlled and reduced, up to now, by the new local political forces. Most of them co-operate in order to maintain regional peace and to profit from new economic development by rebuilding a more consensual discourse closer to the European regional model. The reaction of the state elites has been twofold: firstly, to give a new means of expression to minorities by regional reform aimed at democratising the state, and secondly, to put a brake on the pace of this democratic change so as to keep control of territory and sovereignty.

The reforms (mostly cultural and political) realised by the Solidarity Government remain fluid and rely effectively on the dynamism of private associations and capital and on the peaceful global atmosphere guaranteed by the bilateral treaties. The region of Opole has become a privileged place for German investments, much more so than the Katowice region where the reconversion of the economy is a very long and problematic process. The way freedom is perceived in Poland today is, nevertheless, linked to the democratisation of Russia, to good relations with Germany and to the way they are both willing to become economic partners. Poles have taken advantage of the historic opportunity to organise, with their neighbours, new economic and cultural relationships oriented to West and East. At the same time, in order to protect themselves from both imperialistic designs and from the sort of economic constraints that a new Comecon would create, they seek to provide safeguards with respect to Germany (e.g., in the Visegrad Group of Poland, Hungary and the Czech Republic) in order to integrate Poland more fully into the Central Europe region. Democratisation of the monolithic Polish nation-state, a new porosity of frontiers and new attitudes on the part of a unified Germany towards Poland were the necessary conditions for re-establishing a certain equilibrium inside Upper Silesia and for reducing the risk of the region undermining German-Polish relationships.

The efforts of the two countries to rebuild Silesian identity testifies to the new partnership of the two countries which is now under the direct or indirect control of the CSCE and the EU. Certainly, Upper Silesia has taken advantage of the situation. The risk it takes is that its new development will be seen as a kind of new Germanisation and as a threat to Poles and Poland in the future. Similar fears exist elsewhere on the EU's eastern borders. Nationalist forces in

Poland are very sensitive to these fears and are more and more opposed to the European integration lobbies. Yet, for the moment, all they can do is to slow down the process of integration while trying to maintain a certain balance of forces in Upper Silesia between the new German elite and the Polish one. The encouragement of a new regional discourse is balanced by a slowing down of the reform process. The emergence of a new regional consciousness is a long term process in the wake of such historical turmoil. We have tried to demonstrate that this process has begun in Upper Silesia, in rather favourable conditions, guaranteed by the new international order. But how long will these conditions last?

Notes

This chapter draws on a joint research project "The transition as seen by the Belorussian and German minority in Poland and by the Russian minorities in Estonia, Kazakhstan and Moldavia" carried out for the French Ministry of Research and National Education from 1991 to 1994. The authors have been jointly responsible for fieldwork observations and interviews, discussions, press analysis and the selected bibliography.

1. This reconstruction of Polish history conveniently downplayed the history of the Polish-Lithuanian Commonwealth for roughly four hundred years after 1400 under the Jagiellonian dynasty which at the height of its powers extended to the Black Sea. According to Kubik (1994: 65) Jagiellonian Poland remains "in the collective memory as a glorious multi-ethnic and multinational empire successfully containing the major enemy of Poland in the East - Russia".
2. The size of minority groups varies according to the sources. Currently, the Germans of Poland are estimated at 350,000 according to the official sources, at 700,000 according to the German organisations (Bojar 1993), and at 450,000 according to the Polish Ministry of Culture and Arts.
3. The treaty is based on the 1948 Convention, the final act of CSCE, 1 August 1975, the Copenhagen Document on Human Dimension of 1990 and the Paris Charter for a new Europe, 21 November 1990. The CSCE provides the political basis for legal codification of international norms. Recently, the CSCE has been renamed OSCE, the Organisation for Co-operation and Security in Europe.
4. Poland has signed treaties with Germany, Bohemia and Slovakia, Hungary, Ukraine, the Belorussian Republic, Latvia, Estonia and Romania.

References

Berlinska, D. and K. Frysztacki. 1991. Der Problem der deutschen minderheit in Oberschlescin. In *Information zur Raumentwicklung* Heft 7/8, Rèumliche: Probleme der Auslënderintegration: 469-480.

Biuletyn Biura do Spaw Mniejszosci narodowych przy Ministerstwie Kultury i Sztuki. 1994. Mniejzosci narodowe w Polsce w 1993, r. Warsawa s. 11.

Bojar, H. 1993. Minorities in Poland yesterday and today. Unpublished paper, University of Warsaw, Department of Sociology.

Brubaker, R. 1993. L'Eclatement des peuples et la chute des empires, approche historique et comparative. *Actes de la Recherche en Siences Sociales* 93/98: 3-19

Chlebowczyk. J. 1980. The language and national borderland in east-central Europe in the 18th and 20th Centuries: the problem of their development. In W. Zielinski (ed.). *Z Problemov integracji spoleczno-politycznzj na Gornym Slasku przed II wojna swiatowa* (Some problems in socio-polical integration in Upper Silesia before World War II.) Katowice: W. Zelinski.

Davies, N. 1984. *Heart of Europe, a short story of Poland*. Oxford: Oxford University Press.

Dulczewski, Z. 1970. Regionalizacja w pracy spoleczno-wychowawczej nauczyciela. In *Ziemie Zachodnie w polskiej literaturze socjologicznej*. Posnan: Wybor tekstow.

Joint Polish-German report on the implementation of the bilateral treaty of 17 June 1991 regarding the German minority in Poland and the Polish group in Germany. 1993. Papcr presented to the CSCE seminar: *Human dimension on national minorities*. Warsaw, May.

Lepesant, G. 1993. La politique allemandc à la frontière Germano-Polonaise et à Kaliningrad, premiere approche. *Cahiers de l'Observatoire de Berlin, notes de conjoncture*. 20: 20-47, Centre Français de Recherches en Sciences Sociales: Berlin.

Kazanecki, P. 1993. National minorities in Poland and Polish State policy towards them. Unpublished paper presented to CSCE Seminar: Human Dimension Seminar on National Minorities. Polish delegation for the CSCE seminar on case studies, Warsaw, May.

Kubik, J. 1994. *The power of symbols against the symbols of power: the rise of Solidariy and the fall of state socialism in Poland*. University Park, PA: Pennsylvania State University Press.

Mach, Z. 1993. Myth and cultural construction of time among a resettled population. *The Polish Sociological Bulletin* 2: 131-38.

Michalczyk, T. and S. Zagorny. 1993. Opole Silesia as a border region. In M.S. Szczepanski (ed.). *Dilemmas of regionalism and the region of dilemmas: The case of Upper Silesia*. Katowice: University of Silesia.

Nawrocki, T. 1993. The institutional setting of regional revindication movements. In M.S. Szczepanski (ed.). *Dilemmas of regionalism and the region of dilemmas: The case of Upper Silesia.* Katowice: University of Silesia.

Rykiel, Z. 1993. Upper Silesia as a cultural border region. In M.S. Szczepanski (ed.). *Dilemmas of regionalism and the region of dilemmas: The case of Upper Silesia.* Katowice: University of Silesia.

Schatz, J. 1994. The last true Communist. *Ethnopolitics in Poland (Nationalities papers, special issue)* 22: 129-163.

Simoncini, G. 1994. The polyethnic state: national minorities in inter-bellum Poland. *Ethnopolitics in Poland (Nationalities papers, special issue)* 22: 5-28.

Skurnowicz, J.S. 1994. Soviet Polonia, the Polish state and the new mythology of national origins 1943-1945. *Ethnopolitics in Poland (Nationalities papers, special issue)* 22: 93-110.

Szczepanski, M. S. 1993. *Regionalizm Gorno slaski w spolecznej swiadomosci.* Sociologiczne studium przypadku, Mars. Unpublished research report: 43pp.

Waskiewicz, A. 1994. German-Polish relations as reflected in the proceedings of the bilateral Polish and West German text-book committee. In R. Grathoff and A. Kloskwoska (eds.) *The neighbourhood of cultures.* Warsaw: Institute of Political studies, Polish Academy of Sciences.

Wierzycka, L. and M. Holuszko. 1993. Some remarks on national minorities in Poland: the protection of their rights, achievements and failures. Unpublished paper presented to CSCE seminar: Human Dimension on National Minorities. Warsaw, May.

Wodz, J. 1990. *Haute Silésie, l'espace déchiré.* University of Silesia, Katowice, Poland.

Wozniak, P. 1994. Blut, Erz, Kohle: A thematic examination of German propaganda on the Silesian question during the interwar years. *East European Quarterly* 28 (3): 319-334.

9 At the edge of Europe: Crossing and marking the Mediterranean divide

Henk Driessen

Nador (Morocco), 5 February 1992: Approximately 300 Moroccans board two small fishing boats to cross the Mediterranean. Their aim is to enter Spain through the backdoor. During the night at sea some twenty men die from asphyxiation in the packed holds of the boats. The bodies are thrown into the sea. Later, in view of the Spanish coast, at least two other passengers drown trying to swim ashore. The Coastal Guard of Almería, in eastern Andalucía, arrest seventy-three of the persons on board, recover two corpses, and confiscate the two fishing boats.

Madrid, 13 November 1992: A group of Latin American immigrants sit down to their evening meal in an abandoned disco bar on the outskirts of Madrid which they use as a shelter. Four hooded men burst upon the scene and open fire, killing one woman and wounding one man. Like thousands of other immigrants, this woman from the Dominican Republic worked as a maid in one of the nouveau-riche households of the capital. The police believe this attack is the work of the extreme right. Some weeks later a member of the Civil Guard is arrested as one of the alleged killers.

These tragic events are part of wider processes in Europe, i.e., the integration of the European Union, the dismantling of internal borders, the tightening of control at the external borders, and a growing antagonism toward immigrants. In 1991 Spain joined the Schengen Group and began to apply the same visa requirements as the other member countries for the admittance of people from Africa, in particular the Maghreb. In early January 1991 dozens of bodies of immigrants were found washed up on the beaches of Tarifa, a town in the south-west of Andalucía that is only thirteen kilometres from Morocco. The Spanish media likened the Straits of Gibraltar to the Rio Grande and applied the terms for clandestine immigrants from Mexico such as "wetbacks" (*espaldas mojadas*, or simply *los mojados*) to those who illegally crossed the Mediterranean frontier. In the course of 1992 thousands of Africans tried to make the passage in skiffs. The "wetbacks" of Tarifa became international news.[1]

The European Commission put pressure on Spain and Morocco to intensify their role as gatekeepers of the "new Europe". Large investments were made to reinforce border controls on both shores of the Mediterranean. Instead of the long-heralded year of hopes and promises, "1992" was a year of refugees, illegal immigration, and racist attacks on immigrant communities of Third World origin.[2]

The Mediterranean has recently become more than just a border between Latin Europe and North Africa. Since Greece and Spain joined the European Union, the Inner Sea has been turned into a frontier and a major concern of Western Europe, perhaps more so than at any other moment in modern history. New metaphors are invented to designate the reinforced North-South divide: "the new wall of shame", the "gold curtain" (Goytisolo 1992: 17, 19), and the "European Wall". The Straits of Gibraltar are redubbed as the "moat of fortress Europe". This re-marking of Spain's southern border not only changes the political and economic relations in the region but also cultural categories such as Europe, Mediterranean, immigrant, asylum and refugee. In this chapter, I will probe an ethnography of Spain's southern border by focusing on interlocking events at the international, national and local levels and indicate how these events are articulated through cultural categories.[3] In doing so, I suggest that the redefinition of the external Mediterranean border of the European Union has implications for Spanish and Moroccan sovereignty. The regulation of cross-border migration is part of a network of international agreements that limit state sovereignty and challenge the core of the ideology of the nation-state, i.e., citizenship and national identity.

Boundaries

The problem of boundaries in a globalising world is imperative, pressing, and relevant both from a theoretical and a political point of view. "The question of boundaries is the first to be encountered; from it all others flow," wrote Fernand Braudel (1972: 18) in his monumental work about the Mediterranean. Edmund Leach, pointing out a major theme of British structuralism, stressed that: "whenever we make category distinctions within a united field, either spatial or temporary, it is the boundaries that matter" (1976: 35). Why are boundaries, borders, frontiers and contact zones so important and fascinating?

The main reason is that they are by definition ambiguous, a source of anxiety and conflict. It is in border zones where societies are most vulnerable, where identities are made and unmade, where cultural categories shift and change. The control of state boundaries is basically a protection of national sovereignty and identity, a control of the "us-them" divide.

While Spain and Morocco are well-defined states that have shared ethnic, religious, and linguistic boundaries with each other since 1956 when Morocco became independent, these boundaries have never been stable nor unequivocal. There are tensions between the two states. The Spanish enclaves on the Moroccan coast are a thorn in the flesh of King Hassan II, the Moroccan government and many Moroccans; the fishing grounds in the Mediterranean and Atlantic seas have been a source of tension between the two states since the eighteenth century; the same holds true for traffic in contraband drugs and illegal border-crossing. Moreover, with one-and-a-half million expatriates Morocco has a sizeable presence in the countries of the European Union. The Moroccan government tries to control this expatriate population through Moroccan associations and mosques in France, Belgium and the Netherlands. In 1983 Morocco officially applied for membership in the European Union stressing its status as a Mediterranean nation. Morocco was insulted when its application was not taken seriously by the European Commission. It is not surprising that the Moroccan government reacted furiously when Spain announced visa requirements for Moroccans. This was considered to be degrading. The image of Spain in Moroccan newspapers is correspondingly negative. The major topics are Basque terrorism, illegal fishing of Spanish boats in Moroccan territorial waters, drug abuse, maltreatment of Moroccan immigrants, the enclaves of Melilla and Ceuta, and traffic accidents (del Pino 1990: 262-3). These topics all convey a notion of disorder. Spanish actions which are perceived harmful to Moroccan interests are immediately classified as racist.

In cultural terms the boundary between Spain and Morocco is thus not as hard and fast as is suggested by the lines on maps. From an anthropological perspective, a border or frontier is better conceptualised as a shifting space in which peoples with different identities and cultural backgrounds meet and deal with each other (Krupat 1992: 4-5). One of the basic questions of a border ethnography is the way strangers are treated. In the modern era of nation-states strangers are aliens - legal or illegal, permanent or temporary immigrants and refugees. Whereas anthropologists have devoted considerable research to all kinds of legal migration, the problems of illegal border crossing and refugee-related issues have so far only received little attention.[4] Yet, the new immigration has become one of the major predicaments of the European Union, especially in terms of the entry of illegal migrants, their mobility, and their social rights once they are in the European Union. This increasing immigration constitutes a major challenge to politicians and scholars alike.

Like Italy, Greece and Portugal, Spain has a long history of emigration. In the 1960s more than one million Spaniards left their country to work in Western Europe. But now it has become a country of immigration. As a peninsula with thousands of kilometres of coastline its borders are porous. In the late 1980s more immigrants from Africa arrived on Spain's shores with the aim of staying there than ever since the fall of the Muslim kingdom of Granada in 1492. This has clearly taken the Spanish government by surprise.

Immigrants, legislation and policy in Spain

Since the mid-1980s there has been a remarkable emphasis on European Union co-ordination of the right of asylum in view of the abolition of internal border controls on 1 January 1993 (which has been partly postponed for political and practical reasons) and the failure of national asylum policies (Hailbronner 1990: 347). The Schengen Agreement of 1985 between Germany, France and the Benelux countries was the beginning of an overall European Union policy: it provided for the general abolition of all controls at common borders, for measures to protect internal security and to prevent the influx of "illegal non-European Community immigrants", and finally for the co-ordination of visa policies, entry regulations and asylum procedures.

Immigrants, who were pushed out of Latin America, Asia and Africa by civil war, dictatorship, economic disaster and lack of opportunity, and attracted to Spain by the fast economic growth of the 1980s, have been a relatively new experience in this country. Reliable figures are difficult to obtain and sources contradict each other. In 1989 there were approximately 482,000 legal and 300,000 illegal "aliens" in Spain (de Lucas 1992: 84). The largest group of illegal residents were Latin Americans (100,000), followed by Moroccans (75,000) and Filipinos (50,000). Legal immigrants from Western Africa numbered only 5,770 (Robin 1992). Immigrants of all categories constituted less than two per cent of the total population and only 0.7 per cent of the active population.[5] Between 1979 and 1988 18,000 people applied for the status of refugee, of whom 2,770 were recognised. In 1989 there were 3,800 applications and 181 ceded (de Lucas 1992: 89). Another source indicates that in 1990 15,000 people benefited from the law on refugee status and asylum either as applicants or as recognised political refugees (Escobar Hernandez 1992: 69).

The overwhelming majority of clandestine immigrants who were able to regularise their presence under the restricted amnesty programme of 1991 were young men between twenty and thirty-five, who left behind a wife and children in their native country, entered Spain on a tourist visa, lived in rented rooms, spoke some Spanish, worked in the service sector, and earned a salary of about 100,000 pesetas per month. More than 40,000 of these legalised aliens were living in Catalonia, almost the same number in Madrid, 15,000 in Andalucía, and 16,000 in Valencia and Murcia.[6]

In December 1991 two protest demonstrations against aliens' legislation were organised by the *Emigrantes Marroquies en España* (Moroccan Immigrants in Spain) in Madrid. They demanded legalisation of residence for all immigrants, carrying the following slogan: *La Ley de Extranjería, fascista porquería* (The Aliens Law: Fascist Filth). According to the president of this

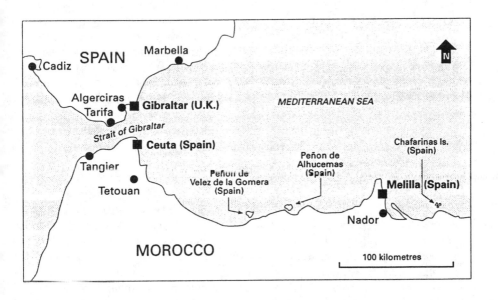

Map 9.1
The Spanish-Moroccan frontier

183

organisation only the presence of one quarter of the 200,000 clandestine Moroccan residents had been regularised.[7]

In 1984 the Spanish Parliament passed a Law on Asylum and Refugee Status, one of the most liberal in Europe. However, one year later an Aliens Act was passed that considerably restricted the residence of foreigners, introduced new obstacles in the procedure for acquiring the Spanish nationality, and provided the police with new instruments for expelling foreign residents. This Act provoked violent protest among Moroccan immigrants in the Spanish enclaves of Melilla and Ceuta (Driessen 1992: 171-76; Carabaza and de Santos 1992: 106-08). Considerable political controversy in Spain also resulted (de Lucas 1992: 83), due largely to the Act's separation of political asylum from refugee status which introduced a fundamental ambiguity in the treatment of aliens[8] There is one fundamental difference between the granting of asylum and recognition of refugee status: asylum automatically gives access to residence and work permits, while refugee status does not. The latter is a kind of permanent liminal condition. One of the consequences is that people who already enjoy refugee status frequently begin a new procedure to obtain asylum because this is the only official road to full civil rights. Most illegal immigrants end up in a vicious circle: without a work permit from the Ministry of Labour they have no access to a residence permit and without a residence permit from the Ministry of the Interior they will not get an employment permit. The only alternative left to them is to enter the black labour market and join the subproletariat of' undesired aliens.

In order to prevent abuse, the Law on Asylum and Refugee Status includes the principle of immediacy for those foreigners who entered the country illegally. They have a maximum period of fifteen days to make a request for refugee status which in itself grants a foreigner the right of temporary residence in Spain. Since Spain's adherence to the Schengen Agreement, the government has adopted a very restrictive and rigid immigration policy. However, the treatment of immigrants differs according to cultural, national, and, in a veiled way, racial background, ranging from lenient treatment in the case of Latin Americans to strict treatment bordering on interdiction in the case of North and Black Africans (de Lucas 1992: 89). Official attitudes may also be contradictory. For instance, Spanish governments have implemented a long-standing policy of friendship vis-à-vis the Arab world while at the same time North African immigrants are discriminated against by state agencies. Many Spaniards express a strong sense of contempt for Arabs in general and Moroccans in particular. They are all referred to by the pejorative term of *moros*.

There are also more fundamental contradictions which Spain shares with the other European Union countries. On the one hand, the government pays lip-service to the fundamental right of asylum, based on Western notions of freedom, openness, and hospitality, while on the other hand it tries to prevent immigrants who seek economic opportunities rather than political asylum from entering the country. As elsewhere there is a determined drive among politicians and bureaucrats to set economic refugees apart from political ones. The Spanish government justifies its policy by pointing out that it is impossible to absorb new people in a time of rising unemployment. For example, in 1992, almost a quarter of the active population of Andalucía was unemployed; about twenty-five per cent of them did not receive any state support at all (*El País* 3 April 1992). In 1994 the employment situation has deteriorated further: now one out of three Andalusians is unemployed.

Paradoxically, the vast majority of non-registered immigrants find work on the illegal labour market. Unemployment fraud is rampant and there is a large-scale shadow economy (Franklin 1992: 19). Opposed to the political rhetoric of an *invasión de indeseables* (invasion of undesired people), many interest groups in Spain welcome a cheap and submissive labour force. Indeed, many sectors of the national economy would hardly exist without illegal workers. Finally, the definition of the concepts of asylum and refugee are being debated and contested not only in Spain but in the European Union at large.[9]

At the edge of Europe

Tarifa where the Mediterranean and Atlantic seas meet is Europe's southernmost town. A town of 15,000 inhabitants, it is located twenty-five kilometres south-west of Algeciras close to the national highway from Málaga to Cádiz. It has a coastline of forty kilometres. Given the proximity of its long sandy beaches to Morocco, only 13 kilometres away or less than one hour by ferry, it has become one of the favourite places for clandestine entry into Spain. On a clear night one can see from Tangier the lights of Tarifa across the Straits of Gibraltar. The main point of orientation for the guides ferrying new immigrants to the promised lands of Europe are the bright lights of a petrol station along the national highway, two kilometres out of town. From the European side, the view of the Moroccan coast on the horizon is a constant reminder to the *tarifeños* that there is another world over yonder. For most of them the small physical distance is a wide ideological and cultural gap.

During 1991 and 1992 Tarifa became known in the national and international media for its African "wetbacks" or "boat people" who crossed the Straits, sometimes with tragic consequences as the town's cemetery testifies. In early January 1991 six corpses were found on one of Tarifa's beaches.[10] Later that month the Coastal Guard of Algeciras arrested thirty illegal immigrants (twenty-three from Liberia, three from Senegal, two from Mali, one from Gambia, and a Moroccan guide). One group of thirteen was discovered by a patrol boat wading ashore naked with a bundle of clothes on their heads. The Moroccan guide and owner of the boat had received 20,000 pesetas per passenger before they boarded on a beach close to Tangier. Later that night the Civil Guard arrested another seventeen Africans along the highway between Tarifa and Algeciras. None of them had documents, all were men between twenty and thirty, and most of them said they had fled the civil war in Liberia hoping to find work in Spain or France. A police spokesman said that, following the principle of first asylum, the Liberians would be sent back to a refugee camp in Abidjan, Ivory Coast.[11]

When it became known that from May 1991 a Spanish visa would be required for all visiting Africans, the police and customs officers of Algeciras were hardly able to handle the enormous rush of Moroccans who at the last moment wanted to get into Spain. Thousands were refused admittance and sent back. Since there was no relief centre in the port of Algeciras, refused Moroccans who arrived on the last evening ferry had to spend the night on board the ship. During one of those nights a furious mob wrecked and looted the ferry. A slogan painted on the ferry expressed the hatred stirred up by the visa requirement: *Españoles, de pequeños maricones y de grandes cabrones* (Spaniards: small pansies, big cuckolds).

At the beginning of May, several Moroccans attempted a new way of escaping police arrest by jumping into the water just before the ferry moved into the port of Algeciras, a highly dangerous escapade in which two of them drowned.[12] The municipal authorities of Algeciras announced the construction of a *Centro de Acogido de Inmigrantes* (Centre for Immigrants). At that time, the ten Spanish consulates in Tunisia, Algeria and Morocco sounded the alarm because of being besieged by tens of thousands of potential immigrants.

The number of Africans trying to enter Spain at Tarifa's beaches increased dramatically at the beginning of 1992. Compared to those who entered Spain on tourist visas in the late 1980s, these border-crossers are generally destitute. They lacked the means to buy false visas and airline tickets and had to spend their last money on the nocturnal passage from Morocco to Tarifa. During a visit to Tangier in March 1992 I was taken to a street in the old centre where in tea-houses and cheap boarding-houses smugglers and passengers meet to negotiate the fare for the nocturnal passages. They openly haggled over prices which oscillated between 40,000 and 60,000 pesetas. One of the prospective immigrants was a young man from Somalia. He told me that he wandered, mostly on foot, through Ethiopia, Sudan, Egypt, Libya, Tunisia, Algeria before arriving at Tangier ("because I knew that from this city there is a shortcut to Europe"). He lived in a cheap boarding house, worked illegally as a worker in the construction of tourist apartment blocks and hoped to save enough money to cross over. He believed that there was abundant work in Europe and got irritated when I told him about the unemployment, exploitation, xenophobia and economic recession throughout Europe.[13]

Upon entering Europe, these immigrants own nothing but the clothes they wear. If they have identity cards or passports, they often destroy them or leave them behind. This is not only done for tactical reasons — to make it more difficult for the Spanish authorities to send them back — but also because they desperately wish to begin a new life with a new identity. Having landed on the beaches of Tarifa, they have to reach Algeciras before dawn because their appearance makes them conspicuous to the Civil Guard who cruise the highway between Tarifa and Algeciras in search of new immigrants. Sometimes they succeed in hiding until the following night or in getting a ride from a truck driver. From Algeciras they try to get to the cities of Málaga, Madrid, Valencia, and Barcelona where they are less noticeable. Many of them say they have friends, acquaintances, or the names of contacts in Spain or France.

Towards the end of 1991 the situation in the Algeciras district grew so critical that a centre for clandestine immigrants had to be opened in Tarifa in a section of a building on the outer quay of the port, a point far removed from the town. When I arrived in Tarifa in the second week of March 1992, about seventy-five Africans were being held there in legal and social quarantine. The weather was calm after several days of Levanter storm. During that weekend dozens of Africans crossed the Straits. Thirty-five were caught at various spots in the municipal territory of Tarifa. When I approached the building where they were being held, the inmates called to me in French through the barred windows where their laundry was hung out to dry, appealing for help. After a few minutes a Civil Guard in the neighbouring office noticed me and ordered me to go away.

In early spring members of the Spanish Parliament were becoming aware of the bad conditions under which the new immigrants were being held in the Algeciras district. A senator from Cádiz interrogated the Minister of the Interior about the situation in the Andalusian ports.[14] A few days later a member of parliament for the Socialist Labour Party paid a visit to the centre of *inmigrantes ilegales acogidos en Tarifa* (the illegal immigrants hosted in Tarifa) accompanied by the mayor and two councillors. He declared to the press that the Africans, who asked for cigarettes and games to kill time, were being treated well "notwithstanding the fact that they are liable to punishment because of their illegal entrance into the country". The politicians left their own packets of cigarettes as a gesture of goodwill: "The mayor went to the café next door to buy two cartons of cigarettes which he distributed among the *acogidos* who showed their gratitude". During a press conference the member of parliament expressed his concern about the increase of illegal immigration in particular "in view of the deteriorating political situation in Algeria" (which he likened to the situation which sent waves of Albanian refugees to Italy).[15] Other interested parties were kept away from the Centre which shows how politically delicate the problem of illegal immigrants already was. Access to the centre soon became an issue of local and national political controversy.[16]

At the end of March 1992 "thirty illegal immigrants of African nationality" were released after having been detained for forty days, the maximum period according to the Aliens Act. Each one of them received an edict of expulsion signed by the provincial Governor. When the Africans left the Centre, they were abandoned to their fate. Lacking financial means, they had to go to the

187

Red Cross to ask for help. Members of the Algeciras Refugee Aid Group, the Red Cross, journalists, and a few inhabitants collected money for food and transport. Most of these immigrants claimed to know contact persons in cities throughout Spain who would be able to get them a job. All of them left Tarifa. They had the right to lodge an appeal against their expulsion within forty days. A few days later I met two of them hanging around and looking for work in the port of Algeciras. They told me they were determined to stay in Spain. Fifty-two men were still languishing in the Tarifa Centre.[17]

The vast majority of the inhabitants of Tarifa remained indifferent to the immigrants. Nevertheless, some feared that these immigrants were a threat to their standard of living. Only a very few inhabitants were really interested in the fate of the immigrants and willing to help them in one way or another. Among them were a few older people who knew the hardships of migration from personal experience. A cowherd whom I met in the hills of Tarifa was one of them. He told me that the immigrants sometimes lost their way and came to his farm for help and work. He said he sometimes helped them with food, shelter, and clothes.

In Algeciras, a city of 100,000 inhabitants, where during the summer hundreds of thousands of Moroccan migrants from all over Europe take a ferry to their native country for a holiday, there is a small group of people committed to the plight of immigrants. Their main work is to denounce abuses and provide information about the "problem of illegality" during meetings and on posters and pamphlets. Their direct opponents are a group of racists who paint anti-alien slogans on the walls, such as ¡No a la inmigración de color a España! (No to coloured immigration to Spain!), ¡Moros, no! (No Moors!), and ¡Moros, fuera!" (Moors Out!).

Overall, the fate of the clandestine border crossers is grim. An immigration officer at Algeciras told me that during the first ten months of 1992 about 2,000 of them were caught along the coast of Cádiz province. More than eighty per cent were Moroccans, five percent Algerians and the rest sub-Sahara Africans.[18] The majority who escaped the Coastal, Civil, and National Guards go into hiding in the large cities where they become part of a floating underclass of non-persons. Many immigrants hire themselves out below minimum wages or go into street peddling along the Costa del Sol where ambulant trade is forbidden by the municipal councils. I frequently saw how they were being chased by the local police.[19] But many of these young men are born survivors who have an admirable amount of stamina, flexibility and creativity.

Take the case of Seku, a young man from Mali whom I met in Málaga. In 1989 he came to Spain on a tourist visa leaving his wife and two children behind. He sold watches and wood carvings for a friend who had a residence permit and who regularly flew back home to buy cheap goods. After a while Seku found a job as an electrician, the trade he had learned in his native country. In 1991 he applied for a residence permit. He likes to return to his native country only for holidays and to see his family. Most of these young men are frontiersmen *par excellence*. If it is true that the internal frontier pattern with its constant shifts and crossings lies at the core of African political culture (Kopytoff 1987, Nyerges 1992), there is no radical break between the experiences of these young men and historical patterns. Whereas their forebears regularly crossed internal frontiers of chiefdoms and kingdoms for a mixture of reasons — adventure, poverty, persecution, war, famine — today young Africans cross the external frontier between Africa and Europe in search of what they call "freedom" — a concept they do not use in a strict political meaning but in the wider sense of freedom resulting from a reasonable standard of living.[20]

To cross the Mediterranean frontier into Europe to do heavy and dirty work is a rite of passage for many young Moroccans, an initiation into manhood[21] The majority of Moroccan immigrants work as undocumented day labourers in agriculture engaged in activities such as picking olives in Jáen, and strawberries, tomatoes and melons in Huelva, Málaga and Almería. In his desire to taste freedom and a Western life style, Mustafa, twenty-three years old, lives as a land labourer on isolated farms in Málaga, sometimes visits the city to have a good time. He has not been in contact with his family for almost three years. He likes to drink whisky and boasts of a Spanish girl-friend. He told me that other boys leave Morocco mainly to escape military service. Some of them have made a little money by smuggling small quantities of hashish or marijuana. Cannabis grown in the Rif and Jbala is worth more than three times its value if sold across the Mediterranean sea along the Costa del Sol.

Immigration, however, is not as exclusively a male phenomenon as it was before. There is a growing number of Moroccan girls and young women in Spain. They dust and clean for the newly rich in Málaga, Madrid, Valencia and Barcelona. Approximately fifty per cent of all Moroccans in Madrid are women and most of them work in the domestic service sector. Within the largest organisation of Moroccans in Spain, a women committee has been founded mainly for the *chachas* (from *muchachas*, girls or domestic servants) as they call themselves. The president of this committee, a married woman with two children, pointed out that "Women in Morocco are defamed when they leave for Europe to work. . . . In Spain we have to fight for documents, in Morocco for equal rights for women" (*El País* 21 May 1991: 3). When I discussed the visa measure with a Moroccan man, he explained to me that "visa requirements should only apply to women in order to prevent them from coming over to Europe to earn a living but not to men who come with dignity to work or to visit relatives." This man implied that most Moroccan women who work in Spain are prostitutes.[22]

Frontier markers

The experiences of events with regard to the Euro-African frontier are articulated through categories which define "us" and "them". Politicians and journalists frequently write and talk about immigrants, refugees and asylum seekers in terms of "invasion", "new invasion", "flood", "being deluged with refugees", and "the avalanche from the South".[23] These terms are derived from a vocabulary of natural disaster and war. It is a rhetoric that expresses and evokes fear. Such notions are not only current in right-wing political circles but have gained a wider circulation in the media, the streets and cafés. They are linked to the general notion of a demographic explosion on the southern shores of the Mediterranean, a widespread fear of Islamic fundamentalism and an invasion of Muslims from the Maghreb.

Such notions reveal attitudes, emotions and ideologies, as does the designation of "undesirables", which I heard several times being used by Spanish bureaucrats and ordinary citizens. Other categories such as "illegal aliens" or "wetbacks" are also dehumanising, the former because it makes immigrants akin to outlaws, the latter because it defines persons in terms of a humiliating experience. The concept of "undocumented", which is mostly used by bureaucrats, reduces humanness to the possession of certain documents. The word *acogido*, which is widely employed by the media, is ambivalent. It means both guest, with an emphasis on uninvitedness and dependency, and inmate of a poorhouse. Ordinary Andalusians simply use the pejorative terms *moro* or *negro* for all immigrants from Africa, regardless of their origin and official status. These categories are often implicitly linked to criminality, in particular with regard to the smuggling and use of drugs, abuse of alcohol and fighting.[24] Rightist newspapers and politicians make an explicit connection between increasing immigration and what they call "the reserve army of delinquency", playing upon the sentiments of many Spaniards for whom drugs and insecurity are a daily preoccupation. Almost everywhere along the coast from Málaga to Tarifa one can hear a cry for more police to fight criminality and to maintain territorial sovereignty. The spread of anti-immigrant graffiti is another manifestation of this trend. There are at least two reasons for the emergence of an anti-immigrant mood: unemployment is again on the rise though not because of immigration as rightist politicians claim. The second reason is the increase, perceived as steep, of legal foreign residents in Spain from 334,000 in 1987 to 540,000 at the end of 1991. This mainly occurred because the government allowed large numbers of illegal residents to legalise their status. This perceived explosion of immigrants should be considered against the background of almost four centuries of non-immigration.

How are cultural categories such as "Spain", "Europe" and "the Mediterranean" used as symbolic markers of the southern frontier? Spaniards in general and Andalusians in particular are preoccupied with Europe almost to the point of obsession. The widespread use in Spain of "Europe" as a cultural category and of symbols such as the flag of the European Community are striking when compared to other countries of the European Union, such as the Netherlands. This concern with "Europe" is linked to cultural identity and the feeling by many Spaniards, not only intellectuals and politicians, that they have to catch up with Western Europe after decades of dictatorship and underdevelopment. They are now eager to compare their country and its regions with Morocco, which they see as corrupt, backward and dictatorial. The southern neighbour represents what Spain no longer is but what it used to be thirty years ago. This negative attitude towards Morocco and its inhabitants is outspoken and widespread. "Europe" stands for democracy, modernity, rationality and prosperity and Spaniards wish to become once and for all part of the European core.[25] Closing off the borders to the south and erecting *el muro de Europa* (The wall of Europe) is an integral part of Europeanising Spain.

However, the situation is more complex than a simple opposition of Spain and Morocco. The Spanish government not only embraces European identity but also cherishes its ambition as a major Mediterranean power and mediator between Europe and the Arab World. Andalucía, the southernmost area of Spain, reflects this ambiguity. It is the region where the non-European past of Spain is most visible, where several new mosques have been built recently, where the wealthy sheikhs of the Gulf States and Saudi-Arabia have constructed their summer palaces, and where some Christians are converting to Islam. One faction of the Andalusian autonomist movement celebrates the Moorish past as a vital part of regional identity, while another faction rejects the Moorish roots as distant past. Regional politicians and economists dream of Andalucía as a California-in-Europe. But how does the highest unemployment rate of Spain and of the European Union fit into this dream?

The Hispano-African frontier, however, is not only constructed from the inside out but also from the outside in. The position of Morocco is equally marked by ambivalence and contradictions. "Europe" is part of daily discourse as both experience and image. Almost every Moroccan family has kin and friends living in Europe. Crossing the Mediterranean is an obsession for many young Moroccans. The image of a European paradise and the dream of becoming part of it places a heavy burden on family life.

There is a strong tendency, both on the European and African sides, to define the Mediterranean frontier in religious terms. In Morocco the notion of "Europe" is inseparable from the notion of "Christian" in the same way that "Moroccan" and "Muslim" are used interchangeably (Munson 1984: 43-56). In Islamic terms "Europe" stands for wickedness, impurity and greediness, whereas "Morocco" is a symbol of spiritual superiority and purity. This is the vocabulary used by fundamentalist leaders to attract followers among the unemployed, students, and schoolboys who hang out in the streets. On the other hand, for many young Moroccans "Europe" is primarily a secular notion

191

meaning opportunity, liberty and the good life. These men are so desperate to cross over to Europe that they are willing to risk their lives.

In 1986 Morocco suffered economically as a consequence of the admission of Spain and Portugal to the European Community. The Moroccan minister responsible for the relationships with the European Community argued as follows: "How can Europe not include Morocco? Spain is only fourteen kilometres away. The southern standard of living in the Mediterranean cannot suffer because of the north. In classical terms this is a setting for war. How can you make one of the great corridors of commerce of history into a barrier, a fortification? This could result in conflict". Another Moroccan minister stated that "The Mediterranean is part of our civilisation, and geopolitically Morocco is a Mediterranean country" (cited in Fox 1991: 307-8).

However, the term "Mediterranean" is rarely used in daily discourse. The way Moroccan politicians employ it as a cultural category to stress proximity and affinity to Europe is contradicted by the history of Moroccan state formation and the geo-political distribution of power within Morocco. Mediterranean Morocco has been a forgotten frontier for centuries. The dominant image of this area in the rest of Morocco, especially in the Atlantic plains which constitute the economic and political heart of the country, is one of poverty, smuggling, kif, cut-throats, emigration and subordination (Zaim 1990: 5). The "real" Morocco begins south of the Rif and Tangier, not only in the eyes of many tour operators in Western Europe but also according to the Moroccan political elite.

"Mediterranean" is also used in a positive way by an increasing number of young Berbers in northern Morocco and by Riffians abroad, particularly by those who are aware of and profess their Berber identity. These people employ "Mediterranean" as a category of opposition to Arab domination. As frontiers people and border-crossers Riffians are more oriented towards Europe than towards Rabat. By seeking a living on both sides of the Mediterranean, they straddle the frontier like Jews, Greeks, and Armenians did in the past.[26] In sum, the Mediterranean emphasis is a recent one in Morocco, an indirect effect of the incorporation of the southern Europe into the European Union.

Conclusion

The Mediterranean sea is in the process of being transformed into a relatively closed frontier between the European Union and Africa. It is erected with the aim to keep out immigrants and drugs and reinforce internal unity and identity. An analysis of the course of events following the Spanish accession to the Schengen Agreement clearly shows that the Spanish authorities and people at local, regional and national levels are unable to deal with the new situation of increased illegal immigration. The Spanish state alone is unprepared to act as the border patrol of Europe's external border. In fact, the European Union needs Morocco's co-operation for this task of gate keeping.

It would seem that Spain and the citizens of the "New Europe" must live with the fact that large numbers of North and Sub-Saharan Africans will continue to enter their territories without the required travel documents. The majority of these border crossers go underground and become part of a shadow economy and society. New internal boundaries are emerging between established residents and marginal outsiders. The failure of the European Union to design a common position and strategy in face of this immigration problem not only brings to light the strong tendency of member states to cling to their national sovereignty, but also the persistence of political and cultural divisions and categories which can be traced back to the sixteenth century. People from southern Europe are still considered to be somewhat lesser Europeans by the core countries of the Union, whereas North-Africans and Turks are on the other side of the frontier that demarcates and defines Europe proper. The irony, however, is that since the 1950s millions of Mediterranean people are living, working, dying, and being born in the European core countries. The Mediterranean has become an integral part of Europe. Its presence is likely to increase.

Finally, the issues of illegal immigration and the policing of the external Mediterranean border of the European Union point out a contradiction with regard to national sovereignty. It has become clear that no single country in the European Union is capable of regulating migration flows without influencing those in neighbouring countries. The regulation of cross-border migration is thus a supra-national political process which inevitably limits state sovereignty. The new immigration is only one manifestation of an increasingly complex world with which the nation-state alone cannot cope.

Notes

This article is largely based on field research in Algeciras, Tangier, Tarifa, Ceuta and Gibraltar in March-April 1992 and June 1993.

1. See "The Short Cut", *The Economist* 9 December 1992; "Les Boat People de Gibraltar", *L'Express* 23 October 1992; "Les naufragés de la migration vers le Nord", *Le Monde Diplomatique* December 1992. This topic was also covered by Dutch television.
2. Given the ideological and political connotations of concepts used by politicians and the media, there is a need for a more neutral term to refer to immigrants who enter Western Europe illegally and reside there without legal status. Although I realize that there is nothing more transient and volatile than "new", I propose to use the term "new immigrants" for lack of a better concept. It is important to differentiate the new immigrants from earlier generations of

labour migrants because conditions in the countries of origin and destination have changed drastically over the past two or three decades (for one recent view of new immigrants in the United States, see Lamphere 1992).

3. Very little is known about aliens in Spain. The same is true for the Muslim population. In a recent overview of Muslims in Western Europe there are ten lines devoted to the Spanish situation: "In Spain, there is clearly a substantial presence of North African Muslims. Most of them are there, however, without documents, so little can be stated with any certainty. It appears that many may be temporary, working in the tourist industry on the Mediterranean coast. Spain is, of course, also a transit country for North Africans travelling back and forth to France. Individual Spanish Muslims have claimed that after the end of the Franco regime, many secret Muslims have declared themselves publicly, suggesting a tradition going back to the *reconquista*" (Nielsen 1992: 87). This author neglects the Spanish literature on the subject. Had he consulted Spanish sources he would have known that there are strong indications that the vast majority of Muslim immigrants want to stay, and that most of them work in agriculture, domestic service, construction and peddling. Since Franco's death thousands of Spaniards have converted to Islam. They stress the legacy of Al-Andalus.

4. Exceptions are, among others, Loizos (1981), Conover (1987), Hirschon (1989), Chierici-Cassagnol (1991) and Gold (1992). Also see the *Journal of Refugee Studies* and the *Journal of International Refugee Law*. The main reason for this relative neglect is the very delicate nature — politically, ethically, methodologically — of studying this problem in an ethnographic way. Scholars of law and political scientists have devoted far more attention to the problem of refugees than anthropologists. See Harrell-Bond and Voutira (1992) for a recent overview of refugee research.

5. According to Actis et al. (1991) there were 75,000 Moroccans living in Spain, 61,000 as illegal residents. Sixty per cent lived in the provinces of Catalonia and Madrid. Figures provided by the Ministry of the Interior after the amnesty programme of 1991 under which more than 125,000 illegal immigrants legalized their presence, amounted to 540,000 legal aliens (1.4 per cent of the total population), of whom 77,000 are Moroccans. More than half of the alien population are retired and aged people from Northwest Europe who live along the Costa del Sol (*El País* 15 December 1991: 20). According to non-governmental organizations, after the amnesty more than 294,000 illegal residents remained in Spain because they did not fulfil the conditions of having a job or business, of possessing a passport, and having proof of residence in Spain before May 1991.

6. *El País* 13 December 1991: 26.

7. These reports have been taken from *El País* 8 December 1991: 14-5; 9 December 1991: 19; 13 December 1991: 26; 16 December 1991, *Ciudades*: 1. Note that the estimates of the immigrant population by non-governmental organizations are much higher than the figures provided by the government.

8. The best discussion of the Spanish Aliens Act is Escobar Hernandez (1992). Escobar Hernandez judges Spanish policy and legislation as relatively lenient, liberal and benevolent, while De Lucas (1992) holds it to be highly restrictive.

9. There is an urgent need to refine the concept of refugee, which in its original definition is intimately linked to political persecution, in order to take into account victims of civil-ethnic wars and mass displacements as a result of economic misery in places such as former Yugoslavia, Romania and Albania. The difference between an immigrant and a refugee may be a matter of degree rather than essence. Migrants often leave their homes for a combination of political, economic, religious, and personal reasons.

10. This section on events is largely based on newspaper clippings from the national daily *El País* and from *Europa Sur* (Southern Europe), a daily newspaper based in *el campo de Gibraltar*, the district to which Tarifa belongs (together with Algeciras, Los Barrios, Castellar de la Frontera, Jimena de la Frontera, La Línea de la Concepción, and San Roque). In a booklet about this district used in the secondary schools of the area it is proudly depicted as: "This is our land. A piece of Andalucía. The beginning and the end of Europe. Gate of the Mediterranean and the Strait of Gibraltar" (Fernández Mota 1990: 13).

11. *El País* 30 January 1991, *Ciudades*: 1.

12. *El País* 2 May 1991: 16; 4 May 1991: 16.

13. In December 1992, the European Union's Council of Ministers gave its officials the green light to negotiate with Morocco one of the closest partnership treaties ever drafted by the Union and a non-European country. Before this decision was taken, Hassan II tried to show his good will by promising to clamp down on corruption, drug smuggling, and illegal immigration (*The Economist* 9 January 1993: 44). Indeed, in late 1992 some of the networks by which migrants from sub-Saharan Africa found their way illegally into Europe were broken up. In Tangier a new Chief of Police was appointed, and black Africans were rounded up and held in the bullring which served as a provisional prison camp (*Le Monde Diplomatique* December 1992: 23). Thousands of soldiers were deployed to guard the beaches of northern Morocco. When I returned to Tangier in June 1993 it seemed that sub-Saharan Africans had almost vanished from its streets.

14. *Diario de Cádiz* 7 March 1992: 12.

15. *Europa Sur* 11 March 1992, front-page report.

16. The secretary of the local *Juventudes Andalucistas* (Andalusianist Youth) complained to the local newspaper how he was denied access to the "illegals" when he went there to give the inmates food as a gift from his political association. The Guards had received orders not to accept goods on behalf of the inmates (*Europa Sur* 12 March 1992: 1). At the weekend following this visit thirty-four Liberians, Senegalese, South Africans and Ethiopians were arrested at different places along the highway between Tarifa and Algeciras. The Tarifa Centre became overcrowded (*Europa Sur* 17 March 1992: 20).

17. *Europa Sur* 29 March 1992: 13.

18. Also see *Le Monde Diplomatique* December 1992: 22.

19. They become part of the "shadow economy" which refers to those economic activities not included in official statistics and therefore withdrawn from government regulations and taxation. The "informal sector" consists of that part of the shadow economy in which small units produce for the market or render services. The "underground economy" is the world of tax evasion, economic crimes, fraud and unregistered labour (Evers 1991).

20. Some authors evoke "African character": "the Africans' relative indifference to rootedness in physical space, permanent attachment to a particular place"; "the general African 'adventurousness': the eagerness to see new places, the curiosity about other societies, the avidity for travel, the readiness to migrate" (Kopytoff 1987: 22-3). There is a risk of stereotyping in such sweeping statements.

21. Hart (1976: 94) argues in his monograph about the Aith Waryaghar of the central Rif that "Labor migration has become such a deeply rooted pattern of economic behavior that one can indeed say that it has in effect become the socio-economic institution that has replaced the bloodfeud".

22. Muslim women are pre-eminent boundary markers in contact zones. See, for instance, the study of women in the Spanish enclave of Ceuta where gender constructions also encompass the symbolic dimensions of geographical locations (Morocco, Spain, Christian and Muslim Ceuta) and the different religious identities ascribed to them (Evers Rosander 1991: 273).

23. "La avalancha del Sur es imparable," *El País* 27 August 1992: 14.

24. Compare the negative stereotypes of Moroccan workers in Gibraltar (Stanton 1991). Official figures show that seventeen per cent of the inmates in Spanish prisons are foreigners, while the latter make up only two per cent of the Spanish population. About twenty per cent are Moroccans, almost all convicted for drug traffic (*El País* 16 March 1992: 16).

25. Douglass (1992: 67) argues that "'Spain' and 'Europe' are symbols in a dialogue about world view and the quality of life. They are, in effect, moral categories. One is the opposite of the other." She focuses on the role of the Spanish bullfight in this dialogue and concludes that while for many Spaniards the bulls are inherently unEuropean, for a minority they add an extra quality to Spanish Europeaness. A booklet (*El Libro de España*) written by a sociologist as a gift to the official guests of the Spanish pavilion at the World Exhibition, concludes that Spain is now as modern as the other Western European countries. Yet, according to this scholar, Spain is also different because of another rhythm of day and night, intense sociability, widespread smoking, the strong influence of Catholicism, and the enormous popularity of games of chance. The author argues that Spain is a modern country where traditions are still important.

26. I am particularly grateful to Rachid Ahmed Raha for discussing this point with me.

References

Actis, W. et al. 1991. *La inmigración magrebi en España*. Madrid: Cáritas.

Baldwin-Edwards, M. and M.A. Schain (eds.). 1994. Special issue on the politics of immigration in western Europe, *West European Politics* 17.

Braudel, F. 1972. *The Mediterranean and the Mediterranean world in the age of Philip II* (vol. I). New York: Harper & Row.

Carabaza, E. and de Santos, M. 1992. *Melilla and Ceuta. Las ultimas colonias*. Madrid: Talasa.

Chierici-Cassagnol, R.M. 1991. *Demele, 'making it'. Migration and adaptation among Haitian boat people in the United States*. New York: AMS Press.

Conover, T. 1987. *Coyotes. A journey through the secret world of America's illegal aliens*. New York: Vintage Books.

Douglass, C.B. 1992. 'Europe', 'Spain', and the bulls. *Journal of Mediterranean Studies* 2: 67-76.

Driessen, H. 1992. *On the Spanish-Moroccan frontier. A study in ritual, power and ethnicity*. Oxford/New York: Berg Publishers/St. Martin's Press.

Escobar Hernandez, C. 1992. Asylum and refugee status in Spain. *International Journal of Refugee Law* 4: 57-71.

Evers, H. D. 1991. Shadow economy, subsistence production and informal sector: Economic activity outside of market and state. *Prisma* 51: 34-46.

Evers Rosander, E. 1991. *Women in a borderland. Managing ethnic identity where Morocco meets Spain*. Stockholm: Stockholm Studies in Social Anthropology.

Fernández Mota, M. 1990. *Nuestra comarca. Guía escolar del Campo de Gibraltar*. Algeciras: Ediciones Bahía.

Fox, R. 1991. *The inner sea*. London: Sinclair-Stevenson.

Franklin, D. 1992. Spain: Mitteleuropa on the Med. *The Economist* 25 April: 5-24.

Gold, S.J. 1992. *Refugee communities. A comparative field study*. London: Sage.

Goytisolo, J. 1992. Constructing Europe's new wall. From Berlin to the Strait". *Middle East Report* 22: 17-20.

Hailbronner, K. 1990. The right to asylum and the future of asylum procedures in the European Community. *International Journal of Refugee Law* 2: 341-361.

Harrell-Bond, B.E. and Voutira, E. 1992. Anthropology and the study of refugees. *Anthropology Today* 8: 6-11.

Hart, D.M. 1976. *The aith waryaghar of the Moroccan rif. An ethnography and history*. New York/Tucson: Wenner-Gren/The University of Arizona Press.

Hirschon, R. 1989. *Heirs of the Greek catastrophe. The social life of Asia Minor refugees in Paraeus*. Oxford: Clarendon Press.

Kopytoff, I. (ed.). 1987. *The African frontier. The reproduction of traditional African societies.* Bloomington: Indiana University Press.

Krupat, A. 1992. *Ethnocriticism. Ethnography, history, literature.* Berkeley: University of California Press.

Lamphere, L. (ed.). 1992. *Structuring diversity: Ethnographic perspectives on the new immigration.* Chicago: Chicago University Press.

Leach, E. 1976. *Culture and communication. The logic by which symbols are connected.* Cambridge: Cambridge University Press.

Loizos, P. 1981. *The heart grown bitter. A chronicle of Cypriot war refugees.* Cambridge: Cambridge University Press.

Lucas, J. de. 1992. *Europa: Convivir con la diferencia? Racismo, nacionalismo y derechos de las minorías.* Madrid: Tecnos.

Munson, H. Jr. 1984. *The house of Si Abd Allah: The oral history of a Moroccan family.* New Haven: Yale University Press.

Nielsen, J. 1992. *Muslims in western Europe.* Edinburgh: Edinburgh University Press.

Nyerges, A .E. 1992. The ecology of wealth-in-people: Agriculture, settlement, and society on the perpetual Frontier. *American Anthropologist* 94: 860-81.

Pino, del D. 1990. *Marruecos entre la tradición y el modernismo.* Granada: Universidad de Granada.

Robin, N. 1992. L'espace migratoire de l'Afrique de l'ouest. *Hommes et Migrations* 1160: 6-15.

Stanton, G. 1991. 'Guests in the dock'. Moroccan workers on trial in the colony of Gibraltar. *Critique of Anthropology* 11: 361-79.

Zaim, F. 1990. *Le Maroc et son espace méditerranéen. Histoire économique et sociale.* Rabat: Confluences.

10 Sovereignty, identity and borders: Political anthropology and European integration

Thomas M. Wilson

The Single European Market was intended to be a transformative step towards "European," i.e., European Community (EC), now European Union (EU), economic and political integration. The completion of the EU's internal market was supposed to create a Europe without frontiers (European Communities - Commission 1987), in which international borders, which presented barriers to the movement of people, goods and capital, would become anachronistic. This EU road to socio-economic harmony has been diverted through Maastricht on the way to the Intergovernmental Conference of 1996, however, while the proposed therapeutic effects of supranationally-directed economics diminish in scale before the monstrous aspects of ethno-nationalist war in the Balkans. Nonetheless, if the wider European economic integration is to succeed, and if true political unity in the nominal European Union (EU) is to be achieved, they must do so in the everyday lives of the citizens of the fifteen EU states. "1992" — the date which came to symbolise the completion of the internal market — is fast receding in the public consciousness, but it stands as the most recent attempt in the European Communities to achieve greater economic integration, and, by extension, greater social, cultural, and political cohesion. As such, the processes of completing the internal market, still far from over in 1995, have had a number of direct and indirect effects on local, national, and transnational perspectives on the future of the sovereignty of the nation and the state in an expanding EU, and on definitions of sovereignty and social and political identities in this "new Europe".

This chapter examines some perspectives in the growing anthropological interest in European international (i.e., interstate) borderlands and peoples in order to shed some light on ways in which anthropological research and writing can enhance wider social science concerns with identities, sovereignty and European integration. Political anthropology is increasingly concerned

199

with local and national identity formation which, in European studies, has meant the exploration by anthropologists of a variety of the dialectical relations between "top-down" and "bottom-up" cultural constructions of nation, state and supra-national entities. As a result, the growing anthropology of the EU is interested in the overall role of culture, i.e., configurations of symbols and action in society, in wider relations of political and economic institutions and policy. Borderlands are seen by anthropologists as areas of cultural contest and integration, in which national identity and citizenship are often not the same thing, and where states and many of their people dispute widely held beliefs about state sovereignty through symbolic and other means.

Political anthropology, nation and state

The social and cultural anthropology of the nation and the state in Europe has a long and uneven record. From the beginning of political anthropology in North America and Europe, there has been an important and deep interest in the origins and the institutions of the state, as both an evolutionary achievement and in terms of the impact of the people and policies of the so-called "nation-state" on the localities and communities which have been the research focus of anthropologists world-wide. Some anthropologists date the start of classical political anthropology to the studies done of centralised and acephalous societies in Africa before the Second World War (many of which were published in Fortes and Evans-Pritchard 1940), but any attempt to define the study of politics in anthropology by setting it off as independent from the mainstream historical interests of anthropology does injustice to its intellectual development (for the best overview of the history of the many types of anthropological studies and ideas of politics, see Vincent 1990).

Suffice to say that modern political anthropology has long been concerned with the relations between localities and other levels of sociocultural integration. Much of this interest was a product of anthropologists' experiences of rapid social change in World War II and the consequent break-up of the empires. Such processes of international violence and political disintegration have continued to define the parameters of the anthropology of politics, especially in Europe. By the 1960s, many influential anthropologists were calling for the study of the many formal and informal ways in which communities at the village and neighbourhood levels are tied to the organs and representatives of political formations of much greater size and power. These new political anthropologists demanded that the state and its actions be the focus of anthropological research, and that the analysis of the structure and function of the state at local levels should be complemented by the study of political process between localities and their wider regions and states. In terms of the social anthropology of Europe, this new attention to the ebb and flow of political relationships beyond the local community was meant to put an end to the "tribalization" of European communities (Boissevain 1975; see also Wolf 1966).

Such calls for the reordering of the political anthropological agenda in Europe and elsewhere notwithstanding, most anthropologists of Europe continued to study rural villages and urban communities in ways which ignored the people and institutions that represented the state at local levels, or, alternatively, they rather simply studied these state agents and institutions at local levels, often viewing the state as an external entity which existed to have a variety of effects on local life. As a result, few anthropological studies of politics in Europe have had an impact on scholarly debate outside of the discipline. This is not to say that there is little of value for sociologists and political scientists, among others, in macro-level analyses of European society and culture done by anthropologists (in such notable works as Wolf 1982) or in the more traditional approach to politics as represented in local community studies (for example, see Blok 1974; Kertzer 1990), in regional studies (Schneider and Schneider 1976; Schneider et al. 1972), at national frontiers (Cole and Wolf 1974), or in comparative studies of political rituals (Kertzer 1988) and political symbols (Kubik 1994). But most studies of politics in anthropology address the theories, models, hypotheses, and disciplinary contexts of the field itself, and are written for audiences of anthropologists, in ways which often make anthropology inaccessible to outsiders, and as impenetrable as any of the other social sciences is to outsiders. This is an unfortunate situation, precisely because few ethnographic studies of modern Europe can successfully isolate themselves from the national and state politics which are integral to the everyday lives of the people of whatever community, however "community" is defined, who are the focus of the anthropologist's gaze. As Sydel Silverman has pointed out (1979: 414), in reference to the anthropological uses of history in European research, a caution which I suggest is just as accurate for the anthropology of politics in Europe:

Although anthropology has a distinctive approach, the work of disciplines that border on it cannot be set aside in advance on the grounds that they deal with different aspects of reality. Nor can matters be settled by defining other fields in such a way as to exclude the anthropologist's interest.

The political anthropology of the nation and the state in Europe is relatively unknown outside of anthropology itself because of the actions of anthropologists, but these actions find parallels in the other social sciences, where scholars define their fields in ways which exclude their interest in social anthropology.

As a result of the various ways in which anthropologists have approached political studies in Europe, there have been a number of notable omissions in the political anthropological literature. Foremost among them have been anthropological studies of state and popular sovereignty, and studies of

201

citizenship and its relation to a variety of social and political identities. The reasons for the absence of citizenship and sovereignty studies in anthropology are relatively simple to deduce. Because the "nation" is too large a group to study through participant observation, its many ideologies and identities at national or state levels have been very difficult to discern at local levels, especially when local identities and actions seem to dominate anthropological hypotheses. Thus, the professional culture of anthropology has tended to favour the replication of locality studies and the testing of theories which make local communities microcosms of their associated "cultures". As a result of this tacit assumption of the representativeness of localities, anthropologists have been much more comfortable constructing theories about culture than they have been discussing political movements, ideologies and identities at levels of the nation and the state. The fact that "culture" is no less slippery a concept to anthropologists than the "nation" is to political scientists is seemingly lost on most scholars in the relevant field (as discussed in two very different but parallel ways by Clifford 1988 and Connor 1978).

Simply put, anthropologists will wax poetic about culture but often avoid the mildest musing about the nation and nationalism, or they refer to "national culture" when discussing ways in which local social and cultural systems fit into wider levels of integration beyond the locality. Reference to national culture often masks an uncritical view of the nation, and suggests little critical investigation into the definitions of the nation, and into ways in which local communities fit into the often competing matrices of nations and states (uncritical perspectives on the nation and the state such as these in social anthropology make the creation of an anthropology of the European Union very difficult, a point to which I shall return below). In fact, in many anthropological perspectives on national culture, the nation is seen to be coterminous with the state, with national culture ending at the limits of state sovereignty.

Broad stroke assessments such as the one I have just proposed run the risk of excluding the many exceptions to the rule. For example, Handler (1988), Kapferer (1988), Spencer (1990), and Verdery (1991) have brilliantly moved from the local to the national, to analyse national and other political cultures in ways which clearly address nations as political and cultural entities, which have particular relationships with the state in which they reside and which they help to define. Geertz (1963, 1973) and Wolf (1982) have in very different ways examined the origin and development of new and old national cultures in Europe and in the post-imperial world. But the majority of anthropologists writing on national cultures has tended to avoid the examination of ways in which nations and states define their own political identities and structures, from the top down so to speak, in the terms understandable and accessible to other social scientists. Thus citizenship and sovereignty were long absent from the anthropological lexicon.

Although this situation is changing, it does so only slowly. This is in part a reflection of wider changes in the theoretical context of social science in general, and of social and cultural anthropology in particular. In recent years, with some important exceptions, most anthropological studies of "nations" have been part of a general disciplinarian turn to the study of the conditions of post-modernity. In other words, anthropologists have begun to use post-modern perspectives to revise their perceptions of the peoples of the world, in order to take into account the perceived momentous impact of international capital, transnational societies, and global culture. Although nominally about power, postmodern anthropology has made the anthropological study of states and the territorialization of political power extremely difficult and rare, principally because of its hegemonic notion that there is no longer a fixed relationship between space, place, time, and culture (for a provocative analysis of the politics of difference that results from this perspective, see Gupta and Ferguson 1992). In the new social science of metaphorical borders and boundaries, in which all people are seen to be cultural minorities negotiating their role in social and political systems seemingly adrift in a cultural hyperspace, a shifting but seemingly permanent interstitiality, no national culture is bounded in the traditional sense of being coterminous with the state. Much of this perspective is not new. It is one of the arguments of this chapter, and the book on the whole, that culture has never been limited by the borders of nation and state, and that the understanding of culture and power at and across international frontiers will enhance our vision of sovereignty and the state. Nevertheless, postmodern perspectives on transnational populations can do much to inform our notions of the everyday lives of the powerful and powerless at borders as well as in metropolitan centres.

Although the changes in theoretical and methodological direction which are characteristic of this "new ethnography" are widespread and immensely popular in anthropology, on both sides of the Atlantic, they have not completely excluded other anthropologies of politics, including those which are very much embedded in place and time. Overall, in fact, the modernist and post-modernist perspectives in political anthropology share a concern with culture and power, although they may not share definitions of either or of ways one might best be able to understand them (for an excellent review of the present state of the anthropology of power, see Gledhill 1994). Regardless of theoretical persuasion in anthropology, the importance of studying the relationship between culture and power is especially apparent in the investigation of national and other cultural identities at international borders.

Anthropology and borders in the European Union

As predicted a decade ago, the EU has shifted the problems of boundaries and borders to another level or levels (Coakley 1982:47). The internal and external forces of greater EU integration — either in "widening" or "deepening" the EU (Bull 1993) — are having an impact on a wide range of aspects of the EU as a social system. Frontiers have been changed but not removed in the EU's drive to a common market, and the cultural identities of the people of the borderlands reflect these changes, but only in part (Wilson 1993b). The degree to which border cultures adapt to the EU, including the degree to which traditions and customs survive, albeit in modified form, remains an exciting and daunting problematic for social scientists. Throughout this New Europe, border cultures continue to be important forces in the perceptions, if not the shaping, of regional and national identities. Some scholars beyond anthropology have begun to view national borders not only in terms of their roles as the political symbols of state and nation, or as the locales of international disputes, but as zones of border cultures which have been "motive forces" in the construction and definition of their associated nations and states (see, e.g., Sahlins 1989: 3,8). Many people in and outside of the academy, including decision-makers of the public and private sectors, cannot seem to keep up with the pace of change, which is gripping the EU from its borderlands to its boardrooms. In fact, the EU has gained such momentum in its citizens' lives over the last decade that "reality is outpacing theory" (Jones and Platt 1992: 2).

An anthropology of border lives and border cultures can inform debates about local and national definitions of cultural membership and identity. Ethnographic analyses of the many cultural inventions which are constructing the EU in its villages, workplaces, and neighbourhoods, as well as the anthropological investigation of the dialectics between localities and nation-states, may provide needed scholarly correctives to the wide perspective, macro-level social science that is a by-product of EU-building. Past attempts in political science and sociology to avoid defining international borders beyond the strictest spatial and legal terms have failed because of their poor sense of the complexities of local and national culture(s) (see, e.g., Tägil 1982: 18-19).

This is especially evident in the overall investigation of cultural meaning and perception at and across borders. Anthropology, perhaps more than any other social science, concentrates on the symbolic construction of social life. Although cultural boundaries exist for all social groups, the anthropological attention to the meanings people ascribe to national cultures have particular salience at international frontiers and borders, in areas where the state has invested a great deal in order to impose its definitions of boundary. The anthropological investigation of culture at international borders highlights many ways in which state-building and nation-building are two very different processes, in which the state's projection of its "own" national culture may be at odds with the lived experiences of a variety of its populations. In other words, anthropologists consider trans-frontier "cultural systems" to be as important and vital as trans-frontier political systems. Some social scientists, in recognising the convergence in Europe in the social, economic, and political forms of cross-border culture, are perhaps too quick to dismiss or overlook cultural divergence. Take, for example, this view:

> The legacy of the past still gives a distinctive appearance to most countries but there is increasing homogenisation of the appearance of urban, industrial and commercial developments as a result of technical and economic changes. The international boundary no longer constitutes a sharp break in the cultural landscape. This is a reflection of the economic and social realities of contemporary Europe (Anderson 1982:14).

It would be foolish to disagree totally with this observation, but it would be just as foolhardy to ignore or minimise the sharp breaks which persist in a cultural landscape which is unseen and unknown to outsiders. Although the forms of cross-border cultures are converging, to include many of the signs and symbols, such as in dress, language, transportation and communication, which once marked difference, the meanings local groups attach to those forms may not. In fact, they may symbolise cultural contestations. "This is because, whilst the *form* of symbols may be common to those who bear the same culture, the *meanings* of the symbols, their contexts, may differ" (Cohen 1987:13, emphasis in original).

For example, at the Irish border a Europe without frontiers is not a Europe without cultural and national barriers to integration, many of which begin and end at international borders (Wilson 1993b). EU drives towards a brave new world of free market capitalism may bypass groups of people, regions, or entire nations, who may also experience greater economic integration as the exaggeration of cultural difference, or the accentuation of nationalism. Because EU-building is a process of the redistribution of wealth, in which the opportunities to accumulate wealth, power and prestige will change for many groups of people throughout the fifteen member states, it is certain that there will be economic and political "winners" and "losers", just as there has been since the formation of a Common Market. Many of these people identify the EU as the source of their good fortune or their decline. At the Irish border, in which extremely strongly felt and expressed national identities are perceived by locals to be unchanged by any construction of European identity, the EU is seen largely in economic terms. This is not surprising, given the long and violent history of Irish and British nationalism in the region, and because the British state in Northern Ireland has consistently portrayed the EU as principally an economic market. The result is a borderlands where, partly as a result of EU initiatives to provide much-needed injections of capital, the EU is judged almost entirely in terms of its economic impact. In this region, at least, the projection by British elites of the meaning of EU integration has predominated over the social and political interpretations of the same process put forward by EU elites.

This contest between elites reinforces one of the points of this chapter and volume, that international borders are cultural battlegrounds between and among states and the EU over the limits to power and sovereignty. The economics of integration result in the reconfiguration of nation-state politics, and the EU is now seen by interested parties in the member states to be an actor in this. But even when the EU's role in economic restructuring is not evident, the wider processes of integration remain factors in the maintenance or decline of state power. The long-predicted break-up of Britain (see Nairn 1977, for the clearest warning of this) may be the unintended result of over a decade of Tory economics, which have been accelerated by the technocratic legislation of the liberal democratic EU (see, e.g., the review of resurgent Scottish nationalism in McCrone 1991). Anthropological studies of border populations — both within Europe and elsewhere — should encourage political debates over what has increasingly become an extremely problematic area for any new Europe: the construction of cultural and national identities (see Donnan and Wilson 1994b, which includes a number of anthropological case studies of border cultures in Europe, Asia and Africa).

The EU, i.e., its leaders, institutions, member state governments and administrators, and many of its private economic sectors, have been forced by events in the former Yugoslavia and Soviet Union, in Northern Ireland and in the Basque lands to face their political "identity gap." For too long the cultural and political construction of self, localities, regions, and "minority" nations, have been ignored or tolerated by EU elites, in an effort to homogenise European "national" (i.e., nation-state) cultures through the wonders of free market forces, which are presumed by architects of policy to be simultaneously levelling and uplifting.

On the surface this process parallels that of "nation-building" in each of the states, in which the cultures (presumed to be) internal to the state are to be homogenised into a national culture. Here too borderlands have often proved to be difficult areas for the state to achieve this, precisely because the cultural landscapes of border zones transcend the borderline. But the congruity of the twin processes of cultural homogenisation in EU- and nation-building is a superficial one because the state has invested itself in strengthening the definition of the national "we" versus "them". Thus, while EU elites attempt to integrate and homogenise national cultures, the borders of states still stand as simultaneous markers of homogeneity and heterogeneity. Perhaps the external borders of the EU function in this way too.

The result of this dual process of homogenisation, as the EU and its member states are all too aware, yet practically dare not mention for fear of increasing national and racial violence within their borders, is the realisation that the differences far outmatch the similarities within the social system that is the EU. The perceived inequities and grievances of EU minorities (i.e., races, classes, women, workers, interest groups, and nations striving for self-determination, among others) are powerful forces that much of the econocentric legislators of the EU are not addressing. For example, many people in the British Isles question the UK's opting out of the Social Charter. Some suggest that this government policy is evidence of the power of elitism, conservatism, and capitalism at large in the New Europe. Debates currently rage in Westminster on the question of a European single currency, which may, in fact, jeopardise the UK's role in the post-Maastricht EU. If the Tory government is swayed by its party's Eurosceptics, many people of the left, both in and outside of Britain, will see anti-integration Conservative policy as a victory for the economic and political right. The new right of Europe is clearly a product of forces that have also given rise to the EU's New Europe. Ironically, much of the support the new right movements of Germany and France enjoy at the grassroots level may result from fear of what the EU is doing in the everyday lives of its people.

Identity and sovereignty

The anthropological study of local communities in Europe is primarily one of everyday life and the values and behaviours which constitute local culture and society. Anthropological perspectives on local life do not end at the boundaries of villages and neighbourhoods, however. As I suggested above, anthropological studies of localities are often implicitly about wider and more inclusive levels of sociocultural integration, from the region to the world-system. Some anthropological studies explicitly link the local to the national and the international. All anthropological perspectives share a common concern with culture, comparison and the methods, usually but often mistakenly lumped together under the rubric of "participant observation", of long-term field research among small communities of people. The anthropological gaze often picks out aspects of local life which other social sciences miss, in part because anthropologists are looking at and for different things. As a result, anthropologists and other ethnographers can provide a number of correctives to the research conducted by other social scientists, who use methods designed to elicit wider comparative data. Such insights into local life can be extremely helpful to scholars, policy makers and other societal leaders who seek to construct complete pictures of the impact of policy at local levels, in the everyday lives of their fellow citizens.

Although a review of the many facets to the anthropology of the EU is beyond the scope of this chapter, a principal theme which has emerged in anthropological studies of European integration has been that of identity formation and its relationship to political and social action (for wider reviews of the anthropology of the EU, see Wilson 1993a, 1995). Anthropological interest in cultural identities is not surprising, but the ways in which they are being linked to wider political and social phenomena in Europe may help to construct more complete pictures of the sociological impact of integration at local levels in the EU, and, in return, help to provide a portrait of policy successes and failures. Paralleling this concentration on identities (i.e., national, class, gender, regional, religious, and local identities, among others) has been an increasing anthropological interest in the frontiers of polity and identity at international borders in Europe. Much of the analysis of cultural identities at borders has been in terms of symbolic constructions of group and individual boundary maintenance, following in the paths so well established by Barth and Anthony Cohen. Missing in these recent accounts of borderlands cultures has been the role of sovereignty in national identity. I agree with Ulf Hedetoft's assessment of sovereignty in Europe as being both a political ideal and reality, as well as a cultural self image (1994: 17):

> in theory, as well as in the popular mind, sovereignty is an unquestioned axiom, belonging equally to the world of politics and to the world of culture and identity. In fact, sovereignty is a central building block in the wall of national identity. It links people and state within a well-defined authority space, where [people] . . . refuse to recognise any important distinction between sovereignty as an attribute of the state and as their own cultural property.

Constructions of identity such as these clearly have a great deal to do with the popular association of nation with state, in which the boundaries around the cultural or ethnic community of the nation are coterminous with their self-governed state. Regardless of the many scholarly debates about the origin, development, definition, and future of both the nation and the nation-state (debates to which this volume seeks to contribute), most of the people of Europe are not as critical. Whether one is in Belfast or in Bucharest, threats to the state are perceived by many to be threats to their way of life and their sense of community. In this perspective, a diminution of the sovereignty of the state and its government is a loss of popular sovereignty, and a threat to citizens' national identity. Although the connections between sovereignty, identity, nation and state may be clearest when the people of the state or their territory are physically threatened by an external aggressor, their essential relationship in the eyes of the people may be just as strong when their government, in their name and at their behest, rclinquish or share aspects of their sovereignty in agreement with other peoples, nations and states. This is the case in the EU, where many groups of people among the member nations perceive the EU as a political organisation which diminishes national state sovereignty, and who resist the EU's efforts at the creation of a "European identity" as directly at odds with their own, superordinate national identities.

Nowhere are the debates about the maintenance of national sovereignty and identity more salient in the EU than at international borders. At the Irish border, i.e., that land border between the Republic of Ireland and Northern Ireland, part of the United Kingdom, national identities predominate, even to the extent that European identity is often scoffed at by some as little more than a role to be played in order to get a grant from the EU. This is not to say that national identities are homogeneous at this border, or that the international borderline divides nations. Irish nationalists, especially those who want a united Ireland in which Northern Ireland and the Republic would be joined in one state, are found on both sides of the border. In fact, the majority of people who live at the Northern Ireland side of the border are nationalists. Their nominal adversaries, those who wish to remain loyal to the British crown and way of life and those who want to maintain Northern Ireland's political union with the British state, see their national identity as British. The numbers of loyalists and unionists who live in the border areas of Northern Ireland are in decline. Part of this demographic change is due to the migration of these people away from areas with majority nationalist populations. Some of these loyalists see themselves to be victims of "ethnic cleansing" (at least they have claimed this since the term became popular in press reports of the Balkans). Both nationalists and loyalists have one thing in common, the belief in the primacy of their own distinct national identities. Many people have expressed to me in interviews, in a variety of ways, that they may be European by the accidents of history and geography, but they are Irish or British by race, spirit, inclination and choice.

Such strongly held views, the product of hundreds of years of nationalist and sectarian strife, are complicated by the legislation and the projected images of an EU-Europe. Although nationalists and loyalists on the Northern side of the Irish border subscribe to the view that their national identities are their most important political and cultural ones, things are not so clear on the southern side, where the vast majority of people, in what is one of the most homogeneous states in Europe, may be deemed to be nationalist. But their nationalism is not the same thing as their fellow Irish nationalists across the border, due to historical and regional divergence. At both the border and in the Ireland's cities people recognise and remark upon the curious development that southern Irishmen, and the Republic in general, are clearly more "European" than those in Northern Ireland. By this, I infer people to mean that the Republic and its people are more committed members of the EU. At a conference of Irish and British community leaders and scholars held in Belfast to discuss Irish, British and European identities a few years ago, no one in a seminar of fifty people disputed this notion. Nevertheless, although people in the Republic may see themselves as more European than many of their Irish and British neighbours, this does not necessarily weaken their perspective that they share national culture with Irish nationalists in Northern Ireland. In this respect, the cultural landscape transcends the political border, but does so in a way that allows some Irish nationalists to seek to redefine those borders, in a sense to put up even stronger national barriers around their own "reunited" state.

Overall the EU has had a very mixed impact on local and provincial politics at the border, especially in Northern Ireland. In everyday politics at the county council or local district council levels (i.e., those of the Republic and Northern Ireland respectively) the EU seems to be having little effect. This is largely due to the ethnonationalist politics of border life, which clearly take precedence over any other type of identity politics. The seeming lack of an EU dimension to border political life is also a result of the relatively negligible effect which EU programmes have had on patronage and clientelist local politics (a long-standing feature of the politics of the Republic in particular). In Northern Ireland, in fact, the money which flows directly from Brussels pales in comparison to the subvention which every aspect of public life receives from London, which has been sustaining the province through twenty-five years of war. This is not to say that the EU has been uninfluential in Northern Irish life, but a close reading of the political symbolism which marks both sides of the Irish border gives credence to the argument that the EU has had little effect on borderlands' political cultures (for a review of some of these political symbols at the Irish border, see Wilson 1994). However, many symbols and signs are deceptive, and often are not as clear as one might expect because they are embedded in other sociocultural formations. For example, the use of the EU's symbols (such as the "European" flag and the prefix "Euro") in local consumer advertising and marketing may not be perceived by entrepreneur or consumer to be evidence of transformations in the context of political life, but they may indeed be just that. This depends, of course, on the resonance such symbols have in other areas of local life over time, which, like much that is suggested in this chapter, must become a matter for empirical research if the EU is to understand what it *means* to its people. Returning to the point made above, the form of the nationalist symbols involving flags, colours, road signs, graffiti, and parades may not have changed much in the last generation, but their content has been evolving along with the new European dimensions to Irish and Northern Irish politics. The extent to which these symbols take on a European content, or give birth to new symbols of political action, remains to be seen.

However, the fact that the manifestations of EU-inspired political change at the Irish border are not self-evident does not mean that they are not occurring or transformative, or that some people do not recognise the EU's political impact. Ask any local politician on either side of the border about the EU and a dramatic reply will be forthcoming, that may be decidedly positive or negative, but is rarely noncommittal. These politicians recognise the shift in budgetary powers away from their capitals to Europe (this is especially evident, in my experience, among local politicians in the Irish Republic), a process that reflects the mutual dependencies of economics and politics that have changed the parameters of local government and politics. Thus, although the political transformations that are due to EU policies are as yet relatively unclear to most residents of the Irish borderlands, the EU is playing an increasingly important role in regional and national political culture. For example, over the last decade many nationalists, especially among the leadership of the Social Democratic and Labour Party, have put forward plans for the future of Northern Ireland which clearly have European dimensions. Such plans, however, have not met with the approval of many other nationalists or of unionists. Nonetheless, the role of Northern Ireland as a region in Europe has increasingly become a topic of discussion among Irish elites, giving credence to the idea that the EU has impinged upon the consciousness of many Irish and British people by providing alternative models of regional and state relations. A number of Northern Irish people, like some Scots, Welsh and northern English, recognise that the region can establish and sustain direct relations with other regions and states through the organs of the EU, thereby bypassing the institutions of the British state. Such deliberate moves have implications for the sovereignty of the state, and may very well test the fortitude of the United Kingdom.

Attempts to redefine regionalist politics within the state through the use of institutions and movements which are based in Europe, and which arise out of the new dialectics of European integration, raise the question of the extent to which EU-building is splintering the identification of the citizen with the state. If in the past state-building has succeeded in creating a fusion of national identity with citizenship and sovereignty, then any political system which claims the right to offer alternative citizenship thereby diminishes the sovereignty of the state and dilutes that aspect of national identity. In sum, the EU makes alternatives to the nation-state more plausible, viable and attainable. The EU also provides the basis for the revitalisation and transformation of identities beyond the national. The tension between the state and the EU can be found in the new identity politics throughout the member states, and much of this tension is due to the inability of both the state and the EU to control the meanings which people attach to the symbols and actions of both. As I have argued above, it is perhaps in this area of symbols, culture and identity that anthropology has the most to offer the social science of the new Europe.

The political anthropology of European communities chronicles peoples' perceptions of the policies, policy-makers, and institutions which they see as most important in the structuring of their lives. Statistical reports like the *Eurobarometer* are incomplete pictures of the ways in which Europe is perceived and culturally constructed in the lives of Europeans. EU and other leaders are often quoted as wanting to close the "democratic deficit" which apparently exists at European levels, but despite their efforts they are often surprised by the reactions of voters and the actions of other social and political movements, as, for instance, in the recent Danish and Norwegian votes (even if these votes may not have surprised some local, regional and national elites in Scandinavia).

Although many regions and social movements attempt to use the state and the EU against each other, it is also clear that throughout the EU, in the local tally sheet of costs and benefits, the EU is becoming associated, at a political, governmental, and administrative level, with the strengths and weaknesses of national governments. The EU is inheriting political traditions, in each member state, that are not of its making or choosing. Among these are citizens' dependence on the welfare state. As states today fail to provide for all of their citizens' welfare, law-makers increasingly blame the EU for its legislative constraints and insensitivity. In this way they attempt to avoid responsibility for unemployment, industrial and agricultural development, crime, terrorism, drugs, and racism. At the same time, some politicians claim credit when the EU does something perceived to be "right" in their regions or nations, e.g., when structural funds pay for transportation and communication improvements.

Although the EU has had, and will increasingly have, a role to play in the development of EU-wide social and economic policies, and is thus rightly seen to be a new and powerful actor in national politics, the meanings which people attach to its policies in each of the member states are sure to be problematical for scholar, policy maker and citizen. Many of the meanings the EU will have in everyday life will be filtered through state interpretations of EU policy. Some of these state messages portray the EU as a threat to local and national. economics. Debates in Britain over the single currency and the future of the Bank of England after monetary union are about economic and political sovereignty as well as the British way of life. In part as a result of state-influenced media images of "Europe", people throughout the EU are using the ballot box, community and occupational organisations, political parties, and the media to show their opposition to EU institutions and integration. Others, like French and Irish farmers, have also protested in less pacific ways.

Rising unemployment is the issue of primary importance to the people who perceive the EU to be the supranational political system that is increasingly pre-eminent over their national governments. After the border region of Lille voted against France's ratification of the Maastricht treaty, one journalist concluded that the region had "sent an unequivocal message that work comes before European dreams" (Cohen 1993: 3). Unemployment has all but devastated the Lille region, where the decline of the steel industry is locally seen to be partly a result of European integration. Industrial zones like Lille, which formerly enjoyed national subsidisation and protection, are to be pressured even more in the run-up to economic and political integration that is promised in the Maastricht treaty. Lille, like many other border regions of the EU, was expected to profit from the 1992 project, but a world recession and increased free market competition have led to the region's rising unemployment, which recently topped 13% (Cohen 1993: 3). Lille sees itself as a loser in the competition for scarce resources that results from the economic side of European integration. The major towns of the Irish border region have unemployment rates which are double that of Lille, and nothing in the near future on the regional, national, and international scene is likely to alleviate the social problems associated with so many unemployed. Although it may be wrong to blame the EU for economic woes in an underdeveloped and peripheral region of the UK and Ireland, many people of the region wonder about the EU's role in their national and local economic problems.

Conclusion

This chapter is a call for the EU, and the scholars of the EU, to become more involved in both the frontier regions and the borderlands of all of the EU's peripheral regions, because it is there, among many key areas of the EU (such as in the capital cities of the member states and the conference rooms of the Eurocracy), that the battle for the hearts and minds of "the Europeans" must be won if the EU as a sociocultural system is to develop in support of further political and economic union. As one scholar pointed out a decade ago, the problems of internal and external frontier regions are too often seen by the EU to be economic problems that will be "solved with the advent of the improved levels of integration" (Strassoldo 1982: 133). As he rightly indicated, even the successes of EU integration may lead to other problems, perhaps even intensifying some typical frontier problems at the borders with non-EU states (Strassoldo 1982: 133). The decision makers in the 1992 and post-Maastricht processes may be repeating these errors of economic bias. The polysemic constructions of the border cultural landscapes in the New Europe of the EU will remain problematical — for "us" and "them," however defined — for as long as any construction of "nation," "ethnicity," and "region" have salience in modern political discourse. This is to say, of course, for a very long time into the foreseeable future.

The new Europe of the EU can be seen as a "Europe of the Borders", since the new definitions of border in a "Europe without frontiers" make the very notion of borders just as fluid, and expansive, as a "Europe of the Regions." If, as is suggested in the introduction to this volume, we perceive borders to be the specific geopolitical state boundaries, the borderlines, and frontiers are overlapping zones of an often contested cultural landscape, then perhaps EU-building results in a Europe of more frontiers, not fewer. Europe is currently experiencing social transformations that threaten a wide range of nationalisms and internationalisms. There is little to suggest that such processes will not continue:

> There will be more borders in this future world, not fewer -- more kinds of division, a cacophony of contrasts and conflicts previously repressed and distorted. There are depths to this sea-change that theory will take a long time to get to grips with (Nairn 1992: 30).

This chapter portrays some of the ways that local people are being caught up in an EU "sea-change," which is reconstructing many aspects of both Europe and locality throughout the EU. As such, it seeks to add to a growing anthropological interest in issues of cultural and national identity at international borders throughout Europe (see, for example, Driessen 1992; Donnan and Wilson 1994a), which is based on long-standing anthropological concerns with the cultural construction and maintenance of ethnic and community boundaries (as inspired by the work of such scholars as Barth 1969; Cohen 1982; 1986) and the political economy of border communities (see, for example, Cole and Wolf 1974; Douglass 1977). The biggest problem facing anthropologists who wish to study the EU is to recognise and chronicle the dialectics between the social and political levels of locality, region, state and supranation. This is especially problematic when elites at all of these levels persist in portraying the EU as principally an organisation of economic integration.

That the EU is much more than this should be clear to all. As former EU Commission president Jacques Delors said, "it is hard to love the single market." The EU interprets him to mean "that if the goal was eminently desirable the means of getting there were decidedly unglamorous" (European Communities-Commission 1992a: 15). The EU is faced with the policy objective of making people more aware of both its achievements and their possible roles in the new society being created, without turning these people into opponents. For some, this objective will not be attained. The question remains whether a minority or a majority of people, at any or all levels of sociocultural life in the EU, will resist this "Europeanising process." It may be safe to say that resistance to the EU juggernaut will be easily overcome, but my research at the border and elsewhere in Ireland suggests that this may be a cavalier assumption, dangerous in any political system. The images and rhetoric of "ethnic cleansing" have been commonplace in Northern Ireland; many local people recall with not a little irony that the Bosnians and the Serbs "got along fine" with each other for years. The message for the architects of either a wider or a deeper EU is clear: ignore national identities at your own risk.

The EU has put forward a number of metaphors about itself in its efforts to make integration understandable and acceptable to the new "citizens" of Europe. Many of these "official" metaphors privilege the actions of building and construction. In one official publication dealing with economic aspects of the New Europe the single market was portrayed as a motorway, begun in 1985 and due to open in 1993 (European Communities-Commission 1992a: 21), while in another guide the EU presents itself as a house that Europeans are building, albeit only the basement and ground floors are completed (European Communities-Commission 1992b:7). These metaphors may have unpredictable meanings among EU citizens who can no longer find employment in the transportation and construction industries. And if the people of the EU are questioning the costs of Europe in their daily lives, their nation-states cannot be far behind with their queries. The jobs crisis in Europe today is only one detour that the EU must negotiate on its own "integration and union" motorway.

Anthropologists have a role to play in the scholarship of the EU, especially in the issues of culture and identity (Wilson 1993a; Wilson and Smith 1993). I agree with the assertion (Shore and Black 1992: 10-11) that in order to integrate theory and practice in their studies of the EU, anthropologists should "study up" and focus on the cultures of power among EU institutions (as done, for example, in Abélès 1992). This chapter champions a wider concern, however. An anthropology of the EU must explore the EU's institutions and processes as they are experienced in everyday life, at every level of society and culture throughout the member states and even beyond the EU's borders. In order to integrate the EU into their lives, as both an idea as well as a set of institutions and laws, people are symbolically constructing the EU in more ways than its leaders may wish. Because the EU also constructs itself, through often complex processes of image-building, it seeks to influence the ways it is perceived in its citizens' daily lives. But the images and their meanings cannot be controlled in the public spheres of the EU and the state. What may appear to be clear-cut images of economic union are being used by national elites to strengthen borders, while others, for example among Irish nationalists, use the imagery of integration as a weapon against the British state's notions of its sovereignty. Much of the EU's imaging (which may also be an imagining, an attempt to create a new "imagined community of Europeans," in a way reminiscent of nation-building [Anderson 1991]) is at the levels of symbolic culture, e.g., "European" flag, passport, and anthem. Much of the EU's production of the symbolic culture of European integration is more implicit, done through its representatives' day to day administrative activities. For instance, the EU, through its commissioners and other public servants, goes to great lengths to appear disinterested in the EU's assault on the power of both its nation-states and their politicians. They push the concept of "subsidiarity", which is as much a symbol of decentralisation as it is a policy objective of delegated authority. But the implicit message is that there will be some important policy decisions which will inevitably be taken at the centre, in the EU's administrative heartland. This is very much a process of political centralisation, and a challenge to the sovereignty of the state.

A Europe without frontiers is, of course, one with many remaining cultural boundaries and legal and political borders. But the EU recognises that the symbols of a common market pave the way for its achievement. To continue the EU's metaphor of highway construction, the invention of a Europe without frontiers also entails the construction of a series of signposts, for a journey to a destination which is not yet clear. If the meanings of these signposts continue to be contested, which is certain in this post-Maastricht recession, so too will the destination. While the Europe of the EU is being invented in its capitals, it is simultaneously being constructed by the experiences of its people. A new Europe will be a product of the dialectical relations which result.

Notes

This essay is based in part on field research that I have been conducting intermittently since 1991, at the eastern end of the Irish border. This research has been funded by the United States National Endowment for the Humanities, the Wenner-Gren Foundation for Anthropological Research, the British Council, and the Queen's University of Belfast.

References

Abélès, M. 1992. *La vie quotidienne au Parlement Européenne.* Paris: Hackette.

Anderson, B. 1991. *Imagined communities.* London: Verso.

Anderson, M. 1982. The political problems of frontier regions. *West European Politics* 5 (4): 1-17.

Barth, F. 1969. Introduction. In Barth, F. (ed.). *Ethnic groups and boundaries: The social organization of cultural difference.* Boston: Little Brown.

Blok, A. 1974. *The Mafia of a Sicilian village, 1860-1960.* Oxford: Basil Blackwell.

Boissevain, J. 1975. Introduction: Towards a social anthropology of Europe. In Boissevain, J. and Friedl, J. (eds.). *Beyond the community: Social process in Europe.* The Hague: Department of Educational Science of the Netherlands.

Bull, M. 1993. Widening versus deepening the European Community: The political dynamics of 1992 in historical perspective. In T. M. Wilson and M. E. Smith (eds.). *Cultural change and the New Europe.* Boulder: Westview Press.

Clifford, J. 1988. *The predicament of culture.* Cambridge, MA: Harvard University Press.

Coakley, J. 1982. National territories and cultural frontiers: Conflicts of principle in the formation of states in Europe. *West European Politics* 5 (4): 34-49.

Cohen, A. P. 1982. *Belonging.* St. John's, Newfoundland: Memorial University.

_____. 1986. *Symbolising boundaries.* Manchester: Manchester University Press.

_____. 1987. *Whalsay: Symbol, segment and boundary in a Shetland Island community.* Manchester: Manchester University Press.

Cohen, R. 1993. Price of European unity is reckoned in lost jobs. *The New York Times*. 10 January: 3.

Cole, J. W., and Wolf, E. R. 1974. *The hidden frontier: Ecology and ethnicity in an Alpine valley*. New York: Academic Press.

Connor, W. 1978. A nation is a nation, is a state, is an ethnic group, is a . . . *Ethnic and Racial Studies* 1 (4): 379-88.

Donnan, H. and Wilson, T. M. 1994a. An anthropology of frontiers. In Donnan, H. and Wilson, T. M. (eds.). *Border approaches: Anthropological perspectives on frontiers*. Lanham, MD: University Press of America.

_____. 1994b. (eds.). *Border approaches: Anthropological perspectives on frontiers*. Lanham, MD: University Press of America.

Douglass, W. A. 1977. Borderland influences in a Navarrese village. In Douglass, W. A., Etulain, R. W., and Jacobsen, Jr., W. H. (eds.). *Anglo-American contributions to Basque studies: Essays in honor of Jon Bilbao*. Reno (Nevada): Desert Research Institute.

Driessen, H. 1992. *On the Spanish-Moroccan frontier: A study in ritual, power and ethnicity*. Oxford: Berg.

European Communities - Commission. 1987. *The European Community — 1992 and beyond*. Luxembourg: Office for Official Publications of the European Communities.

_____. 1992a. *The Single Market in action*. Luxembourg: Office for Official Publications of the European Communities.

_____. 1992b. *From Single Market to European Union*. Luxembourg: Office for Official Publications of the European Communities.

Fortes, M. and Evans-Pritchard, E. E. 1940. *African political systems* London: Oxford University Press.

Geertz, C. (ed.). 1963. *Old societies and new states*. Glencoe: Free Press.

_____. 1973. *The interpretation of cultures*. New York: Basic Books.

Gledhill, J. 1994. *Power and its disguises: Anthropological perspectives on politics*. London: Pluto.

Gupta, A., and Ferguson, J. 1992. Beyond 'culture': Space, identity, and the politics of difference". *Cultural Anthropology* 7 (1): 6-23.

Handler, R. 1988. *Nationalism and the politics of culture in Quebec*. Madison: The University of Wisconsin Press.

Hedetoft, U. 1994. The state of sovereignty in Europe: Political concept or cultural self-image. In S. Zetterholm (ed.) *National cultures & European integration*. Oxford: Berg.

Jones, D. and S. Platt 1992. Introduction. Borderlands Supplement. *New Statesman and Society*. 19 June: 2.

Kapferer, B. 1988. *Legends of people, myths of state: Violence, intolerance and political culture in Sri Lanka and Australia*. Washington: Smithsonian Institute Press.

Kertzer, D. 1988. *Ritual, politics, and power*. New Haven and London: Yale University Press.

_____. 1990. *Comrades and Christians: Religion and political struggle in Communist Italy*. Prospect Heights, Ill: Waveland Press.

Kubik, J. 1994. *The power of symbols against the symbols of power: The rise of Solidarity and the fall of state socialism in Poland*. University Park, PA: The Pennsylvania State University Press.

McCrone, D. 1991. Politics and society in modern Scotland. In G. Day and G. Rees (eds.) *Regions, nations, and European integration*. Cardiff: University of Wales Press.

Nairn, T. 1977. *The Break-up of Britain: Crisis and neo-nationalism*. London: New Left Books.

_____. 1992. Does tomorrow belong to the bullets or bouquets. Borderlands Supplement. *New Statesman and Society*. 19 June: 30-32.

Sahlins, P. 1989. *Boundaries: The making of France and Spain in the Pyrenees*. Berkeley: University of California Press.

Schneider, J. and P. Schneider. 1976. *Culture and political economy in Western Sicily*. New York: Academic Press.

Schneider, J., P. Schneider, and E. C. Hansen. 1972. Modernization and development: The role of regional elites and noncorporate groups in the European Mediterranean. *Comparative Studies in Society and History* 14: 328-350.

Shore, C. and A. Black. 1992. The European communities and the construction of Europe. *Anthropology Today* 8 (3): 10-11.

Silverman, S. 1979. On the uses of history in anthropology: The *palio* of Siena. *American Ethnologist* 6: 413-436

Spencer, J. 1990. Writing within: Anthropology, nationalism, and culture in Sri Lanka. *Current Anthropology* 31 (3): 283-300.

Strassoldo, R. 1982. Frontier regions: Future collaboration or conflict? *West European Politics*. 5 (4):123-135.

Tägil, S. 1982. The question of border regions in Western Europe: An historical background. *West European Politics*. 5 (4):18-33.

Verdery, K. 1991. National ideology under socialism: Identity and cultural politics in Ceauçescu's Romania. Berkeley: University of California Press.

Vincent, J. 1990. *Anthropology and politics: Visions, traditions, and trends*. Tucson: University of Arizona Press.

Wilson, T. M. 1993a. An anthropology of the European Community. In T. M. Wilson and M. E. Smith (eds.). *Cultural change and the New Europe*. Boulder: Westview Press.

_____. 1993b. Frontiers go but boundaries remain: The Irish border as a cultural divide. In Wilson, T. M. and Smith, M. E. (eds.). *Cultural change and the New Europe: Perspectives on the European Community*. Boulder and Oxford: Westview Press.

_____. 1994. Symbolic dimensions to the Irish border. In Donnan, H. and Wilson, T. M. (eds.). *Border approaches*. Lanham, MD: University Press of America.

____. 1995. The anthropology of the European Union. *ECSA Newsletter* 8 (1): 12-15.

Wilson, T. M. and M. E. Smith (eds.) 1993. *Cultural change and the New Europe: Perspectives on the European Community.* Boulder: Westview

Wolf, E. R. 1966. Kinship, friendship, and patron-client relations in complex societies. In M. Banton (ed.). *The social anthropology of complex societies* London: Tavistock.

____. 1982. *Europe and the people without history.* Berkeley: University of California Press.

Index

227

229

Maribor 135
Mazey, S 33
McCrone, D 206
Mecklenburg-Western Pomerania 38
Mediterranean 14,21,74,78,83, 91- 92,100,142,179-196
Meegan, R 112
Mexico 180
Michalczyk, T 155,162-163
Middle Ages 158
Middle East 117
Milan 77-78,81,85,139,142
Millan, B 26,31,33,35,40
Millar, P 14,
Milstatt declaration 54,57
Milward, A 118
Monitoring Committees (EU) 44
Moore, T 114
Morocco 14, 179-196
  Jbala 189
  King Hassan II 181,195
  Moroccan Immigrants in Spain 183
  Moroccans 8
  Nador 179
  Rif 189,192
    Aith Waryaghar (Central Rif) 196
      Riffians 192
  Spanish enclaves 181
  Tangier 185-186,192,193
Morrow, D 53,56
Morton, P 125
Moscow 142
Muller, W 6
Munich 139
Munson, H 191
Music, V B 142
Muslims
  immigrants 194
  in Africa 194

in Western Europe 194
  women 196
Mustafa 189
Nagorno Karabakh 117
Nairn, T 206,213
Napoleon 151
NATO 64
Nawrocki, T 165-167
Nazism 160
  Nazi
    occupation 162
    propaganda 159
    regime 169
    neo- 6
Netherlands (Holland) 30,37-38, 40,181,191
  Dutch 22,24
  German border regions 36
  government 36,38
  Low Countries 23
  Ministers of Trade and Industry 38
  Ministry of Transport and Public Works 36
    of the Flemish Community 36
New Left 77
Nielsen, J 194
Nijkamp, P 13,
Nile 36
North America 3,4,200
  American imperialism 161
  Anglo-American relationships 130
North Rhine-Westphalia 29,32
North Sea 91
North-South co-operation 66
Northern Ireland, *see Ireland, Ulster,* 6,42,117-131,205-211, 214
  B-Specials 119
  Civil Rights Movement 117